Mometrix
TEST PREPARATION

NYSTCE

Technology Education (118) Test Secrets Study Guide

DEAR FUTURE EXAM SUCCESS STORY

First of all, **THANK YOU** for purchasing Mometrix study materials!

Second, congratulations! You are one of the few determined test-takers who are committed to doing whatever it takes to excel on your exam. **You have come to the right place.** We developed these study materials with one goal in mind: to deliver you the information you need in a format that's concise and easy to use.

In addition to optimizing your guide for the content of the test, we've outlined our recommended steps for breaking down the preparation process into small, attainable goals so you can make sure you stay on track.

We've also analyzed the entire test-taking process, identifying the most common pitfalls and showing how you can overcome them and be ready for any curveball the test throws you.

Standardized testing is one of the biggest obstacles on your road to success, which only increases the importance of doing well in the high-pressure, high-stakes environment of test day. Your results on this test could have a significant impact on your future, and this guide provides the information and practical advice to help you achieve your full potential on test day.

Your success is our success

We would love to hear from you! If you would like to share the story of your exam success or if you have any questions or comments in regard to our products, please contact us at **800-673-8175** or **support@mometrix.com**.

Thanks again for your business and we wish you continued success!

Sincerely,
The Mometrix Test Preparation Team

> **Need more help? Check out our flashcards at:**
> **http://MometrixFlashcards.com/NYSTCE**

TABLE OF CONTENTS

Introduction

Thank you for purchasing this resource! You have made the choice to prepare yourself for a test that could have a huge impact on your future, and this guide is designed to help you be fully ready for test day. Obviously, it's important to have a solid understanding of the test material, but you also need to be prepared for the unique environment and stressors of the test, so that you can perform to the best of your abilities.

For this purpose, the first section that appears in this guide is the **Secret Keys**. We've devoted countless hours to meticulously researching what works and what doesn't, and we've boiled down our findings to the five most impactful steps you can take to improve your performance on the test. We start at the beginning with study planning and move through the preparation process, all the way to the testing strategies that will help you get the most out of what you know when you're finally sitting in front of the test.

We recommend that you start preparing for your test as far in advance as possible. However, if you've bought this guide as a last-minute study resource and only have a few days before your test, we recommend that you skip over the first two Secret Keys since they address a long-term study plan.

If you struggle with **test anxiety**, we strongly encourage you to check out our recommendations for how you can overcome it. Test anxiety is a formidable foe, but it can be beaten, and we want to make sure you have the tools you need to defeat it.

Secret Key #1 – Plan Big, Study Small

There's a lot riding on your performance. If you want to ace this test, you're going to need to keep your skills sharp and the material fresh in your mind. You need a plan that lets you review everything you need to know while still fitting in your schedule. We'll break this strategy down into three categories.

Information Organization

Start with the information you already have: the official test outline. From this, you can make a complete list of all the concepts you need to cover before the test. Organize these concepts into groups that can be studied together, and create a list of any related vocabulary you need to learn so you can brush up on any difficult terms. You'll want to keep this vocabulary list handy once you actually start studying since you may need to add to it along the way.

Time Management

Once you have your set of study concepts, decide how to spread them out over the time you have left before the test. Break your study plan into small, clear goals so you have a manageable task for each day and know exactly what you're doing. Then just focus on one small step at a time. When you manage your time this way, you don't need to spend hours at a time studying. Studying a small block of content for a short period each day helps you retain information better and avoid stressing over how much you have left to do. You can relax knowing that you have a plan to cover everything in time. In order for this strategy to be effective though, you have to start studying early and stick to your schedule. Avoid the exhaustion and futility that comes from last-minute cramming!

Study Environment

The environment you study in has a big impact on your learning. Studying in a coffee shop, while probably more enjoyable, is not likely to be as fruitful as studying in a quiet room. It's important to keep distractions to a minimum. You're only planning to study for a short block of time, so make the most of it. Don't pause to check your phone or get up to find a snack. It's also important to **avoid multitasking**. Research has consistently shown that multitasking will make your studying dramatically less effective. Your study area should also be comfortable and well-lit so you don't have the distraction of straining your eyes or sitting on an uncomfortable chair.

 The time of day you study is also important. You want to be rested and alert. Don't wait until just before bedtime. Study when you'll be most likely to comprehend and remember. Even better, if you know what time of day your test will be, set that time aside for study. That way your brain will be used to working on that subject at that specific time and you'll have a better chance of recalling information.

Finally, it can be helpful to team up with others who are studying for the same test. Your actual studying should be done in as isolated an environment as possible, but the work of organizing the information and setting up the study plan can be divided up. In between study sessions, you can discuss with your teammates the concepts that you're all studying and quiz each other on the details. Just be sure that your teammates are as serious about the test as you are. If you find that your study time is being replaced with social time, you might need to find a new team.

Secret Key #2 – Make Your Studying Count

You're devoting a lot of time and effort to preparing for this test, so you want to be absolutely certain it will pay off. This means doing more than just reading the content and hoping you can remember it on test day. It's important to make every minute of study count. There are two main areas you can focus on to make your studying count.

Retention

It doesn't matter how much time you study if you can't remember the material. You need to make sure you are retaining the concepts. To check your retention of the information you're learning, try recalling it at later times with minimal prompting. Try carrying around flashcards and glance at one or two from time to time or ask a friend who's also studying for the test to quiz you.

To enhance your retention, look for ways to put the information into practice so that you can apply it rather than simply recalling it. If you're using the information in practical ways, it will be much easier to remember. Similarly, it helps to solidify a concept in your mind if you're not only reading it to yourself but also explaining it to someone else. Ask a friend to let you teach them about a concept you're a little shaky on (or speak aloud to an imaginary audience if necessary). As you try to summarize, define, give examples, and answer your friend's questions, you'll understand the concepts better and they will stay with you longer. Finally, step back for a big picture view and ask yourself how each piece of information fits with the whole subject. When you link the different concepts together and see them working together as a whole, it's easier to remember the individual components.

Finally, practice showing your work on any multi-step problems, even if you're just studying. Writing out each step you take to solve a problem will help solidify the process in your mind, and you'll be more likely to remember it during the test.

Modality

Modality simply refers to the means or method by which you study. Choosing a study modality that fits your own individual learning style is crucial. No two people learn best in exactly the same way, so it's important to know your strengths and use them to your advantage.

For example, if you learn best by visualization, focus on visualizing a concept in your mind and draw an image or a diagram. Try color-coding your notes, illustrating them, or creating symbols that will trigger your mind to recall a learned concept. If you learn best by hearing or discussing information, find a study partner who learns the same way or read aloud to yourself. Think about how to put the information in your own words. Imagine that you are giving a lecture on the topic and record yourself so you can listen to it later.

For any learning style, flashcards can be helpful. Organize the information so you can take advantage of spare moments to review. Underline key words or phrases. Use different colors for different categories. Mnemonic devices (such as creating a short list in which every item starts with the same letter) can also help with retention. Find what works best for you and use it to store the information in your mind most effectively and easily.

3

Secret Key #3 – Practice the Right Way

Your success on test day depends not only on how many hours you put into preparing, but also on whether you prepared the right way. It's good to check along the way to see if your studying is paying off. One of the most effective ways to do this is by taking practice tests to evaluate your progress. Practice tests are useful because they show exactly where you need to improve. Every time you take a practice test, pay special attention to these three groups of questions:

- The questions you got wrong
- The questions you had to guess on, even if you guessed right
- The questions you found difficult or slow to work through

This will show you exactly what your weak areas are, and where you need to devote more study time. Ask yourself why each of these questions gave you trouble. Was it because you didn't understand the material? Was it because you didn't remember the vocabulary? Do you need more repetitions on this type of question to build speed and confidence? Dig into those questions and figure out how you can strengthen your weak areas as you go back to review the material.

 Additionally, many practice tests have a section explaining the answer choices. It can be tempting to read the explanation and think that you now have a good understanding of the concept. However, an explanation likely only covers part of the question's broader context. Even if the explanation makes perfect sense, **go back and investigate** every concept related to the question until you're positive you have a thorough understanding.

As you go along, keep in mind that the practice test is just that: practice. Memorizing these questions and answers will not be very helpful on the actual test because it is unlikely to have any of the same exact questions. If you only know the right answers to the sample questions, you won't be prepared for the real thing. **Study the concepts** until you understand them fully, and then you'll be able to answer any question that shows up on the test.

It's important to wait on the practice tests until you're ready. If you take a test on your first day of study, you may be overwhelmed by the amount of material covered and how much you need to learn. Work up to it gradually.

On test day, you'll need to be prepared for answering questions, managing your time, and using the test-taking strategies you've learned. It's a lot to balance, like a mental marathon that will have a big impact on your future. Like training for a marathon, you'll need to start slowly and work your way up. When test day arrives, you'll be ready.

Start with the strategies you've read in the first two Secret Keys—plan your course and study in the way that works best for you. If you have time, consider using multiple study resources to get different approaches to the same concepts. It can be helpful to see difficult concepts from more than one angle. Then find a good source for practice tests. Many times, the test website will suggest potential study resources or provide sample tests.

Practice Test Strategy

If you're able to find at least three practice tests, we recommend this strategy:

UNTIMED AND OPEN-BOOK PRACTICE

Take the first test with no time constraints and with your notes and study guide handy. Take your time and focus on applying the strategies you've learned.

TIMED AND OPEN-BOOK PRACTICE

Take the second practice test open-book as well, but set a timer and practice pacing yourself to finish in time.

TIMED AND CLOSED-BOOK PRACTICE

Take any other practice tests as if it were test day. Set a timer and put away your study materials. Sit at a table or desk in a quiet room, imagine yourself at the testing center, and answer questions as quickly and accurately as possible.

Keep repeating timed and closed-book tests on a regular basis until you run out of practice tests or it's time for the actual test. Your mind will be ready for the schedule and stress of test day, and you'll be able to focus on recalling the material you've learned.

Secret Key #4 – Pace Yourself

Once you're fully prepared for the material on the test, your biggest challenge on test day will be managing your time. Just knowing that the clock is ticking can make you panic even if you have plenty of time left. Work on pacing yourself so you can build confidence against the time constraints of the exam. Pacing is a difficult skill to master, especially in a high-pressure environment, so **practice is vital**.

Set time expectations for your pace based on how much time is available. For example, if a section has 60 questions and the time limit is 30 minutes, you know you have to average 30 seconds or less per question in order to answer them all. Although 30 seconds is the hard limit, set 25 seconds per question as your goal, so you reserve extra time to spend on harder questions. When you budget extra time for the harder questions, you no longer have any reason to stress when those questions take longer to answer.

Don't let this time expectation distract you from working through the test at a calm, steady pace, but keep it in mind so you don't spend too much time on any one question. Recognize that taking extra time on one question you don't understand may keep you from answering two that you do understand later in the test. If your time limit for a question is up and you're still not sure of the answer, mark it and move on, and come back to it later if the time and the test format allow. If the testing format doesn't allow you to return to earlier questions, just make an educated guess; then put it out of your mind and move on.

On the easier questions, be careful not to rush. It may seem wise to hurry through them so you have more time for the challenging ones, but it's not worth missing one if you know the concept and just didn't take the time to read the question fully. Work efficiently but make sure you understand the question and have looked at all of the answer choices, since more than one may seem right at first.

Even if you're paying attention to the time, you may find yourself a little behind at some point. You should speed up to get back on track, but do so wisely. Don't panic; just take a few seconds less on each question until you're caught up. Don't guess without thinking, but do look through the answer choices and eliminate any you know are wrong. If you can get down to two choices, it is often worthwhile to guess from those. Once you've chosen an answer, move on and don't dwell on any that you skipped or had to hurry through. If a question was taking too long, chances are it was one of the harder ones, so you weren't as likely to get it right anyway.

On the other hand, if you find yourself getting ahead of schedule, it may be beneficial to slow down a little. The more quickly you work, the more likely you are to make a careless mistake that will affect your score. You've budgeted time for each question, so don't be afraid to spend that time. Practice an efficient but careful pace to get the most out of the time you have.

Secret Key #5 – Have a Plan for Guessing

When you're taking the test, you may find yourself stuck on a question. Some of the answer choices seem better than others, but you don't see the one answer choice that is obviously correct. What do you do?

The scenario described above is very common, yet most test takers have not effectively prepared for it. Developing and practicing a plan for guessing may be one of the single most effective uses of your time as you get ready for the exam.

In developing your plan for guessing, there are three questions to address:

- When should you start the guessing process?
- How should you narrow down the choices?
- Which answer should you choose?

When to Start the Guessing Process

Unless your plan for guessing is to select C every time (which, despite its merits, is not what we recommend), you need to leave yourself enough time to apply your answer elimination strategies. Since you have a limited amount of time for each question, that means that if you're going to give yourself the best shot at guessing correctly, you have to decide quickly whether or not you will guess.

Of course, the best-case scenario is that you don't have to guess at all, so first, see if you can answer the question based on your knowledge of the subject and basic reasoning skills. Focus on the key words in the question and try to jog your memory of related topics. Give yourself a chance to bring the knowledge to mind, but once you realize that you don't have (or you can't access) the knowledge you need to answer the question, it's time to start the guessing process.

It's almost always better to start the guessing process too early than too late. It only takes a few seconds to remember something and answer the question from knowledge. Carefully eliminating wrong answer choices takes longer. Plus, going through the process of eliminating answer choices can actually help jog your memory.

Summary: Start the guessing process as soon as you decide that you can't answer the question based on your knowledge.

How to Narrow Down the Choices

The next chapter in this book (**Test-Taking Strategies**) includes a wide range of strategies for how to approach questions and how to look for answer choices to eliminate. You will definitely want to read those carefully, practice them, and figure out which ones work best for you. Here though, we're going to address a mindset rather than a particular strategy.

Your odds of guessing an answer correctly depend on how many options you are choosing from.

Number of options left	5	4	3	2	1
Odds of guessing correctly	20%	25%	33%	50%	100%

You can see from this chart just how valuable it is to be able to eliminate incorrect answers and make an educated guess, but there are two things that many test takers do that cause them to miss out on the benefits of guessing:

- Accidentally eliminating the correct answer
- Selecting an answer based on an impression

We'll look at the first one here, and the second one in the next section.

To avoid accidentally eliminating the correct answer, we recommend a thought exercise called **the $5 challenge**. In this challenge, you only eliminate an answer choice from contention if you are willing to bet $5 on it being wrong. Why $5? Five dollars is a small but not insignificant amount of money. It's an amount you could afford to lose but wouldn't want to throw away. And while losing

$5 once might not hurt too much, doing it twenty times will set you back $100. In the same way, each small decision you make—eliminating a choice here, guessing on a question there—won't by itself impact your score very much, but when you put them all together, they can make a big difference. By holding each answer choice elimination decision to a higher standard, you can reduce the risk of accidentally eliminating the correct answer.

The $5 challenge can also be applied in a positive sense: If you are willing to bet $5 that an answer choice *is* correct, go ahead and mark it as correct.

Summary: Only eliminate an answer choice if you are willing to bet $5 that it is wrong.

Which Answer to Choose

You're taking the test. You've run into a hard question and decided you'll have to guess. You've eliminated all the answer choices you're willing to bet $5 on. Now you have to pick an answer. Why do we even need to talk about this? Why can't you just pick whichever one you feel like when the time comes?

The answer to these questions is that if you don't come into the test with a plan, you'll rely on your impression to select an answer choice, and if you do that, you risk falling into a trap. The test writers know that everyone who takes their test will be guessing on some of the questions, so they intentionally write wrong answer choices to seem plausible. You still have to pick an answer though, and if the wrong answer choices are designed to look right, how can you ever be sure that you're not falling for their trap? The best solution we've found to this dilemma is to take the decision out of your hands entirely. Here is the process we recommend:

Once you've eliminated any choices that you are confident (willing to bet $5) are wrong, select the first remaining choice as your answer.

Whether you choose to select the first remaining choice, the second, or the last, the important thing is that you use some preselected standard. Using this approach guarantees that you will not be enticed into selecting an answer choice that looks right, because you are not basing your decision on how the answer choices look.

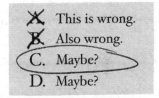

This is not meant to make you question your knowledge. Instead, it is to help you recognize the difference between your knowledge and your impressions. There's a huge difference between thinking an answer is right because of what you know, and thinking an answer is right because it looks or sounds like it should be right.

Summary: To ensure that your selection is appropriately random, make a predetermined selection from among all answer choices you have not eliminated.

Test-Taking Strategies

This section contains a list of test-taking strategies that you may find helpful as you work through the test. By taking what you know and applying logical thought, you can maximize your chances of answering any question correctly!

It is very important to realize that every question is different and every person is different: no single strategy will work on every question, and no single strategy will work for every person. That's why we've included all of them here, so you can try them out and determine which ones work best for different types of questions and which ones work best for you.

Question Strategies

☑ READ CAREFULLY

Read the question and the answer choices carefully. Don't miss the question because you misread the terms. You have plenty of time to read each question thoroughly and make sure you understand what is being asked. Yet a happy medium must be attained, so don't waste too much time. You must read carefully and efficiently.

☑ CONTEXTUAL CLUES

Look for contextual clues. If the question includes a word you are not familiar with, look at the immediate context for some indication of what the word might mean. Contextual clues can often give you all the information you need to decipher the meaning of an unfamiliar word. Even if you can't determine the meaning, you may be able to narrow down the possibilities enough to make a solid guess at the answer to the question.

☑ PREFIXES

If you're having trouble with a word in the question or answer choices, try dissecting it. Take advantage of every clue that the word might include. Prefixes can be a huge help. Usually, they allow you to determine a basic meaning. *Pre-* means before, *post-* means after, *pro-* is positive, *de-* is negative. From prefixes, you can get an idea of the general meaning of the word and try to put it into context.

☑ HEDGE WORDS

Watch out for critical hedge words, such as *likely, may, can, sometimes, often, almost, mostly, usually, generally, rarely,* and *sometimes.* Question writers insert these hedge phrases to cover every possibility. Often an answer choice will be wrong simply because it leaves no room for exception. Be on guard for answer choices that have definitive words such as *exactly* and *always.*

☑ SWITCHBACK WORDS

Stay alert for *switchbacks.* These are the words and phrases frequently used to alert you to shifts in thought. The most common switchback words are *but, although,* and *however.* Others include *nevertheless, on the other hand, even though, while, in spite of, despite,* and *regardless of.* Switchback words are important to catch because they can change the direction of the question or an answer choice.

10

⊘ Face Value

When in doubt, use common sense. Accept the situation in the problem at face value. Don't read too much into it. These problems will not require you to make wild assumptions. If you have to go beyond creativity and warp time or space in order to have an answer choice fit the question, then you should move on and consider the other answer choices. These are normal problems rooted in reality. The applicable relationship or explanation may not be readily apparent, but it is there for you to figure out. Use your common sense to interpret anything that isn't clear.

Answer Choice Strategies

⊘ Answer Selection

The most thorough way to pick an answer choice is to identify and eliminate wrong answers until only one is left, then confirm it is the correct answer. Sometimes an answer choice may immediately seem right, but be careful. The test writers will usually put more than one reasonable answer choice on each question, so take a second to read all of them and make sure that the other choices are not equally obvious. As long as you have time left, it is better to read every answer choice than to pick the first one that looks right without checking the others.

⊘ Answer Choice Families

An answer choice family consists of two (in rare cases, three) answer choices that are very similar in construction and cannot all be true at the same time. If you see two answer choices that are direct opposites or parallels, one of them is usually the correct answer. For instance, if one answer choice says that quantity x increases and another either says that quantity x decreases (opposite) or says that quantity y increases (parallel), then those answer choices would fall into the same family. An answer choice that doesn't match the construction of the answer choice family is more likely to be incorrect. Most questions will not have answer choice families, but when they do appear, you should be prepared to recognize them.

⊘ Eliminate Answers

Eliminate answer choices as soon as you realize they are wrong, but make sure you consider all possibilities. If you are eliminating answer choices and realize that the last one you are left with is also wrong, don't panic. Start over and consider each choice again. There may be something you missed the first time that you will realize on the second pass.

⊘ Avoid Fact Traps

Don't be distracted by an answer choice that is factually true but doesn't answer the question. You are looking for the choice that answers the question. Stay focused on what the question is asking for so you don't accidentally pick an answer that is true but incorrect. Always go back to the question and make sure the answer choice you've selected actually answers the question and is not merely a true statement.

⊘ Extreme Statements

In general, you should avoid answers that put forth extreme actions as standard practice or proclaim controversial ideas as established fact. An answer choice that states the "process should be used in certain situations, if..." is much more likely to be correct than one that states the "process should be discontinued completely." The first is a calm rational statement and doesn't even make a definitive, uncompromising stance, using a hedge word *if* to provide wiggle room, whereas the second choice is far more extreme.

11

☑ Benchmark

As you read through the answer choices and you come across one that seems to answer the question well, mentally select that answer choice. This is not your final answer, but it's the one that will help you evaluate the other answer choices. The one that you selected is your benchmark or standard for judging each of the other answer choices. Every other answer choice must be compared to your benchmark. That choice is correct until proven otherwise by another answer choice beating it. If you find a better answer, then that one becomes your new benchmark. Once you've decided that no other choice answers the question as well as your benchmark, you have your final answer.

☑ Predict the Answer

Before you even start looking at the answer choices, it is often best to try to predict the answer. When you come up with the answer on your own, it is easier to avoid distractions and traps because you will know exactly what to look for. The right answer choice is unlikely to be word-for-word what you came up with, but it should be a close match. Even if you are confident that you have the right answer, you should still take the time to read each option before moving on.

General Strategies

☑ Tough Questions

If you are stumped on a problem or it appears too hard or too difficult, don't waste time. Move on! Remember though, if you can quickly check for obviously incorrect answer choices, your chances of guessing correctly are greatly improved. Before you completely give up, at least try to knock out a couple of possible answers. Eliminate what you can and then guess at the remaining answer choices before moving on.

☑ Check Your Work

Since you will probably not know every term listed and the answer to every question, it is important that you get credit for the ones that you do know. Don't miss any questions through careless mistakes. If at all possible, try to take a second to look back over your answer selection and make sure you've selected the correct answer choice and haven't made a costly careless mistake (such as marking an answer choice that you didn't mean to mark). This quick double check should more than pay for itself in caught mistakes for the time it costs.

☑ Pace Yourself

It's easy to be overwhelmed when you're looking at a page full of questions; your mind is confused and full of random thoughts, and the clock is ticking down faster than you would like. Calm down and maintain the pace that you have set for yourself. Especially as you get down to the last few minutes of the test, don't let the small numbers on the clock make you panic. As long as you are on track by monitoring your pace, you are guaranteed to have time for each question.

☑ Don't Rush

It is very easy to make errors when you are in a hurry. Maintaining a fast pace in answering questions is pointless if it makes you miss questions that you would have gotten right otherwise. Test writers like to include distracting information and wrong answers that seem right. Taking a little extra time to avoid careless mistakes can make all the difference in your test score. Find a pace that allows you to be confident in the answers that you select.

⊘ KEEP MOVING

Panicking will not help you pass the test, so do your best to stay calm and keep moving. Taking deep breaths and going through the answer elimination steps you practiced can help to break through a stress barrier and keep your pace.

Final Notes

The combination of a solid foundation of content knowledge and the confidence that comes from practicing your plan for applying that knowledge is the key to maximizing your performance on test day. As your foundation of content knowledge is built up and strengthened, you'll find that the strategies included in this chapter become more and more effective in helping you quickly sift through the distractions and traps of the test to isolate the correct answer.

Now that you're preparing to move forward into the test content chapters of this book, be sure to keep your goal in mind. As you read, think about how you will be able to apply this information on the test. If you've already seen sample questions for the test and you have an idea of the question format and style, try to come up with questions of your own that you can answer based on what you're reading. This will give you valuable practice applying your knowledge in the same ways you can expect to on test day.

Good luck and good studying!

Fundamentals of Technology and Engineering Education

History and Impact of Technology

IMPACT OF SCIENTIFIC AND TECHNICAL INNOVATION

Scientific and technical innovation has played a major role in enhancing productivity, increasing a society's wealth, and raising its standard of living. After a new innovation comes about, it must spread to other people and groups in order to be effective. This process is known as **diffusion**, and is illustrated using an **s-curve**, also known as a **diffusion curve**, which tracks an increase in revenue or productivity over time. An s-curve represents the product life of an innovation. During the early stages of product life, an innovation must establish its usefulness and experiences a very slow growth in terms of revenue and productivity. The middle stages of product life see rapid increases in growth, and the latter stages of product life involve gradual decline. Product improvements may extend the lifespan of an innovation, but it will inevitably fall off. Consequently, companies are always seeking new innovations to replace older ones.

RESOURCE MANAGEMENT

Resource management seeks to allocate an organization's resources in the most efficient and economical ways possible—that is, the goal of resource management is the **optimization** of resource usage in a project. Resources include money, employees, inventory, production, and information technology, and are allocated using a variety of processes and techniques. One such technique is **resource leveling**, which balances usage by eliminating inventory shortages and excesses. To avoid shortages and thereby reduce conflict, management should take care when scheduling multiple activities at the same time. If concurrent activities require more of one resource than is available or make use of the same person, they should be rescheduled. In many cases, management may be forced to delay an activity until the resource becomes available. If this activity is part of the critical path, the project may be delayed.

STIMULATING COMPETITIVENESS AND CREATING NEW GOODS AND SERVICES

Technological innovation provides a number of benefits to the marketplace. It can introduce new products, which are simply those with which customers have no prior experience. Technological innovation can also introduce an improved or more efficient means of production or commodity handling. In many cases, these new products or means of production will open up new markets and require the discovery of new sources of raw materials. This often stimulates the economy by creating additional competition and breaking up existing monopolies. Technological innovation is often the result of the pursuit of better quality; new market formation; new regulations; need for replacement parts or services; decreased availability of materials; increased labor costs; increased production costs; etc.

MAJOR SCIENTIFIC AND TECHNOLOGICAL INNOVATIONS

The **automobile** was granted a patent in 1885. Karl Benz, who is widely regarded as the inventor of the gasoline-powered car, placed the first automobiles into production during the same year.

The **airplane** was developed in 1903 by Wilbur and Orville Wright. They used various principles of aerodynamics, such as drag and lift, to develop the first power and controlled flight.

15

The **integrated circuit** was developed in 1958 by Jack Kilby of Texas Instruments and Robert Noyce at Fairchild Semiconductor. It led to the development of the microchip by enabling semiconductor devices to perform the same functions as vacuum tubes. It revolutionized electronic equipment, leading to the development of personal computers, cellular phones, and various digital devices.

The **internet** came about with the first TCP/IP protocol, which was developed in 1983 by Robert E. Kahn and Vince Cerf.

RELATIONSHIP BETWEEN TECHNOLOGY AND SOCIETY AND CULTURE

Technology and culture have a **synergistic relationship** which began with the simple tools developed during the dawn of man and continues today with modern technologies such as computers and various other electronic devices. This relationship is **cyclical and codependent** with each party exerting influence over the other. Funding for technological development comes from two primary sources in most modern cultures and societies: Private business and enterprise, or government programs. Once new technology is developed, it **influences** social attitudes and beliefs, which, in turn, influence the implementation of new technology. For instance, key values and beliefs that derive from this codependence between technology and culture are the notions that human productivity should work to achieve higher levels of efficiency and that technology drives social progress. According to these beliefs, humankind is improving as long as technology is improving.

CONSERVATION AND SUSTAINABILITY

Conservation is the effort to reduce energy and material consumption by reducing usage and making more efficient use of existing resources. New technology can facilitate conservation in a variety of ways. Renewable energy sources (geothermal, hydroelectric energy, wind power, etc.), building techniques that take advantage of the local climate, and vehicles that consume less gas (such as hybrids) all help lower energy consumption. Real-time energy metering helps consumers to better understand the impact of their energy usage.

Sustainability determines the length of time over which an ecological system will endure. Sustainable systems are those that will remain healthy and productive for a long time. Technology is often a means of increasing energy efficiency and conserving natural resources so that the human environment can become more sustainable.

BIOTECHNOLOGY

Biotechnology is the technological application of biology. It uses living organisms and bioprocesses to create products or processes, and has numerous applications in the following fields:

- **Medicine** – includes drug production, gene therapy, gene testing, and pharmacogenomics (i.e. determining an individual's response to drugs based on inherited genetic traits).
- **Agriculture** – includes enhancing crop yield, increasing nutritional attributes of food, improving crop durability, producing new substances in crop plants, and reducing dependence on agrochemicals.
- **Biological engineering** – uses physics, chemistry, and mathematics to solve life science problems.
- **Bioremediation and biodegradation** – create organisms for purposes of removing environmental contamination.

- **Cloning** –two main types: reproductive, which brings a fully developed life into the world, and therapeutic, which involves using stem cells.
- **Human Genome Project** – seeks to discover all human genes and create a reference sequence for the human genome.

Biotechnology often makes use of mathematical biology, which models complex biological processes using various types of math: graph theory, calculus, probability theory, statistics, linear algebra, abstract algebra, combinatorics, algebraic geometry, topology, dynamical systems, differential equations and coding theory.

GOVERNMENT REGULATION AND FACILITATING TECHNOLOGICAL DEVELOPMENT

Historically, the government has served a role not only in funding technological research but also in regulating its usage and side effects. One example of such regulation is the FDA, or Food and Drug administration. When selecting which types of research to fund, the government will choose those that offer the greatest benefit to mankind. However, the presence of different interest groups competing for resources can complicate the selection process. In reality, both the populace-at-large and special interests hold tremendous influence over governmental policy. The government also assumes a regulatory role in technological development, especially regarding the environment and the protection of ecological systems. The government is responsible for assigning liability to corporations whose products cause harm.

MATERIAL DISPOSALS, AND ENVIRONMENTAL EMISSION MONITORING AND CONTROL

Materials disposal is carried out using a variety of technologies and techniques:

- **Incinerators** – subject solid waste to the process of combustion in order to convert it into residue and gas. This generates heat, gas, steam, and ash.
- **Landfills** – eliminate solid waste by burying it.
- **Recycling** – reprocesses discarded materials (e.g., aluminum cans, glass bottles, newspapers, cardboard boxes, paper) into their constituent materials, and reuses them.
- **Sustainability methods** – include biological reprocessing, such as composting and anaerobic digestion, and energy recovery, which processes waste into fuel.

Environmental emission monitoring and control is performed by continuous emission monitoring systems, which use gas analyzers to test air samples for certain types of emissions, such as carbon dioxide, carbon monoxide, sulfur dioxide, mercury, etc. Federal programs use these systems to ensure compliance with emission standards, such as the acid rain program and other EPA standards.

MEDICAL AND AGRICULTURAL TECHNOLOGY

Medical technology includes any device, procedure, pharmaceutical, or system whose purpose is improving health, preventing sickness, and diagnosing or treating disease. Medical technology covers a vast number of healthcare products, which often make use of mathematical principles and concepts. For instance, medical imaging machines (CAT, ultrasound, etc.) and pharmacology often make use of trigonometric functions for measurement problems. Mathematical tools such as dimensional analysis are often used to calculate the correct dosage for patients.

Agricultural technology encompasses a wide array of machinery, processes, and systems designed to enhance agricultural production. Agricultural technology also makes use of mathematical principles and concepts. For instance, dimensional analyses are often used to examine complex agricultural-social economic systems. Graph theory provides a means of modeling ecology. And quadratic equations often used to solve economic problems related to agriculture.

PHYSICS

The following concepts and principles of physics have been essential to the development of new technologies:

- **Bernoulli's principle** – states that, when the speed of an inviscid flow increases, the pressure (or potential energy) of the flow will decrease. Consequently, faster moving air creates slower static pressure and higher dynamic pressure. Carburetors and pitot tubes work on Bernoulli's principle.
- **Aerodynamics** – include four forces relevant to flight: thrust, lift, drag, and weight. Thrust is a reaction force explained by Newton's Second and Third Laws. When mass is accelerated in one direction, it will generate an equal force in the opposite direction. Jet engines, propeller blades, and rockets generate thrust by pushing air in the direction opposite to flight. Lift is a force that is generated perpendicular to the oncoming air flow (using Bernoulli's Principle). Airplane wings are designed to take advantage of lift (climbing, descending, banking). Drag is a force that is generated parallel to the oncoming air flow, and opposes the motion of an object. Weight is applied by gravity. In order to achieve flight, all forces must be balanced.

BIOLOGY

Biology includes several fields with an especially strong focus on developing new technologies. One such field is **biological engineering**, which attempts to emulate biological system and, thereby, develop new products or enhance existing biological systems. Biological engineering is responsible for the creation of renewable bioenergy, biocompatible materials, medical devices, diagnostic equipment, and similar technologies. A second field is **molecular biology**. It helped create the therapies and techniques used in gene therapy, which treats diseases by inserting, altering, and removing genes within a person's cells and tissue. Using techniques developed in molecular biology, gene therapy is capable of replacing mutated genes or even modifying and correcting mutated cells. A third field is **pathology**, which uses laboratory equipment to diagnose disease. Another field is **biotechnology**, which uses living organisms and bioprocesses to create products or processes.

CHEMISTRY

An understanding of chemistry is necessary to convert raw materials—such as oil, air, water, minerals, metals, etc.—into usable and marketable materials—such as solvents, soaps, pesticides, cement, etc. The chemical industry consists of numerous businesses that use chemical processes and reactions to create and refine products. Below is a partial list of such products:

- **Petrochemicals** – includes ethylene, propylene, benzene, and styrene.
- **Agrochemicals** – includes fertilizers, insecticides, and herbicides.
- **Polymers** – includes polyester, polyethylene, and Bakelite.
- **Fragrances/flavors** – includes vanillin and coumarin.
- **Inorganic industrial compounds** – includes ammonia, nitric acid, sodium hydroxide, and sulfuric acid.
- **Organic industrial compounds** – includes phenol, urea, and ethylene oxide.
- **Ceramics** – include silica brick and frit.
- **Explosives** – includes ammonium nitrate, nitrocellulose, and nitroglycerin.
- **Oleochemicals** – include lard and soybean oil.
- **Elastomers** – includes polyisoprene, neoprene, and polyurethane.

Safety and Regulations

SDS

An **SDS**, or **Safety Data Sheet** (formerly MSDS), explains the properties of a specific substance, and provides a means of cataloging substances according to their effects and risks. It is an integral component of **workplace safety** as it provides information necessary to the safe handling and storage of the substance. SDS information has sixteen sections: Identification, Hazard identification, Composition/information on ingredients, First-aid measures, Fire-fighting measures, Accidental release measures, Handling and storage, Exposure controls/ personal protection, Physical and chemical properties, Stability and reactivity, Toxicological information, and Other information. They should be present wherever chemicals are being used or kept. SDS data sheets are not necessarily intended for general consumers; rather, they are meant for those who work with chemicals in an occupational setting.

STANDARD PROCEDURES

Standard procedures when working around materials and equipment related to technology include the following:

- Do not bring pets or nonessential personnel.
- Do not consume food or drink.
- Familiarize yourself with the proper operation of all equipment and materials by consulting user guides.
- Wear shoes, shirts, and all other appropriate attire.
- Tie back long hair and remove loose clothing (ties, scarves, dangling jewelry, etc.) so that they do not contact equipment or materials.
- Refrain from dropping equipment.
- Observe appropriate precautions when working around electrical equipment.
- Ensure that all equipment and instrumentation is calibrated correctly.
- Ensure that that power is off before making circuit connections.
- Power untested circuits with adjustable power sources at their lowest levels.
- Be professional in your conduct.

EMERGENCY FIRE PROCEDURES

The following procedures should be undertaken in the event of fire:

- Sound the fire alarm if you will be unable to extinguish the fire on your own or a serious emergency has occurred, such as the release of toxic gas.
- Use a nearby fire extinguisher to extinguish the fire. If possible, extinguish the fire using CO_2 units rather than dry chemical units. CO_2 units often pose less risk to equipment.
- Carry a fire extinguisher with you when going to an area in which a fire might be present.
- When a person's clothing is on fire, roll them on the floor or wrap them in a coat or blanket.
- Immediately leave a building in which a fire alarm has been sounded.

ELECTROCUTION

Electrocution refers to severe injury or death caused by direct exposure to an electric current. The following procedures should be undertaken in the event that someone is being electrocuted:

- Never touch someone who is being electrocuted.
- Turn off power supply if possible. This can be done at the work bench or at a breaker panel.

- If the power cannot be turned off, use a piece of non-conducting material (such as lumber) to separate the person from the energized conductor.
- Ensure that the person is breathing and check for pulse. Administer CPR if necessary. Only qualified individuals should administer CPR.
- Seek medical assistance.

Whenever equipment is damaged, report it to the appropriate personnel for repair. Damaged equipment can be very hazardous. A blown fuse or circuit breaker indicates a faulty circuit; therefore, identify and correct the faulty circuit before resetting the breaker or replacing the fuse.

OSHA

OSHA, or **Occupational Safety and Health Administration**, is a federal regulatory agency that enforces workplace safety and health standards to prevent work-related injuries, illnesses, and fatalities. OSHA applies to most workplaces, and requires the following workplace safeguards:

- **Guards** – must be placed on all moving parts where contact is possible.
- **Permissible exposure limits**, or **PEL** – prevent chemical or dust concentrations from exceeding certain limits.
- **Personal protective equipment**, or **PPE** – require use of respirators, gloves, coveralls, goggles, face shields, and/or other protective equipment when working in certain industrial environments.
- **Lockout/tagout** – requires that energy sources be secured in an off condition when maintenance or repairs are being performed.
- **Confined space** – requires air sampling and use of a buddy system while working in enclosed areas, such as tanks, pits, manholes, etc.
- **Hazard communication** – requires that workers are informed of workplace chemical hazards.
- **Process safety management** – lessens risk of large industrial accidents.
- **Blood borne pathogens**, or **BBP** – prevents workers from being exposed to blood borne pathogens, such as HIV.
- **Excavations and trenches** – must follow certain procedures and use certain safety equipment if they are more than five feet down.
- **Asbestos exposure** – limit occupational exposure to asbestos.

> Review Video: **What is OSHA (Occupational Safety and Health Administration)**
> Visit mometrix.com/academy and enter code: 913559

CAREER AND TECHNICAL EDUCATION COURSE APPROVAL AND RE-APPROVAL PROCESS

According to the Carl D. Perkins Career and Technical Education Improvement Act of 2006, **career and technical education (CTE)** programs in all states must emulate the New York CTE program. In Washington, the CTE program has the following goals:

- Maintaining rigorous academic standards.
- Providing the skills necessary to fill any deficiencies or gaps in Washington's economy.
- Ensuring that all state education reform requirements are aligned.
- Creating and designing good career and technical education programs by building and facilitating relationships with local CTE advisory councils.

The approval/re-approval process for CTE courses can be performed online. Approval requests are due April 15 for first-semester courses and October 15 for the second-semester courses. Additionally, re-approval requests for programs must be received by January 31. Approval and re-approval for specific courses follow a schedule that can be found at the same site.

SAFETY AND HEALTH STANDARDS

The **Safety Guide for Career and Technical Education** contains the most recent instructions and checklists for vocational education curricula. This lengthy document is published by OSPI, and can be found online. It contains a comprehensive list of safety practices and requirements that students and teachers should observe in CTE courses. These practices and requirements include the following:

- Proper floor cleanliness and maintenance.
- Proper maintenance, storage, and handling of power tools, shop machinery, and equipment.
- Required shop equipment.
- Safety rules and standards displayed in plain sight.
- Proper material handling and storage.
- Storage, labeling, and handling of electrical devices and equipment.
- Disposal of hazardous waste.
- Non-asbestos fire blankets.
- Proper safety equipment, such as eyewear and face shields.
- Eye wash stations.
- Proper ventilation.
- Safety Signs.
- Ambient noise level limits.

CAREER AND TECHNICAL EDUCATION CURRICULUM ADVISORY COMMITTEE

The career and technical education (CTE) advisory committee is responsible for **determining and recommending a curriculum** that will best prepare students for passing state assessments and earning a Certificate of Academic Achievement, or CAA. The specific duties of the CTE advisory committee include the following:

- Establishing criteria, processes, and tools that state and district boards will use to identify and evaluate appropriate CTE equivalency courses. These courses should gain equivalent academic credit in the core subject areas of math, science, social studies, English, health/fitness, and art.
- Using these criteria, processes, and tools to determine if existing CTE courses fulfill the equivalency requirements.

TECH PREP ARTICULATION

Tech Prep is a high school program that provides students with technical training, applied academics, and assistance in finding workplace internship and guidance. Tech Prep offers a number of advantages to high school students:

- Provides **college credit**, ultimately saving both time and money. Tech Prep enables high school graduates to bypass entry level courses and enroll in higher level classes. The manner in which college credit and standing are awarded is based on an articulation agreement between the high school and the college program. In most cases, this agreement awards college credit using tests, certification by a high school teacher, or college course completion.

- Prepares high school students for the **rigors of college courses**.
- Prepares high school students for a **career in technical professions**, such as engineering, science, health care, computers, etc. Upon leaving college, tech Prep students often receive better wages and benefits than students who did not take Tech Prep courses.

MEMBERSHIP IN PROFESSIONAL CAREER AND TECHNICAL ORGANIZATIONS

There are many different **professional career and technical organizations**. When deciding which organization to join, the best choice will vary depending on the specific CTE field and personal preference. However, most organizations offer similar benefits, such as the following:

- **Networking and professional development** opportunities through expos, seminars, and webinars. Members have the opportunity to meet and speak with CTE educators, business partners, institutional representatives, and policy makers.
- Helpful **classroom tools**, best practices, and analysis.
- **Partnerships** with and access to industry experts.
- A **news periodical** that keeps members up-to-date on the newest developments in the field.
- **Awards programs** that offer national recognition.
- **Online courses** that may improve career advancement prospects.
- **Job banks**.
- **Connection** to other education worldwide.

PRIMARY BUSINESS MANAGEMENT FUNCTIONS

Business management usually includes the following functions:

- **Planning** – involves creating plans for action based on forecasts over certain periods of time, such as weeks, months, and years.
- **Organizing** – requires the optimization of resource usage so that plans will be successful and can be carried out in the most efficient ways possible.
- **Staffing** – recruits and assigns personnel to the appropriate jobs. This function involves job analysis.
- **Directing** – identifies the specific tasks necessary for plan completion, and getting workers to carry them out.
- **Monitoring** – checks the progress of the project team against the plan, and determines whether it is on schedule.
- **Motivating** – is fundamental and a very important aspect of business management. Workers must be motivated to carry out their specific tasks, and contribute to other functions.

WORK SCHEDULE

A **work schedule** breaks a project down into its most basic work activities. These activities are known as terminal elements and cannot be further divided into smaller tasks. The work schedule will include estimates for the resources, cost, and duration of each activity, and then arrange them by their dependencies and order of completion. To create a work schedule, the project manager must have a **work breakdown structure**, which includes an effort estimate and the resource availability for each task. There is software that can perform much of the work necessary to create a work schedule; however, even when using these applications, the manager must have an understanding of certain key concepts and tools, such as dependencies, resource allocation, earned value, critical paths, and Gantt charts. A **Gantt chart** is a bar chart that shows each terminal element, its duration, and other summary information.

WORKFLOW TRACKING

A **workflow** is an abstraction of work that is performed by a single person or group of people. It depicts a sequence of steps that, upon completion, produces a certain outcome or product. Any workflow must have input, such as information or materials. This input then undergoes a change or transformation in accordance with certain rules. Finally, a workflow will produce an output, which consists of new information or a new product. When monitoring workflow, management may track a document as it passes through each step within the sequence. Workflow plays an important role in issue tracking, the purpose of which is identifying and resolving customer problems. A problem is input into the customer call support center (via a customer complaint), tracked as it passes through all the steps, and then resolved.

SAFETY ASSESSMENTS

A **safety assessment** is a method of quantifying and understanding the hazards and risks associated with certain products and materials, such as hazardous chemicals. Safety assessments incorporate multiple scientific disciplines, and typically involve professional risk assessors hired by the company. Chemical companies, consumer product companies, government agencies, insurance agencies, consulting firms, medical device manufacturers and many others make use of risk assessors. Most safety or risk assessments involve three steps:

- Identify the hazard (i.e. the consequences of exposure).
- Perform a dose-response analysis to determine the dosage necessary to produce a certain response.
- Perform exposure quantification in order to determine the dosage that the population is likely to receive.

The information gained during safety assessments should be incorporated into demonstrations, training, tests, and record keeping.

Technological and Engineering Design

Design Process and Applications

RESEARCH AND CONCEPTUALIZATION

The **research phase** is the first phase of the engineering design process. It involves **locating and examining** information on a specific engineering issue or problem. It may require studying literature and documents on the topic and identifying existing solutions, costs, and market needs. Reverse engineering of similar market products is also a potential avenue of research. Common sources of research information include trade journals, governmental documents, local libraries, the World Wide Web, and interviews with subject matter experts.

The **conceptualization phase** is the second phase of the engineering design process. It involves **identifying potential solutions** for the problem using various techniques of ideation. One popular ideation technique is **brainstorming**, which involves rapidly thinking of and adopting solutions. Another technique is **trigger word**. One person says a word associated with the problem. Hopefully, this word evokes additional words and phrases that can be used to create solutions. Another technique is a **morphological chart**, which includes design characteristics of the problems. Engineers then propose solutions for each characteristic.

FEASIBILITY ASSESSMENT AND DESIGN REQUIREMENTS

The **feasibility assessment phase** is the third phase of the engineering design process. It **determines whether or not the proposed solution is possible** by asking two main questions: Is the project based on an achievable idea? Is the project within the cost constraints of the organizations? These questions are best answered by an experienced engineer with good judgment. He is arguably the most important component of this phase. If the project is feasible, it is sent through the design phase. The **design requirements phase** is the fourth phase of the engineering design process. It **establishes the software and hardware parameters and testability**, maintainability, and other key project requirements. It is carried out concurrently with the feasibility phase.

PRELIMINARY DESIGN AND DETAILED DESIGN

The **Preliminary design phase**, also known as **embodiment design**, is the fifth phase of the engineering design process. It **defines** the overall system design—including schematics, layouts, and diagrams—in a very general way. The design will change as the project proceeds, but these early diagrams will provide guidance in the early stages. Preliminary design phases lead to the detailed design phase.

Detailed design phase is the sixth phase of the engineering design process. It **provides very specific and detailed specifications** (solid models and drawings) on the project. Common specifications include external marking, design life, packaging requirements, operating parameters, test requirements, external dimensions, materials requirements, reliability requirements, external surface treatments, maintenance and testability information, and operating and non-operating environmental stimuli. CAD, or computer-aided design, programs are very helpful during this phase. They increase design efficiency through optimization, which decreases part volume while simultaneously maintaining quality. CAD programs can also perform the finite element method, which calculates stress and displacement. The engineer then determines whether or not these stresses and displacements conform to project parameters.

24

PRODUCTION PLANNING AND TOOL DESIGN AND PRODUCTION DESIGN

The **Production planning and tool design phase** is the seventh phase of the engineering design process. It **establishes a plan** for mass producing the product and identifies the manufacturing tools that should be used. It is during this phase that a working prototype is built and tested for standard compliance. Common tasks include material selection, production process selection, sequence of operation determination, and tool selection.

The **Production phase** is the eighth phases of the engineering design process. It involves **manufacturing** the product and conducting periodic tests of machinery.

INTEGRATED SYSTEMS AND SYSTEMS THINKING

Integrated systems consist of numerous systems working in conjunction. Technology often consists of smaller systems combined together to form larger systems. In this way, systems are the base components of technology. Consider, for example, an automobile. It consists of numerous electronic and mechanical parts. These parts work together to create the subsystems (steering, lighting, combustion, propulsion, etc.) of which the automobile is comprised.

Systems thinking involves viewing a system as a collection of interconnected parts or processes, and then analyzing the cause and effect relationships between those parts or processes. Systems thinking is necessary when creating new products that always perform as intended.

TECHNOLOGY SYSTEMS AND FEEDBACK

A system consists of interrelated components that work together in order to bring about a certain outcome or achieve a specific goal. Systems exist in many different forms—technological, environmental, social, etc. Some systems were created through natural processes while other systems are manmade. As a core concept of technology, systems include the following topics:

- A **technology system** is a manmade system. It combines materials, devices, energy, structures, and information as a means of solving problems or creating products.
- **Feedback** occurs when output produced by a particular event or behavior influences a recurrence of the same event or behavior in the future. There are two primary types of feedback: positive feedback, which increases the occurrence of the event or behavior that produced the output, and negative feedback, which decreases the occurrence of the event or behavior that produced the output. Systems often incorporate feedback components that allow for the system to be changed or refined.

RESOURCES

Resources are required to carry out technological activities. The key resources in technology include the following:

- **Tools and machines** – devices and instruments intended to extend or improve human capabilities. Tools can be handheld or motor-driven, and often perform functions such as cutting, chopping, digging, etc. Machines are structures of moving and unmoving parts that perform work. They function by changing the application of energy. Simple machines include wheels, pulleys, screws, wedges, etc.
- **Processes** – systematic sequences of actions through which humans create, design, invent, produce, control, maintain, and use products and systems. They are the methods through which resources are turned into products.
- **Materials** – include natural resources such as wood and tone; synthetic resources such as plastics, alloys, and concrete; and, mixed resources such as leather, plywood, and paper.

- **People** – include the manpower and labor that goes into performing some task or function related to technology. People are arguably the most important resource.
- **Capital** – is necessary to create products and maintain technological systems. This resource includes money and all other financial instruments.
- **Energy** – the ability to perform work. Technological systems input energy, and though application, convert it into a specific function or product.
- **Time** – must be allocated for the performance of any activity. Because time is limited and is required by all technological activities, it must be used as effectively and efficiently as possible.
- **Information** – includes any data that has been gleaned through reading, listening, observing, researching, or consulting any number of sources. Such data need not be factual, although facts are a type of information. Knowledge is more factual and reliable than information. When being used by technological systems, information should be arranged and presented in a rational and useful way.

In many cases, engineers must choose between resources. This decision will be made by analyzing tradeoffs, or the advantages and disadvantages of using one resource relative to another resource. Tradeoffs may include the cost, availability, desirability, and waste associated with a particular resource.

REQUIREMENTS

Requirements are the criteria and constraints that determine the final design and development of a system or project. They are created by examining the system in terms of concept-generation, marketing, production, use, disposability, and fiscal issues. **Criteria** include the parameters of the system design. They encompass the elements and features that define the system and determine the manner in which it should operate. A common criterion is the level of efficiency at which the system should function. **Constraints** are the limits on system design. They often reflect restrictions on funding, human capabilities, space, material, time, and the environment. Constraints tend to be relative and must be balanced against each other based on the constraint's importance in the system design. Engineers must work within the criteria and constraints of the system design.

QUALITY CONTROL

Quality control makes certain that products meet design requirements and customers receive functional products. It involves setting parameters for the system or product, and then making certain the system or product operates within those parameters. Quality control is an ongoing process in which the materials that enter the system, system operation, and system output are constantly evaluated against an acceptable range. Nonconformances are then identified and corrected. The parameters used by quality control are often based on tolerances and specifications created from engineering standards and marketing research, which collects and examines customer reactions, both good and bad, that influence future designs and iterations of the project.

PROCESSES

A **process** is usually a routine set of procedures through which materials are input and then converted into something more useful, such as a product, a service, or even a different process. In technology and engineering, a process is focused on completing a certain project, and is often described as a set of transformations that occur between input and output. These transformations are defined by their parameters and constraints. New processes are often the result of new technologies, which are the fruits of human creation and innovation. New processes lead to new products and systems that solve problems and enhance human capabilities. We create new technologies to make our lives easier and to increase our happiness and comfort.

OPTIMIZATION AND TRADEOFFS

Optimization is a process through which designers and engineers attempt to make a product or system as efficient and functional as possible. Optimization **improves** the overall system by bettering the performance of specific characteristics. Mathematical models are an important component of optimization. They help engineer to test and predict possible variations in system design.

A **tradeoff** occurs when one characteristic is lost in exchange for another characteristic with a different set of strengths and weaknesses. When optimizing a product, engineers are often forced to make tradeoffs, and must do so with full understanding of the consequences. For instance, in order to achieve a relatively light product weight, an engineer may be forced to use weaker materials.

ISO 9000

ISO 9000 is a set of rigorous international quality standards that are applicable to numerous types of organizations. Maintained by the International Organization for Standardization, ISO 9000 is designed to help companies improve the quality of their products, processes, and services in a systematic and continuous manner. Companies can receive an ISO 9000 certification by meeting certain requirements, including the following:

- Proper **record keeping** system.
- Constant **evaluation** of manufacturing processes to ensure the creation of quality products.
- **Examination** of outgoing products for defects and taking appropriate corrective action when required.
- Method for **continuous improvement**.
- Regular **reviews** of processes and quality systems to ensure efficiency.

Although an ISO 9000 certification does not guarantee a certain level of quality within end products and services, it does guarantee that certain quality and business process are being practiced.

APPLICATION OF QUALITY CONTROL PROCEDURES TO ENGINEERING AND TECHNOLOGY-RELATED SITUATIONS

Quality engineers are responsible for managing, controlling, and addressing product quality. Quality engineers make use of statistical process control tools such as control charts, which identify statistical variations within a process. SPC tools help determine the specific metrics that should be monitored and the method by which they should be sampled. By following the control limits set by these tools, employees can identify nonconforming products and correct or remove them before they pass on to the next production step or the customer. Defects in the production process should be corrected as early as possible; consequently, the quality engineer will work closely with suppliers to ensure conformance and contain potential problems. Additionally, quality engineers are engaged in continuous improvement, such as Six Sigma and lean manufacturing, which seeks to reduce statistical variation and the number of nonconforming products.

ERGONOMICS AND ADA COMPLIANCE

Ergonomics is used to create equipment and devices designed in such a way as to place the least amount of stress possible on the human body and its mental faculties. During the design process, ergonomists must **identify any stressors** (excessive force, unnatural postures, frequent repetition, etc.) that occur while using the equipment or device. If these stressors do not conform to ergonomic guidelines, they must be documented and their statistical variation quantified. Based on these findings, the ergonomist must determine whether there is any correlation between the nonconformances and injuries recorded while using the product and make recommendations to the product engineers.

ADA, or the Americans with Disabilities Act, creates and publishes construction standards intended to help provide disabled persons with better access to buildings. In March 2012, all new construction must comply with ADA standards.

RESEARCH AND DEVELOPMENT

Research and development, or **R&D**, is a systematic and creative process undertaken with the intent of improving knowledge, culture, and society, and developing new applications. R&D is often focused specifically on scientific and technological endeavors, and is carried out by both private industry and government. Most companies will not survive unless they consistently innovate and develop new technologies; consequently, companies with strong R&D departments tend to outperform those without consistent R&D departments. Pharmaceutical companies, on average, spend more on R&D than other companies. They devote much of this funding to researching mechanisms, identifying chemical compounds, proving a concept, fulfilling safety requirements, and discovering delivery methods. In some cases, different companies may form an R&D alliance, in which each party agrees to share their findings and new technology with the other parties. Businesses may form R&D alliances if they lack consistent R&D departments.

TROUBLESHOOTING TECHNOLOGY SYSTEMS

Troubleshooting procedures focus on solving problems that derive from issues other than a user's unfamiliarity with the technology system (as opposed to standard procedures, which focus on familiarizing the user with the system). Such problems include component failures, unforeseen product limitations, and incompatibility. The process of troubleshooting consists of two primary phases:

- **Diagnosis phase** – The user must identify and describe the issues he is experiencing, such as unusually slow performance or failure to complete tasks. These issues are symptoms of underlying problems. The user diagnoses the problem by matching the symptoms to symptoms listed in the troubleshooting procedures.
- **Resolution phase** – After identifying the problems, the user follows a solution path. There may be multiple possible solution paths available to the user, and these paths may vary in complexity.

Diagnosis and resolution are not always separate and distinct processes. Further diagnoses may be required during the resolution phase.

MANUFACTURABILITY, CONSTRUCTION COSTS AND CONSUMER FEEDBACK

Manufacturability determines the ease with which a product can be manufactured. Engineers seek to design for manufacturability—that is, when designing a product, engineers always ensure that there is feasible way in which the product can be produced. Otherwise, it may fail at the manufacturing stage.

Construction costs are estimated by cost engineers, who use scientific principles and techniques. Construction costs encompass a wide array of problems, including business planning and management, project management, planning and scheduling, profitability analysis, cost estimation and cost control.

Consumer feedback can be gathered by interviews, surveys, focus groups, meetings, and many other data gathering tools. Based on feedback from these tools, engineers can recommend and incorporate design revisions that will increase the usability of new products.

EXPERIMENTATION AND INVENTION

New technological innovations often lead to new business models and customer experiences that cannot be tested via conventional market research methods. Consequently, **experimentation** may be the only means of creating a product that will be useful to consumers and, therefore, successful on the market. Experimentation is far less predictable than established business models, but is often necessary to develop new and useful technologies, processes, services, etc.

Invention is the process by which new technologies are developed. New inventions can build off of existing technologies or they can be revolutionary, representing a radical breakthrough. Every new technology is the product of invention. The concept of invention is the basis for patent law. By applying for a patent, the inventor of a new technology can exclude others from using, selling, or importing the technology for the duration of the patent.

MODELS AND MODELING

Models are important to the design process because they help engineers and designers better visualize and understand the final product before it goes into production. There are different types of models. **Physical models**, for example, are physical, three-dimensional copies. They can be smaller than the products they represent (these are often used to test a specific design feature without incurring the expense of a full-sized prototype) or they can be larger (these are often used to provide a better view of smaller components that otherwise may be difficult to see). A **scale model** is a special type of physical model. Regardless of its size relative to the final project, a scale model is always exactly proportional. **Prototypes** are scale models that are the same size as the products they represent. Certain graphics software programs are capable of modeling objects in 3D. Computer modeling may be less expensive than creating a physical model while giving engineers the same benefit of visualization.

ENGINEERING DRAWINGS

Engineering drawings are a specific type of technical representation based on the technical drawing discipline. They include and define all the requirements and critical information of a particular product, such as:

- **Geometry** – includes the shapes of the object and its appearance from various angles.
- **Dimensions** – include the size of the object expressed in standard units, such as inches, centimeters, feet, meters, etc.
- **Materials** – include the components of the product.
- **Finish** – identifies the required surface quality of the product. In most cases, products contained within industrial machines require lower surface quality than consumer products.

Based solely on the drawing, a manufacturer should be able to create the product or component in question. Engineering drawings generally follow certain standardized conventions, such as GD&T, which mandate the use of certain layouts, nomenclatures, interpretations, typefaces, line styles, sizes, etc.

FLOWCHARTS

Flowcharts illustrate the steps within a various algorithm or process. They **offer solutions** to a particular problem, and help document particularly complex processes. Flowcharts consist of various types of shapes: boxes, which contain activities; diamonds, which contain decisions the user must make; and, arrows, which represent the flow of control. Additionally, flowcharts illustrate the following types of activities: start and end, processing steps, inputs and outputs, conditionals, decisions, junctions, and connectors.

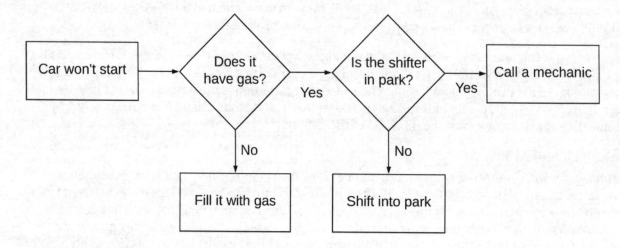

SPREADSHEETS, GRAPHS, AND TIME CHARTS

A **spreadsheet** is a digital simulation of a paper accounting worksheet. There are a number of software applications capable of generating spreadsheets. It contains multiple cells with each cell containing alphanumeric text, numeric data, or a formula that defines how information within the cell will be calculated.

	A	B	C
1	100	200	150
2	50	300	250
3			

In Excel, when the formula "=SUM(A1:A2)" is entered into cell A3, it should display a value of 150.

A **graph** is a visual representation that conveys complex information or concepts in quickly and easily understandable ways. Examples include bar charts, pie charts, column charts, organizational charts, and flowcharts.

Time charts serve as means of planning functions and activities.

Project Planning and Management

PLANNING A COMMUNICATION PROJECT

A basic communication model involves several main components:

- A **sender**
- A **receiver**
- A **medium**
- **Contextual factors**
- The message
- Positive or negative **feedback**

Other factors may include **noise**, elements that interfere with message delivery and **acknowledgement**, as the receiver confirms with the sender that the message was received.

Each of these elements will need to be planned. For a large project, this may include:

- Deciding on the **scope** of the project and defining **goals**.
- Selecting the best **medium** for the project.
- Determining how many **personnel** will be required to perform the setup and actual project.
- Projecting the **cost** of staffing and equipment.
- Setting a **timeline** for completion of the project.

PRODUCING A COMMUNICATION PROJECT

Producing the project may involve:

- **Set-up** – planning and procuring the medium (such as telephone systems or an email distribution software)
- **Hiring** and **training** staff – preparing them to communicate, such as following a telephone script and transcribing answers
- Collecting **data** – this may involve entering data into a software program or spreadsheet for analysis
- **Analyzing** and **reporting** the data – documenting the results of the project and what they mean, including recommendations for action

MANAGING A COMMUNICATION PROJECT

The manager of a communication project ensures that staff are prepared to **communicate** properly and effectively. Staff must have a full understanding of the communication model and the purpose of the project. The manager keeps the project on track, revising the **timeline** if necessary as changes are made. The manager also communicates with **stakeholders** and other involved parties as well as with staff to keep everyone on the same page. The manager helps to compile the collected data into the final **report** and delivers it to the stakeholders.

PLANNING A MANUFACTURING PROJECT

There are several steps to planning a manufacturing project:

- First, clearly define the **goal** of the project. Determine why a new product should be manufactured, who is the target audience, and how to go about producing and marketing it.
- Study the **market**. Check competitors for pricing and market saturation. Take polls and interviews to gauge interest in a new product.

- Run a detailed **cost analysis**. This can include cost of machinery, building, personnel, materials, and advertising. The finished product must sell enough units at a high enough profit to offset these costs and return a profit.
- Create a **timeline**. Calculate how long it will take to design, test, and produce the new product. Plan advertising accordingly so the market is prepared for launch.
- Get **personnel** in place. A manufacturing project will need suppliers, distributors, designers, and advertisers, as well as the actual production team.

PRODUCING A MANUFACTURING PROJECT

Once the planning stage is complete, the actual production can start.

- The first step is to finalize **design**. This will go through stages of testing to make sure it will function appropriately and has the necessary features.
- A **prototype** can then be created. It will be put through rigorous testing to find weaknesses, and a test market may receive prototypes to try out and give feedback.
- Once all the errors are corrected, full production can begin. Contracts should be in place for **suppliers** to bring raw materials. These are processed and then manufactured into the product. Then **distributors** transport them to be purchased.

MANAGING A MANUFACTURING PROJECT

Managing a manufacturing project means handling numerous variables. For a project to run smoothly, needed resources must be available. The manager must be in contact with **suppliers**, ensuring that materials are purchased and delivered regularly to keep up with demand. The manager must also oversee **design** and **production** teams, making sure they are on the same page and that any changes or problems have been communicated. Production must be on pace to meet demand, so the manager should **track progress and demand** and make adjustments as needed (such as hiring more staff or purchasing more machinery). Management of a manufacturing project also includes overseeing **marketing**. This includes advertisements, research, and testing. To keep a product relevant, it may be necessary to make changes or figure out how to make it more cost-effectively. The market constantly evolves, so this requires continual oversight.

PLANNING A CONSTRUCTION PROJECT

When planning a construction project, there are several things that must first be assessed:

- The **location** should be studied. This includes testing soil, checking for geographic dangers such as flood zones, and researching zoning and other local laws.
- The **cost of production** should be projected, along with a **timeline** for completing the project. Cost includes materials, machinery, and personnel, along with other costs such as offsetting the environmental impact.
- The manager should define **roles and responsibilities** and create a schedule with these roles.
- A **quality control and assurance plan** should be developed for ensuring that both work and materials are sufficient for the project's purpose.
- A **communication plan** should also be in place to make sure each team is following the plan and implementing any changes that are made.

PRODUCING A CONSTRUCTION PROJECT

Producing a construction project includes:

- Acquiring all needed **materials** from suppliers. This may include lumber, gravel, metal, concrete, and many other materials, depending on what is being constructed: a building, a road, etc.
- Preparing the **site**. The site may need to be graded or otherwise prepped before construction can start.
- **Building** the project. This may involve many steps. For instance, in a house, this includes laying a foundation, putting up the framework, installing electrical and plumbing, finishing and painting walls, roofing, etc.
- Performing a **quality check** before handing off to the owner.
- **Cleaning** the site of all machinery, excess materials, tools, and trash.

MANAGING A CONSTRUCTION PROJECT

When the project is ready to begin, the manager should do a final review of all **plans** and any related **documents** with stakeholders to ensure that no final changes need to be made. Then the manager can ensure that everyone on the production side has a thorough understanding of roles and what the project entails. The manager should also check with **suppliers** and make sure all materials will be delivered on time and in correct quantities. Throughout the project, the manager oversees progress, checking it against the timeline, and keeps **communication** open between the construction team, suppliers, stakeholders, and other involved parties. The manager also keeps in contact with **city or county personnel**, updating them on progress and ensuring that all is done legally. As changes or delays occur, the manager revises the plan and communicates to all parties. Finally, when the project is completed, the manager officially hands it off to the owner.

PLANNING AN ENERGY, POWER, AND TRANSPORTATION PROJECT

An energy, power, and transportation project requires extensive planning. These projects often involve local, state, and/or federal government contracts, so this may involve numerous tests and precautions to ensure that each part of the project remains in **compliance**. The manager should project the total **cost** of the project, including research and planning, materials, manpower, and tools such as machinery.

PRODUCING AN ENERGY, POWER, AND TRANSPORTATION PROJECT

An energy, power, and transportation project requires several steps:

- All necessary **materials** should be collected from suppliers. This may occur in stages if some supplies will not be needed until later in the project, since some projects can take place over months.
- **Site prep** should be performed, whether this means preparing the ground for building a road or bridge, or to erect wind turbines.
- Following the plan, the project should be **implemented** with frequent reports to stakeholders and government officials.
- The project should undergo **quality checks** and **performance tests** to ensure that it is working properly.

MANAGING AN ENERGY, POWER, AND TRANSPORTATION PROJECT

The manager of an energy, power, and transportation project has the responsibility to **communicate** clearly and frequently between all parties. This often includes government officials as well as stakeholders, suppliers, and the actual production team. The manager should oversee **quality checks** at each stage of production, ensuring that regulations are followed and communicating any necessary changes that are made to the plan.

PLANNING A BIO-RELATED TECHNOLOGY PROJECT

Bio-related technology includes a variety of projects, such as genetically modifying foods or developing renewable fuel sources. This type of project spends much time in the development stage, researching and testing. When planning a bio-related technology project, one must go through several steps:

- Outlining a clear **plan** that describes the goals for the project and how they will be achieved. Many different ideas may be tested and discarded in pursuit of one that will work, so it is vital to have a clear vision for the final product.
- Deciding on the needed **materials** for the project. This may include a lab equipped with various tools and materials to study and test products during development.
- Finding qualified **personnel** to work on the project and **stakeholders** to support the project. The project will need personnel with backgrounds that qualify them to research and develop the specific product. It will also need to be funded and directed by **stakeholders** who see potential in the idea.

PRODUCING A BIO-RELATED TECHNOLOGY PROJECT

Once the planning stage is complete and financial backing is established, the bio-related technology project can begin. Stages of production include:

- **Research and development** – even with a clear idea of what the product should entail, it will need significant research into both the science behind the ideas and other research on the subject.
- **Design** – after research, it is time to begin working on design, creating a blueprint for the prototype. This may go through several iterations and tests before the prototype can be created.
- **Prototype** – a prototype can be created for more testing. Weaknesses and errors are noted so they can be corrected in the next prototype.
- **Working model** – once the prototype has been shown to work as expected, a working model can be shared with stakeholders. It will undergo more testing before obtaining final approval for distribution.

MANAGING A BIO-RELATED TECHNOLOGY PROJECT

Managing a bio-related technology project involves careful oversight. These projects often include handling of hazardous materials so the manager must ensure that safety protocols are followed and appropriate protective equipment is available. The manager communicates between stakeholders and the research and development team. There are often numerous changes, both to the project and the timeline, that must be clearly communicated. The manager must also ensure that all governmental regulations are followed.

Planning a Computer Applications Project

A computer applications project usually involves developing new software. Planning this type of project includes:

- **Researching** the existing software options to see what is available and what is lacking, as well as what features are important to consumers.
- Setting a **goal** for what the project will accomplish and who will use it.
- Making a **timeline** and projecting what **materials and equipment** will be needed.
- Finding the necessary **personnel** (such as coders) to help develop the product.

Producing a Computer Applications Project

Producing a computer applications project involves a significant amount of **research and development**. There will be many stages of **programming**, **testing**, and **debugging** until the software works properly:

- After research, programmers can begin to **code** for the project. This is called **implementation**.
- At various points during coding, the software will be **tested** for bugs and changes will be made as necessary.
- **Documentation** is made throughout, keeping careful records of development and bugs.
- Final tests will be run after the software is completed, before it can be **launched**, or **deployed**.
- Even after distribution, **maintenance** must be done to keep it working and fix any bugs that occur.

Managing a Computer Applications Project

The manager of a computer applications project oversees the development, from market research through production and post-production. The manager **communicates** between different teams and the stakeholders, and works to keep the project on **schedule**. This may include helping to find solutions to programming issues that arise as well as marketing issues. The manager should either remain on the team to head up maintenance issues or hand off the project to another manager for long-term maintenance.

Manufacturing, Construction, and Materials

Marketing and Finance

MARKETING PROCESSES AND TECHNIQUES

Before creating a product, it is necessary to have a plan for marketing it. This requires a thorough understanding of **marketing processes and techniques**. This involves several components:

- **Market research** – it is crucial to have a knowledge of the market before developing and implementing a plan.
- **Target market** – the specific target demographic should be carefully chosen so advertising can be directed toward it.
- **Budget** – once a marketing budget has been decided, it can be allocated to various aspects based on its size.
- **Goals** – goals should be very clearly outlined before marketing, answering questions such as desired sales and customer retention.
- **Competitor research** – it is helpful to scout out the competition, not only to see who you're competing against but to get an idea of what is working for other businesses and what areas are unfulfilled.
- **Timeline** – this may flex as circumstances change, but it is helpful to have a clear plan for the timing of manufacturing, advertising, and so forth.
- **Tracking metrics** – as marketing begins, it is important to keep track of progress (and what is not working) to see trends and concerns.

MANUFACTURING AND FINANCES

Opening and running a business requires a significant capital investment. Ideally much of this is supported by **investors**. These may include individuals who see potential in the business and are willing to help fund the startup in exchange for benefits such as stock and partial ownership. There are also government programs that supply grants or loans for startup.

Costs that must be considered include:

- **Building** – the right building will have sufficient size and layout for the company's specific manufacturing needs. An existing building can be purchased or rented, or a new building erected, but a simple office building will not work. A manufacturing building must be designed specifically for use of machines, etc. Building costs also include electricity, water, and other overhead costs.
- **Labor** – this includes not only regular payroll for the people who will be operating the machines (**direct labor**), but other personnel such as safety inspectors, supervisors, and accounting department (**indirect labor**), and the cost of training new staff and ongoing training.
- **Materials** – these include **direct materials** (the raw materials that are used to create the product) and **indirect materials** (other items that must be purchased to aid in manufacturing, such as lubricant for machines).
- **Machinery** – this includes cost of maintenance and replacement as necessary.

- **Marketing** – to garner business, advertising must be budgeted. This can include traditional print advertisements, emails, radio ads, promos at events, etc.
- **Insurance** – to protect against lawsuits or pay for damages, it is important to purchase business insurance before opening the business.

ECONOMIC FACTORS IN INNOVATION AND PRODUCTION

While business is driven by economics, it is not usually as simple as receiving money from customers and using it to produce more items. When making financial investments, it is necessary to consider the desires and goals of the company's **investors** and the ultimate direction of the company. **Competition** is another factor to consider, as prices may need to be adjusted to compete with other providers. Each decision comes with **risk** and the potential for **reward**, so each aspect must be carefully considered. Some finances must be dedicated to **advertising** and some to **research and development** for a business to stay current.

ECONOMIC AND MARKETING PRINCIPLES

Many factors go into deciding the price that a manufacturer charges for its products. Startup and overhead cost, the ever-changing cost of materials, and competitor pricing must all be taken into account. It is important to calculate the costs and projected **profit margin** and to continually track costs and profits to make sure that pricing is where it should be and to see if changes need to be made to products (adjusting or removing from production if they are not turning a profit). The laws of **supply and demand** greatly affect pricing, not only of manufactured products but also of the raw materials that must be purchased. Some products are **seasonal** and must be planned for accordingly: producing more during the times of greater demand and scaling back at other times.

PRINCIPLES OF PRODUCT DEVELOPMENT

Product development involves many steps:

- **Idea creation** – for a business to keep up in industry, it is vital to develop new product ideas. These ideas should be discussed and researched and experts should be consulted (these can include distributors and suppliers).
- **Market analysis** – research should be done to find what is important to the target audience. Research should be ongoing as these needs can change quickly, especially in the field of technology. To ensure that a product will be profitable, a thorough study of cost is also required. There are many cost factors to take into account, from startup costs of machines and building, to supplier costs, to advertising. Different materials may be cheaper but also lower quality, so one must decide which are best for the ultimate goal of balancing quality and cost for the best possible product.
- **Design** – once it has been decided to go forward with the new product, it is time to develop the design. This typically involves computer models and simulations.
- **Prototype testing** – after the design is complete, a prototype is constructed to see if the design actually works. It may go through several stages of testing and adjusting the design.
- **Test marketing** – the prototype is launched to a select test group of customers to gauge response and get feedback. Any changes can then be made before the official launch.
- **Commercialization** – when the product is finalized, marketing strategies are created to pinpoint and communicate with the target audience and to distribute the product in amounts of projected sales (the company needs to produce a sufficient amount to meet customer demand but not a surplus).

RAPID PROTOTYPING AND MANUFACTURING

Rapid prototyping is an aspect of computer-aided manufacturing. It relies on additive manufacturing technology to **automate** the creation of models, prototypes, and other types of objects. Rapid prototyping is now capable of producing limited numbers of parts that can be used in assembly of the actual product. Additive manufacturing technology is capable of assembling parts in layers based on 3D model information.

Rapid manufacturing, also known as **direct digital manufacturing**, involves producing parts based on information contained in CAD or additive manufacturing files. Rapid manufacturing can make use of most alloy metals as well as different types of polymers. It has applications in a variety of industries, especially automotive, dental, fashion, medical, and any other industry in which midsized complex parts are prevalent.

Manufacturing Industry

CAREERS

- **Manufacturing engineers** improve and streamline the production process by designing manufacturing equipment and systems and finding ways to lower costs and increase profitability.
- **Automation technicians** are responsible for creating, installing and repairing automated systems and equipment.
- **Industrial designers** create designs and improve existing models for a variety of manufactured products, especially commercial, medical, and industrial goods.
- **Quality control engineers** improve the quality of manufactured products. They examine statistical data and find ways to improve product specifications.
- **Product engineers** help design manufactured products. They conduct surveys, talk with customers, and collaborate with other members of the organization as a means of improving product design.
- **Product safety technicians** test products to ensure compliance with safety regulations. These regulations are focused on the mechanical, electrical, and environmental operation of the product.
- **Manufacturing technicians** repair production equipment and facilitate proper equipment functionality. They are integral in maintaining the manufacturing line.

MANUFACTURING INDUSTRIES

Manufacturing includes the following industries:

- **Beverage manufacturing** – includes non-alcoholic beverages and alcoholic beverages produced through fermentation of distillation.
- **Tobacco manufacturing** – includes the creation of tobacco products as well as the stemming and re-drying of tobacco.
- **Leather and allied manufacturing** – produces footwear, tanning, and finishing.
- **Wood manufacturing** – includes sawmills, wood preservation, veneer, plywood, and similar wood products.
- **Paper manufacturing** – creates pulp, paper, paperboard and other paper products.
- **Printing and support manufacturing** – includes newspapers, books, cards, stationary, and other print products. It also includes support services, such as data imaging, platemaking, and bookbinding.
- **Furniture manufacturing** – creates furniture products from wood, metal, glass and similar materials.
- **Electrical equipment, appliance, and component manufacturing** – creates electrical equipment, household appliances and electrical components.
- **Metal manufacturing** – includes iron, steel, aluminum, ferroalloy, aluminum products and mills.

ADDITIONAL INDUSTRIES IN MANUFACTURING

Manufacturing includes the following industries:

- **Transportation equipment manufacturing** – creates vehicles, ships, railroad stock, and products related to transport of goods and people.
- **Food manufacturing** – helps change livestock and agricultural products into consumable products.

- **Petroleum and coal products manufacturing** – uses processes which convert raw petroleum and coal into consumer products.
- **Computer and electronic equipment manufacturing** – creates computers, peripherals, semiconductors, electrical devices, measuring devices and similar electronic devices.
- **Apparel manufacturing** – encompasses two types of businesses: those that knit fabric and then cut and sew it into garments, and those that purchase fabric and then cut and sew it into garments.
- **Chemical manufacturing** – turns raw materials into soap, resins, pharmaceuticals, fertilizer, pesticides, and other usable products.
- **Plastics and rubber manufacturing** – transforms plastic and raw rubber into usable products.
- **Textile mills** – produces yarn and fabric.
- **Textile product mills** – produces textile products other than apparel.
- **Machinery manufacturing** – creates products that generate mechanical force, such as equipment related to mining, turbines and metal working.

JUST-IN-TIME, CONTINUOUS FLOW MANUFACTURING AND TAKT TIME

Just-in-time, or **JIT**, is lean manufacturing technique. It lowers costs and increases profit by reducing or eliminating excess inventory. During procurement, a purchased product is scheduled and received in such a way that inventory levels remain at almost zero.

Continuous flow manufacturing, or **CFM**, is a lean manufacturing technique. It holds that the manufacturing process should produce one piece of material at a time and at a rate determined by customer needs (i.e. takt). It normally includes the following characteristics: poka-yoke (a device or procedure that prevents defects or mistakes from moving to the next step), source inspection, self-checking, successive checks and total productive maintenance.

Takt time is part of lean manufacturing, specifically **continuous flow manufacturing (CFM)**.

> **Takt time** = available production time / rate of customer demand

In CFM, the single-piece flow of materials occurs in a rigid sequence of production steps with various techniques designed to minimize defects. This sequence should form a straight line or U-shaped cells.

INTERMITTENT MANUFACTURING, CUSTOM MANUFACTURING, AUTOMATED MANUFACTURING AND KAIZEN

Intermittent manufacturing produces only those goods necessary to **fulfill customer orders**, not to keep in stock. It normally includes the following characteristics: flexible production facilities, products made in small amounts, process-arrangement of machines and equipment, unbalanced workloads, large in-process inventory and highly skilled workers.

- Custom manufacturing produces goods for a specific person or purpose.
- Automated manufacturing relies on automated machines and equipment to create products. It is closely associated with factory production. Characteristics of automated manufacturing include the following: short lead times, product simplifications, better quality and greater consistency.

- Kaizen is a Japanese word meaning continuous improvement. It involves management in improving operation; focuses on quality; and, uses PDCA improvement cycles. Although kaizen generally occurs on a slow, incremental basis, it can be sped up through a technique known as the kaizen blitz, which uses cross-functional teams to causes rapid workplace improvement.

RESOURCE MANAGEMENT, MANUFACTURING PROCESS MANAGEMENT AND ENTERPRISE RESOURCE PLANNING

- **Resource management** is responsible for identifying and providing the resources necessary to carry out organizational functions. Resources encompass money, personnel, inventory, human skills, equipment, machinery, and information technology. One aspect of resource management is human resources, which allocates personnel to various department and jobs.
- **Manufacturing process management** determines the methods and processes by which products are manufactured. Its goal is increasing efficiency by reducing lead times, using smaller inventories, and reducing production time. Manufacturing process managers often seek more efficient alternatives to the current production process.
- **Enterprise resource planning**, or **ERP**, integrates all business functions and manages the flow of information between those functions and people within the organization and between the organization and its stakeholders. This information includes both external and internal resources, such as human resources, tangible assets, manufacturing, financial assets and materials. ERP often relies on specialized software.

FEDERAL REGULATIONS AND PRODUCT RECALL

Safety and health are regulated by the following federal agencies:

- **Occupational Health and Safety Administration (OSHA)** – enforces worker safety regulations such as eye and ear protection, fire protection and equipment operation.
- **Food and Drug Administration (FDA)** – regulates new products released to the public, especially food, cosmetics, pharmaceutical drugs and health supplements.
- **US Consumer Product Safety Commission (CPSC)** – protects consumers against any products that pose unreasonable injury risks.
- **Environmental Protection Agency (EPA)** – enforces federal laws protecting land, air and water.
- **US Department of Agriculture** – regulates meat, poultry and eggs.

A **product recall** occurs when a company requests that consumers return a defective or potentially harmful batch or production run of a product. It is done to limit liability and prevent bad publicity. Product recalls can be made either voluntarily or at the compulsion of consumer protection laws or federal agencies.

5S PROGRAMS, TOTAL PRODUCTIVE MAINTENANCE AND SMED

5S programs are structured around five basic principles, all of which start with the letter S:

1. **Sort** – separate out and eliminate unnecessary items.
2. **Straighten** – put all items in their proper places.
3. **Scrub** – clean the workplace.
4. **Systematize** – standardize a routine for cleaning and checking.
5. **Sustain** – carry out and improve on previous four steps

The goals of 5S programs are organizing the workplace, eliminating muda (Japanese for waste), creating standardized conditions and keeping discipline.

Total productive maintenance, or **TPM**, increases equipment effectiveness by implementing coordinated group activities and involving all operators in machine inspections, routine maintenance and repair.

Single Minute Exchange of Die, or **SMED**, increases production efficiency by drastically reducing setup change times—or the length of time required to changeover production machinery. It divides changes into two conditions: external setup operations, which include the changeover activities which can be performed prior to shutting down machinery, and internal setup operations, which include the changeover activities which must be performed while the machinery is shut down.

SUPPLY CHAIN MANAGEMENT

Supply chain management, or **SCM**, oversees the entire production process, including raw material acquisition, inventory maintenance, manufacturing of goods and services and their delivery to consumers. SCM encompasses the network of businesses involved in this process. At the organizational level, SCM personnel are responsible for handling supply chain interactions, supplier relationships and business processes. They may use specialized software capable of managing inventory, good receipts, the warehouse, suppliers and sourcing, processing customer requirements and purchases orders, and using integration technology to carry out electronic transactions with supply chain partners. SCM also conducts forecasting and consumption analysis, which seeks to find a balance between supply and demand, make business processes more efficient and predict future needs.

LABELING REQUIREMENTS, WARRANTY AND CONSUMER PROTECTION LAWS

Labeling requirements are imposed by federal agencies, such as the FDA, Federal Trade Commission, and Department of Agriculture. Labels are intended to **educate the consumer** on the contents and characteristics of the product or service before it is purchased.

A **warranty** is a promise between the seller and buyer. The seller promises that the product will meet or fulfill certain conditions, and if it fails to meet these conditions, the buyer may seek some promised remediation. Warranties can be either **expressed** (the seller openly acknowledges the warranty) or **implied** (it exists regardless of whether or not the seller acknowledges it). Examples of implied warranties include warrant of merchantability and warranty of fitness for a particular purpose.

Consumer protection laws protect consumers against harmful or unlawful business practices, and prevent fraudulent businesses from gaining an unfair competitive advantage.

TRADE SECRET, PATENT, COPYRIGHT, AND TRADEMARK

- A **trade secret** is **confidential information** through which **a business gains a competitive advantage**. Access to trade secrets is generally very restricted. They can include instruments, designs, formulas, practices and similar types of data.
- A **patent** is an exclusive right that allows inventors to **protect their inventions** from being copied. A patent is granted by the government in exchange for public disclosure of the invention so that others may use and make it with the patent owner's permission. Once the patent expires, anyone can copy it legally.

- A **copyright** is an exclusive right that **protects expression of an idea**. It prevents anyone from copying, distributing, or adapting an original work except its creator. Copyrights are seldom registered; rather, they come about once the work is created, and apply for a limited time period.
- A **trademark** is a **unique sign** developed and used by a business, such as a company logo. By stamping products with its trademark, the business can distinguish them from competitor products.

Tools in Manufacturing

MANUFACTURING TOOLS AND EQUIPMENT

Manufacturing uses many different tools to create and finish items. Some of these include:

- **Micrometer** – a tool for measuring small components with great precision
- **Milling machine** – this removes excess material from an item with a rotary cutting tool, smoothing the surface
- **Lathe** – this is used for shaping materials such as wood or metal. It rotates and can be used for drilling, cutting, and sanding, among other operations.
- **Jig** – a jig holds a tool in position for precise work
- **Fixture** – this is similar to a jig but secures a workpiece instead of a tool
- **Saw** – several different types of saws can be used in manufacturing, from heavy duty circular saw to a jigsaw or miter saw for fine work
- **Drill** – a drill press or other drilling tool can be used to cut holes in manufactured products
- **Welding machine** – this is frequently needed in manufacturing, to join metal parts together
- **Computer numerical control (CNC) machines** – this is an automated method for manufacturing. The CNC machine is programmed with coded instructions and controls the manufacturing machines to go through the entire manufacturing process.

USE OF MANUFACTURING TOOLS AND EQUIPMENT

To properly use manufacturing tools and equipment, it is important to understand how to work with them. For example, a micrometer is a very precise tool but is useless if one does not know how to read it. A component is placed against one side of the micrometer and a screw is tightened until it just touches the other side of the component. Then the value can be read. For many of the machines, materials must be securely fastened and safety equipment used. For automated equipment, the user must know how to program the machine so that it successfully runs the other machines.

MAINTENANCE OF MANUFACTURING TOOLS AND EQUIPMENT

Tools and equipment should undergo routine inspection and maintenance. Parts can become loose, blades can become dull, and dust and debris can collect in crevices. All of these can lead to manufacturing mistakes or operator harm. Tools and equipment should be regularly **cleaned** and **stored** properly. Power tools should be tested from time to time to make sure they are working properly. Any loose parts should be tightened and dull blades sharpened as needed. Danger items like frayed cords should be replaced.

SAFETY PROTOCOLS FOR MANUFACTURING TOOLS AND EQUIPMENT

Many manufacturing tools involve sharp blades or heavy, moving parts. Additionally, many of them are sanding off tiny pieces of wood or metal that can become airborne. Welding creates dangerous sparks. So it is vital to be properly prepared for working with these tools. This may involve wearing eye and hearing protection, non-slip (and possibly steel-toed) shoes, and keeping hair secured so it cannot be caught in a machine. For welding, a full protective face shield may be required. Operators should be trained on how to use the machines and what safety precautions to take. A safety inspector may visit from time to time to ensure that all are following safety protocols.

FINISHING, HARDENING, ANNEALING, NORMALIZING AND TEMPERING

- **Finishing** involves changing or coating the surface of a material in order to protect or beautify it. For instance, wooden decks are often coated with sealant as a protection from the elements.

44

- **Hardening** increases the hardness of a metal by heating and then rapidly cooling it. This increases internal stresses and, thereby, increases the metal's strength (resistance to deformation) while making it more brittle and reducing its toughness.
- **Annealing** softens a metal by heating and then slowly cooling it. This lessens internal stresses and, thereby, decreases the metal's brittleness and increases its toughness, malleability and ductility (its ability to be shaped, stamped and worked on further).
- **Tempering** is a heat treatment that increases the metal's toughness, decreases its hardness and cracking, and makes it more malleable and ductile.
- **Normalizing** is a heat treatment that returns the metal to its near-equilibrium state. It strikes a balance between strength and hardness.

CASTING, FORMING, SEPARATING, CONDITIONING AND ASSEMBLING

- **Casting** involves pouring a molten or liquid material (such as metal, concrete, plaster or clay) into a mold, and then letting it solidify into the shape determined by the mold. Casting is useful for forming complex shapes.
- **Forming** involves shaping a material using a die and external force. For instance, a person can shape a piece of clay by forming it around a metal cylinder.
- **Separating** involves removing excess material from an object in order to create size and shape. For instance, scissors can cut into a piece of fabric and, thereby, alter its size and shape.
- **Conditioning** involves applying heat, pressure or chemical reactions in order to change the properties of a material. For instance, pottery is baked as means of hardening it.
- **Assembling** involves fastening, bonding, or otherwise joining two pieces together, either permanently or temporarily. For instance, pieces of a plastic model are often glued together.

COMPUTER-AIDED MANUFACTURING AND ROBOTICS

Computer-aided manufacturing, or **CAM**, relies on computer software to **augment the manufacturing process** in some way. Its goal is increasing the efficiency, accuracy, consistency and speed with which products are created. CAM software may guide the tools and machinery that create the products, or it may help coordinate management, planning and other plant operations. CAM can control every step in the production process, from the processing of raw materials to their conversion into consumable products.

Robotics is an aspect of computer-aided manufacturing. Robots are capable of **automating certain manufacturing tasks** and are most prevalent with the automobile manufacturing industry. The most common manufacturing application for robots is materials handling, which involves moving materials and components with the factory. The second most common application is spot welding. More recently, robots have started performing lighter tasks, such as parts installation, packaging (e.g., foods and electronics), and service jobs (e.g., automatic tellers and checkouts).

Manufacturing Materials

WOOD

Wood is used heavily within the manufacturing industries, which uses a variety of natural wood and engineered wood products, such as plywood. Plywood is also formed from sheets of timber glued together. It possesses strong resistance to breaking, shrinkage, warping and cracking. Plywood can be made from softwood, such as pine and fir, or hardwood such as birch. Softwood plywood is used prominently in furniture and house construction, including walls, floors, roofs, fences and wind bracing panels. Hardwood plywood is very strong and resistant, and is used for the most demanding construction applications, such as heavily-trafficked floors, scaffolding, concrete formwork system panels, etc. Wood products are often less expensive and better for the environment than other materials, such as steel or concrete.

MASONRY MATERIALS

Masonry materials include bricks, concrete blocks, stone, marble, travertine, limestone, glass, stucco, tile and granite. In masonry, these materials are stacked and bound together into structures. The binding material is known as mortar. Masonry construction has very high compressive strength (the ability to support weight vertically), but lacks in tensile strength (the ability to withstand twisting and stretching). It is resistant to heat, fire, and projectile impact, but is susceptible to weather wear and requires a strong foundation to support its weight. Masonry uses the following tools:

- **Masonry trowel** – used to level, shape, and spread mortar or concrete.
- **Joint filler** – a compressible material, such as rubber, that is used to fill and keep dry the joints between structural members.
- **Hawk** – holds the mortar or joint compound as it is being applied.
- **Bricklayers hammer** – used during bricklaying.
- **Bull float** – used to smooth the surface of concrete.

PLASTICS

Plastics are a synthetic polymer created from **petroleum and natural gas**. There are two basic types of plastics: **thermoplastics**, which can be remolded numerous times, and **thermosetting plastics**, which undergo irreversible curing. Numerous everyday products are created from plastics, such as grocery bags, storage bags, bottles, jars, food packaging, milk jugs, flooring, window frames, film, polyester fibers, textiles, pipes, gutters, show curtains, lights, straws, household appliances, furniture, siding, dish ware, utensils, tooth brushes, automobile components, and many more. Plastics are fairly inexpensive and easily produced; however, they pose several environmental concerns. They emit pollutants such as greenhouse gases and accumulate in landfills and ocean gyres. Because they are created from a nonrenewable resource (petroleum), their cost will rise as the resource is depleted, and the cost of other petroleum-based products, such as gasoline, will also rise.

METAL ALLOYS

Metal alloys have many different manufacturing applications, ranging from construction to surgical equipment. One of the most commonly used metals is steel, which is produced by alloying iron with carbon—though other materials may be used as well. The tensile strength, hardness, and ductility of steel depend on the amount of carbon within it. Increased levels of carbon increase the alloys hardness while decreasing its ductility (i.e. the alloy is less resistant to twisting and warping). Long steel is used in the creation of high-strength wire, bridges, and building structures. Flat carbon steel is used in major appliances as well as automobiles and boats. Stainless steel is used in

46

mechanical equipment, surgical equipment, and cutting tools. Other common manufacturing metals include aluminum alloys, which feature prominently in the aerospace, shipbuilding, cycling and automotive industries.

COMPOSITES

A **composite** consists of multiple materials that differ widely in their properties and characteristics. Composites can be naturally-occurring, such as wood, or manmade, such as engineered wood, fiberglass and concrete. Fiberglass combines plastic and thin fibers of glass, which provide structural reinforcement. It is lightweight while possessing good tension and compression strength. Fiberglass is used prominently in the manufacturing of storage tanks, pipes, houses, cars, and boats. Concrete is used in a variety of construction applications, but poses several environmental concerns. For instance, paved roadways are one of the major causes of the urban heat island effect, in which a city tends to be hotter than its surrounding area. Concrete surfaces also lead to increased surface runoff, which causes erosion. Additionally, the manufacture of concrete releases carbon dioxide, a greenhouse gas.

Manufacturing Processes and Quality Control

MANUFACTURING PROCESSES

Manufacturing of materials is a multi-step process involving many different techniques and machines. Some of these include:

- **Separating** – when raw materials are mined, they must be separated into their chemical components so they can be used. There are multiple separation processes, depending on what is being separated (e.g., liquids or solids).
- **Casting** – a substance is heated and poured as a liquid into a mold, where it solidifies in the desired size and shape.
- **Molding** – molding is similar to casting but can include not only pouring liquid in a mold, but also soft solids that can be shaped.
- **Forming** – this is a method typically applied to metals to shape them. There are many different ways of forming, such as extruding and forging.
- **Conditioning** – this involves removing defects from metal with a variety of methods (chemical, thermal, or mechanical).
- **Assembling** – the materials are put together so that they can be used in construction.
- **Finishing** – this is one of the final stages in preparing materials and may involve polishing, painting, or dyeing a product.
- **Inspection** – before a product can be sold, it undergoes a quality check.

AUTOMATED SYSTEMS

Increasingly, manufacturing uses a multitude of automated systems, increasing efficiency and accuracy. Some of these include:

- **Robotics** – manufacturing can be improved in both productivity and precision by use of robots. They can be programmed to perform tasks at each stage of production and can work nonstop rather than in shifts like human workers. It can cut costs and simplify procedures.
- **Artificial intelligence** – this can be used to evaluate a manufacturing process, looking for ways to improve efficiency or cut costs in materials, as well as exploring new products and methods.
- **Computer-integrated manufacturing (CIM)** – this involves using computers for the entire manufacturing process. This improves efficiency and cuts down on errors.

MANUFACTURING QUALITY CONTROL PROCEDURES

It is important to check products before distribution to avoid defects or safety issues. There are several steps for quality control:

- First, it is necessary to **define** the product standards so quality can be tested. This includes methods of testing and the number of products from each batch that will be tested.
- Employees must be **trained** in these standards and a system of **reporting** must be established. Additionally, procedures must be established for what to do if defects are found.
- Tools like **statistical process control (SPC)** can track data to identify problem areas and propose solutions.

Construction

CAREERS

- **Civil engineering technicians** assist engineers, architects, and planners in planning, designing, locating and constructing buildings. They estimate material costs and amounts, perform quality control inspections on materials, and conduct suitability tests on soil, concrete, and building materials.
- **Building inspectors** ensure that the structure complies with all applicable codes, such as building, plumbing, electrical and mechanical codes.
- **Safety specialists** maintain safe environments within construction areas. They make sure that hazardous waste is disposed of properly, perform routine inspections on equipment and scaffolding, conduct safety education classes, consult with managers and engineers, and write safety reports.
- **Site managers** ensure that a building project does not exceed budget or the time schedule. They handle any delays, problems, and communication between parties. They are also involved in quality control.
- **Contractors** supervise the entire construction process including the construction of work spaces, homes, schools and other buildings. They write contracts, make bids, estimate costs, perform scheduling, manage labor and ensure safe storage of equipment and construction materials.

TYPES OF CONSTRUCTION

- **Light construction** describes **light frame construction**, which is limited to floor and ceiling joists, rafters and wood stud walls. Light construction is mostly residential; however, it can apply to smaller commercial buildings that do not exceed two stories.
- **Heavy construction** applies to any construction that uses cranes, excavators, and other **large machines**.
- **Civil construction** applies to the construction of **social infrastructure**, such as bridges, dams, irrigation projects, air field surfacing and grazing, sewer and water lines, highways, roadways, sidewalks, curbs, and railroads. In some definitions, heavy construction and civil construction are combined into a single category.
- **Industrial construction** applies to the construction of factories, manufacturing facilities, power plants and processing plants. It requires extensive planning and teams of people with specialized skills in design and construction. Big industrial corporations carry out the majority of industrial construction projects.

BUILDING CODES

Building codes are a set of **construction standards** that determine the manner in which structures are built and repaired. Building codes are established and enforced at the municipal level. They regulate building materials and workmanship quality, such as electrical wiring, sanitation facilities, fire and safety equipment, and similar building aspects. City officials conduct building inspections in order to ensure compliance. If compliance is met, the official will issue a certificate of occupancy, also known as an occupancy permit. This document explains the proper use of the building in sheltering people, animals and property. For instance, in a single-family home, many building codes require an occupancy separation between the living space and the garage, in which flammable substances are kept. If a building has multiple uses (e.g., residential and commercial), building codes usually require that builders place fire barriers, such as fire doors and fire stops, between individual occupancies.

FEDERAL ENVIRONMENTAL REGULATIONS

- The **Clean Air Act of 1970** regulates the **emission of six pollutants**—carbon monoxide, ozone, lead, sulfur dioxide, nitrogen dioxide, and particulate matter—according to the limits established by the national ambient air quality standards, or NAAQS.
- The Clean Air Act Amendment of 1990 regulates 189 additional toxic air pollutants.
- The **Clean Water Act**, or **CWA**, regulates the **quality and pollution content of all navigable waters** in the US, including lakes, rivers, streams, wetlands, ponds, territorial seas and every other small or large body of water. Point source of water pollutions—such has construction sites, factories, and plants—must acquire a national pollution discharge eliminations system, or NPDES, permit through their state regulatory agencies.
- The **Wilderness Act** established the **national wilderness preservation system**, and forbids any road construction, settlement, mechanized transportation, or other forms of development within the boundaries of the system.
- The **Resource Conservation and Recovery Act**, or **RCRA**, regulates **industrial waste** and the manner in which it is generated, stored, treated, transported and disposed of.
- The **Endangered Species Act**, or **ESA**, protects **threatened or endangered species** and their ecosystems on public and private land.

PERMITS

Permits empower their holders to **carry out certain development and construction activities**. Permits are usually granted by a **government agency**, such as the zoning board of appeals, which usually conduct a review of some sort before agreeing to the permit. There are many different types of permits. **Conditional-use permits**, also known as special-use permits, allow for land uses in zones where such land uses may be forbidden under existing ordinances but is generally considered for the common good. For instance, a planner may acquire a conditional-use permit in order to build residencies in an industrial zone. **Nonconforming use permits** are generally granted to structures that do not conform to current zoning ordinances because they were built before the ordinances were passed. **Variance permits** enable a landowner to use his property in a way that directly conflicts with zoning laws. A right of way is a granted by a private landowner. It empowers an agency or individual to use the landowner's property to build or maintain a road, pathway, or utility line.

ZONING

Zoning ordinances determine **the manner in which land can be used in a particular community**. They are designed to maintain public safety and promote public welfare. They are established and enforced by city governments via enabling acts. Zoning ordinances generally divide the community into multiple land-use districts and regulate district use, district size, the kinds of buildings that can be built, building height, setback distance (distance between the structure and streets and walkways), architecture and density (land to structure ratio). Urban areas tend to be high-density. Low density ordinances increase the space between buildings, but contribute to urban sprawl. Most zoning districts are classified as residential, industrial, commercial or agricultural. Zoning ordinances normally contain general provisions, definitions, maps, zoning district delineation and guidelines for enforcement and administration.

ZONING METHODS

- **Euclidean zoning** divides a community into separate land use districts and then limits the kind of development which occurs within each district. Land use districts are designated according to the following uses: residential for single families, residential for multiple families, industrial, and commercial. A single district cannot mix land uses.
- **Euclidean II** zoning allows for mixed land uses within a single district.
- **Cumulative zoning** allows a single land use district to combine less intensive land uses, such as residential, with more intensive land uses, such as commercial. The only stipulation is that residences can only be mixed with light industrial uses (high-tech, warehouses, and other non-polluting industries). Heavy industrial uses must remain by themselves.
- **Exclusive**, or **non-cumulative, zoning** is the dominant contemporary zoning method. It forbids a land use district from incorporating any developments which do not conform to its designated use. Exclusive zoning allows for more excess room than cumulative zoning; consequently, existing businesses have more room for expansion.
- **Transect zoning** divides the development area into six zones. The first zone is the wilderness area. Each subsequent zone is progressively more urbanized. The sixth and final zone is the urban core. Transect-based ordinances encourage mixed land uses within districts, and regulate parking placement, street layout, building height, setback, façade and design.
- **Overlay zoning** superimposes a new zone on top of an existing land use zone and imposes additional requirements and standards.
- **Floating zones** are **unmapped** zoning districts. They enable municipalities to promote certain land uses (apartments, research campuses, etc.) without actually reserving an area of land for such a use.
- **Cluster zoning** imposes **strict density standards** on development, but allows flexibility in setting lot size, setback distances, various characteristics related to individual house lots, street layout, utility sites, and building placement. In cluster zoning, developers can reserve a single high-density area for residences, and leave large amounts of open space for uses such as agriculture, recreation, and preservation.

REZONING, UPZONING, DOWNZONING, VARIANCE AND EXTRATERRITORIAL JURISDICTION

- **Rezoning** is the act of changing the zoning classification of a land use district.
- **Upzoning** is a type of rezoning in which higher density developments are allowed within a land use district.
- **Downzoning** refers to two possible actions: reducing the intensity of development that is allowable within a specific land use district, or increasing the intensity of development so that higher order development is allowed within a land use district. When intensity is reduced, minimum lot sizes are often increased.
- **Variances** allow land uses within particular district that are otherwise forbidden under existing zoning ordinances. Variances are not allowed unless an area of land is caused considerable hardship without the land use.
- **Extraterritorial jurisdiction**, or **ETJ**, is the power of a municipality to enforce zoning ordinances outside its jurisdiction. It is granted by the state.

URBAN ANALYSIS

An **urban analysis** helps determine the kind of development that best fits a certain site. It considers the context and characteristics of a location and identifies the urban design strategies and concepts which are best suited for the construction project. There are six types of urban analysis:

- **Community** – examines census and demographic information, previous planning information from past projects, and the wants and needs of the general public.
- **Continuity** – examines the developments patterns (e.g., buildings that are unique to the community) and changes that have occurred within the community throughout its history.
- **Character** – examines a community's urban form, topography, views, open space, population centers, architectural character, streetscape, and environmental issues.
- **Connections** – determines the accessibility of a community by examining its streets, rights-of-way, parking, traffic problems, transit service, and bicycle and pedestrian services.
- **Regulations and ownership** – reviews and reassesses based on more localized requirements for construction in a portion of a city, such as a neighborhood. Ownership may be a concern in certain areas, such as features which are shared with neighbors or have unclear property definitions.
- **Economic and market setting** – examines the development within the scope of current economic and market trends.

CONSTRUCTION FINANCING

PRIVATE SOURCES

- Private equity comes from individuals and corporations.
- Banks provide loans for construction, such as mortgages. Investment banks offer equity financing.
- Credit companies offer equity financing.
- Real estate investment trusts are groups of developers, lenders and equity investors who pay out over 90 percent of their earnings so that they can avoid corporate income taxes.
- Pension funds provide both debt and equity financing.
- Life insurance companies provide both debt and equity financing.

PUBLIC SOURCES

- Tax increment financing is focused primarily on redevelopment and infrastructure, and it may assist developers as well.
- Special service and assessment areas are special tax districts in which new residents assume most of the financial burden.
- Historic tax credits are available for restoring certified historic structures.
- Tax-exempt bonds offer low-interest loans to industrial and low-income housing developers.
- Home investment partnership program funds are provided to municipalities, who give them to developers for the purposes of building affordable housing.

LAND USE REGULATION

- **Quota systems** place restrictions on the building permits that developers can acquire over a year. The restrictions include both the **number and type of permits**. Quota systems slow the future growth of communities and allow more time to assimilate existing growth. Quota systems are common in rapidly growing areas.
- **Moratorium** restricts or completely stops certain types of development until a more thorough plan can be developed and put in place. This plan must address the expansions of water, utilities, and other necessities.
- **Cost** is the property's value after improvements (i.e. buildings) have been added to it. Cost does not necessarily reflect the property's market value.
- **Cost-benefit analysis** is used to determine which proposed development will generate more value in the future. It compares the benefits and costs of each proposed development.

URBAN ANALYSIS

Economic and market setting analysis examines economic factors that may affect development. The factors include the current state and needs of the local real estate market; the existing market demand for certain land uses and land uses that need to be fulfilled (more office space, additional housing units, factories, etc.); available financing options (banks, tax credits, bonds, etc.); fiscal analysis of the community; and construction projects that are currently going on or have been recently approved.

Regulations and ownership examines zoning and land use regulations, design guidelines, and property ownership, including property boundaries, shapes, sizes and parcel distribution. Design guidelines include windows, doors, building types, signage, roof shapes, planting and other construction elements. Design guidelines are often set by the community, and can be determined by studying drawings and photographs.

CONSTRUCTION SITE MANAGEMENT

Managing a construction site involves the following tasks:

- Supervising, coordinating, and scheduling every design and construction process throughout the project's lifetime, from its inception to the final phases. This includes meeting with owners, engineers, architects and other important personnel.
- Determining the material, tools and labor requirements of the project. Finding the best way to acquire the necessary tools and materials, and overseeing their delivery. Hiring and dismissing workers if necessary.
- Estimating all costs necessary to complete the project.
- Choosing, hiring, and overseeing carpenters, plumbers, electricians, metalworkers, roofers and other specialty trade contractors.
- Ensuring the project stays on time and within budget.
- Overseeing site preparation, which involves clearing and excavating the land, building roads, landscaping and installing sewage systems.
- Overseeing building construction, which involves laying foundation and building the structural framework, floors, walls and roofs.
- Overseeing building system installation, such as fire suppression, electrical, HVAC, and plumbing systems.
- Ensuring compliance with building codes and any other regulations. Acquiring all required building permits and licenses. Scheduling required inspections.
- Ensuring worker safety.

CONSTRUCTION PROJECT INSPECTIONS

Before a building can receive an occupancy permit, it must receive the following inspections:

- **Public work inspections** – ensure compliance with government contracts. Public works include sewer systems, bridges, dams, highways, and streets for compliance with government regulation.
- **Building inspection** – ensures compliance with applicable building codes. It occurs in stages throughout the construction process. Building inspectors examine the following: building plans; soil, including the position and depth of the footings; the foundation after it has been poured; fire suppression system, including sprinklers, alarms, smoke control, and exits; and the completed building.
- **Electrical inspections** – ensure compliance with electrical codes and standards. The main panel, subpanels, junction boxes and all wiring must be completed before an inspection can take place.
- **Elevator inspections** – check all lifting and conveying devices.
- **Mechanical inspections** – check all systems and equipment related to heating, air conditioning, ventilation and refrigeration.
- **Plumbing inspections** – examine the layout of the piping, venting, backflow protection, and fixture settings. They ensure safe drinking water and sanitary waste disposal.

Engineering Principles in Construction

ENGINEERING TERMS AND CONCEPTS

With several different branches of engineering, there are a multitude of terms used by engineers. Some common terms and concepts include:

- **Capacitance** – an object's ability to hold charge.
- **Computer-aided design (CAD)** – using software to virtually create a design for a building or other object.
- **Deflection** – a measure of the displacement caused by a load on some structural element.
- **Density** – the mass per unit volume of a given substance.
- **Elasticity** – an object's ability to resume its original shape and size after being stretched or squeezed.
- **Faraday constant** – the amount of electric charge per mole of electrons.
- **Friction** – the force that creates resistance when two surfaces slide against each other.
- **International System of Units (SI)** – the universal system of measurement for length, mass, electric current, etc.
  - Length – meter
  - Mass – kilogram
  - Time – second
  - Amount of substance – mole
  - Thermodynamic temperature – kelvin
  - Electric current – ampere
  - Luminous intensity – candela
- **Resistivity** – a measure of how powerfully a material conducts (or resists) electrical current.
- **Safety Data Sheet (SDS)** – sometimes called Material Safety Data Sheet (MSDS) or Product Safety Data Sheet (PSDS), these documents give occupational safety and health information for jobsite safety when using particular materials or substances.
- **Shear strength** – a substance's ability to resist shear stress, or force that attempts to cause the substance to separate either horizontally or vertically.
- **Specific gravity** – the ratio of a substance's density to a given standard density (usually water or air).
- **Tensile strength** – the greatest amount of stress a substance can endure before breaking.
- **Torque** – a force that twists to rotate.

ENGINEERING PRINCIPLES IN CONSTRUCTION

Construction is dependent on engineering principles in great detail, from the materials used to the way they are put together. For instance, a material's **shear strength** and **tensile strength** must be calculated and weighed against the amount of weight and stress that will be placed on it. Materials are also chosen based on **resistivity** and **tension** to ensure endurance and safety. Concepts of **wind load** and **fluid dynamics** must be applied to ensure that a building can withstand the elements. Angles of roofs are pitched according to engineering calculations to best work in the region (e.g., more steeply sloped in regions with heavy snowfall and flatter in warmer regions).

STRUCTURES

- An **arch** is a structure that supports weight atop an open space, such as the top of a window. It normally has a semicircular shape but can also have a flat or pointed shape. Arches remove tensile stress and support the entire load as compressive stress.

- A **cantilever** is a projecting structure that receives support at only one end and carries a load at the other end. Examples include diving boards and balconies.
- A **suspension** is a structure that consists of cables supporting a horizontal beam, such as a suspension bridge. The cables are hung from a long, very strong steel cable that is attached to support columns. The structure is supported by tension in the cables and compression in the columns.
- A **truss** is a triangular structure formed by straight beams. A **node** is formed where the ends of the beams connect. The node is also where tensile or compressive forces are absorbed. In a planar truss, the beams form a two-dimensional plan. In a space truss, the beams create a three-dimensional structure.

Tools Used in Construction

CONSTRUCTION DEVICES AND TOOLS

Construction requires a vast array of equipment, ranging from simple measuring tape to heavy machinery.

Measuring devices include:

- **Tape measures** – there are a variety of tape measures, from small tapes to check brief dimensions to long tapes that can measure hundreds of feet.
- **Speed squares** or **protractors** – these are used for making accurate angles, such as roofs and corners.
- **Laser measures** – instead of a manual measuring tape, distance can be measured with a handheld laser device. This is especially useful for long distances, as several hundred feet can be accurately measured without moving.
- **Measuring wheels** – these roll along the ground to measure distance. They are useful for walking a site to check measurements. Some wheels are manual and some are digital and can be used to create a virtual map of an area, complete with dimensions and calculations.
- **Levels** – these are used to make sure construction is perfectly aligned. Levels check both level (horizontal) and plumb (vertical).

Hand tools include:

- **Hammers, screwdrivers, nails, screws, and bolts** – for joining wood and other materials.
- **Trowels and jointers** – for masonry work.
- **Saws** – several different types of saws may be helpful on construction sites, such as handsaws and hacksaws, depending on the material to be cut.
- **Wrenches** and **pliers** – wrenches can be used not only for turning bolts but also for gripping slick pipes and other objects to hold them steady, and pliers also hold objects in places, as well as cutting or bending wire.
- **Chisels** and **files** – these tools can be used on a variety of materials, such as wood and metal, to remove imperfections or layers like paint and to smooth the surface.
- **Utility knives** – these are used for marking wood, scraping, or cutting.

Power tools include:

- **Saws** – there are a variety of power saws such as circular saws and jigsaws for heavy duty cutting.
- **Drills** – power drills are frequently used on the job for drilling holes, installing screws, and tightening nuts.
- **Nail guns** – these are much more efficient than a manual hammer for projects that require many nails.
- **Sander** – a power sander quickly removes layers of paint and varnish, smoothing the surface to prepare it to be finished.
- **Air compressors** – these are used for powering certain other tools such as nail guns and jackhammers.

Heavy equipment includes:

- **Backhoes** – these are primarily for digging or excavating, with a large bucket that scoops dirt and rocks.
- **Excavators** – these are also diggers. They are typically on tracks rather than wheels and can be used for demolition, mining, and drilling, along with digging trenches and holes.
- **Graders** – these are equipped with a wide, flat blade behind the front wheels that drags along the ground to smooth a site.
- **Bulldozers** – similar to graders, these have a large blade at the front, but it is for heavy moving rather than precision grading. Bulldozers are used for clearing rubble, rocks, and dirt off of a site.
- **Dump trucks** – backhoes and other machines empty dirt and rubble into dump trucks to be hauled offsite.
- **Skid steers** – a skid steer is one of the smallest machines you may see at a construction site. It is useful for tight quarters and small loads and its lift arms can be equipped with various attachments for digging, moving, and transporting.

USE OF CONSTRUCTION TOOLS AND EQUIPMENT

Simply having the proper tools for construction is not sufficient without knowledge of how to use them. While many are straightforward, some require training. For **measuring devices**, it is vital to be precise. This is one reason that laser measuring devices are useful, particularly in long distances, since one end of a measuring tape may slip or the altitude may change. A laser device gives a precise, digital reading and can calculate area and volume. Some measuring tools are more challenging to use, such as a protractor or speed square. This can be used with the attached level to find the pitch of a roof. It can also be used to mark angles on a board by marking a vertical angle and then swinging it until the desired angle on the speed square touches the edge of the board.

Many tools have **overlapping functions** or **multiple options**. For instance, there are many types of hammers, depending on the use. The mallet may be steel or rubber, flat or rounded, circular or hexagonal or square. They can be used not only for driving nails, but also shaping metal, dislodging parts, or separating boards. It is important to know which tool is ideal for each function.

Most heavy equipment requires **training** and often **certifications**. Each machine operates differently and an operator must know how to use the various functions, as well as being aware of its particular dangers and required maintenance.

MAINTENANCE OF CONSTRUCTION TOOLS AND EQUIPMENT

Like any equipment, construction tools must be treated properly. **Hand tools** should be stored neatly and in a building or secure container (such as a truck toolbox). While some tools can be stored loose in a toolbag or box, others such as laser measurers should be treated with more care to avoid harm. Most tools have metal parts that are subject to rust so if they become wet they should be cleaned and dried. Tools with joints should be lubricated regularly. Tools with blades should be sharpened regularly. Extra batteries should be carried for tools that require them.

Power tools need additional care, storing them carefully to avoid damage to cords and motors. Tools should be fully cooled before puttting away. Some tools require regular calibration to maintain accuracy. Batteries should be replaced as needed.

Heavy equipment requires regular, continual maintenance. Machines should be cleaned at the end of the day to avoid buildup of dirt and debris. At the beginning of the day, before use, machines should receive a visual inspection. Regular tests should be performed to check operation. Oil changes, tire/track inspection, lubrication, and calibration are other routine preventive measures that should be taken.

SAFETY ISSUES

If tools and equipment are not properly maintained, they could become a safety hazard. A malfunctioning machine could cause serious harm. It is also important to follow safety precautions in using any tool. Even a simple hand tool can cause harm if used incorrectly, and of course large machines could cause serious harm if operated incorrectly or without proper safeguards. A company or jobsite should have specific safety protocols to follow, posted on walls in a building or delivered to workers on a jobsite.

USING CONSTRUCTION TOOLS AND EQUIPMENT SAFELY

Construction sites typically have a safety officer who performs inspections and makes sure all on the site are following safety protocol:

- Everyone should be wearing proper **personal protective equipment (PPE)**, which may include hard hats, reflective vests, safety glasses, and steel-toed boots.
- **Fall protection equipment** should be in place (lanyards, lifelines, etc.) to keep workers from falling while working at heights or over holes. Guardrails or safety nets may also be set up.
- **Hazard communication** should be in place to warn workers about potential hazardous substances and proper handling of them with a Material Safety Data Sheet (MSDS).
- **Ladders** and **scaffolding** are some of the leading sites of construction accidents. Scaffolding should be inspected daily and should include safeguards such as guardrails. Tools should be secured before climbing and never left on a scaffold. Fall arrest systems should be employed. When climbing a ladder, a worker should maintain three points of contact at all times (such as both feet and one hand). Ladders should be placed carefully to avoid slipping and tied off if needed. Tools should be carried in a tool bag rather than in hands.

Construction Materials

STEEL AND PLUMBING SYSTEM

Steel possesses better **compressive strength** and far more **tensile strength** than concrete; however, steel is also far **more expensive**. Steel is stronger and more resistant to rust than most other metals—though its strength depends heavily on the materials with which it has been alloyed. Steel provides the support skeleton for most large buildings, such as skyscrapers. It also reinforces masonry walls, and is used in railroad track construction. The steel industry is one of the leading producers of greenhouse gases.

The **plumbing system** within a building consists of **water supply lines**, which provide usable water, and **drain and vent lines**, which remove waste. Water supply pipes are created from nontoxic materials, such as plastic, brass, or copper. Drain pipes are usually created from plastic, steel, cast-iron, or lead. Lead is toxic and, therefore, cannot be used in water supply lines. Pipes are often joined using a welder, which creates a bond via some molten material.

WOOD AND CONCRETE

Wood is a common building material. In construction, it is found in both its natural state and as an engineered product, such as glue laminated timber. Glue laminated timber consists of several layers of timber glued together into a single, large beam. It is stronger than most forms of solid timber, and is capable of serving as a support beam within a structure. Engineered wood requires smaller diameter trees, which can be farmed. This preserves natural forests.

Concrete is made from cement, cementitious materials, water and chemicals. It is inexpensive compared to other building materials, and is used in the construction of roads, parking lots, foundations, and block walls. Concrete can carry very heavy loads (high compressive strength), but has a very low resistance to stretching and twisting (low tensile strength); consequently, concrete structures are often reinforced with steel. Concrete is also very susceptible to thermal expansion, which causes it to shrink and crack as it ages.

Building, Maintaining, and Repairing Structures

STRUCTURAL DETERMINATION

Urban development plans lay out the construction strategies for **high-density urban development**. Most construction incorporates the following elements: public spaces; restoration of old neighborhoods; compact design, which connects commercial and residential areas; good transit systems; walkways that encourage walking and bike riding; infill development rather than expansion; land use that improves the health and economic well-being of the poor; and affordable housing.

Suburban development plans lay out the construction strategies for **low-density, homogenous suburban areas**, which normally include single-family detached dwellings, office parks, retail centers, employment centers, and recreation areas. These plans facilitate automobile usage and allow for curving streets, lawns, garages, driveways and parking lots

Capital facilities plans lay out the construction strategies for **roads, bridges and sewer lines** within a community over a 5 to 6 year period.

Parks and open space plans lay out the construction strategies for **park and open space systems**, such as play grounds, parks, athletic facilities, community gardens and recreation parks.

ELECTRICAL WIRING SYSTEM

Electrical wires usually consist of conductors that are twisted together and encased in insulating material. The voltage requirements determine the number of conductors that must be twisted together in a single wire. Two common conductors used in electrical systems are copper and aluminum. **Copper** is more expensive but poses fewer problems than aluminum. Copper is the most popular choice in residential structures. **Aluminum** is lighter, cheaper, and better suited to larger wires and circuits. In today's electrical systems, insulation is made from synthetic materials, such as thermoplastic and polymers that act and feel like rubber. The latter has an extremely high resistance to moisture, making it ideal for industrial and utility usage. According to most building codes, electrical systems must be fire-stopped, with sealing closing opening and joints, or fireproofed, which involves increasing the resistance of materials to fire. A building's electrical system includes junction boxes, through which electrical power can be rerouted.

Information and Communication

Drafting

TOOLS AND MATERIALS FOR SKETCHING AND TECHNICAL DRAWING

It is important to be prepared both to make hand sketches and to make computer drawings. Typically one first creates a simple sketch to visualize something (top view, front view, side vies, and 3D isometric view). Then the technical drawing can more easily be created.

Some tools and materials that are used for sketching include:

- **Paper** (it is handy to keep a sketchpad, but sheets of plain paper or graph paper will work as well)
- **Mechanical pencil** and **eraser**
- **Technical pens** (these are available in a variety of widths)
- **Ruler**
- **Compass**
- **Drawing board** (many people sketch without this, but it is useful for securing paper and ruler; preventing slipping, smudging, or tearing; and includes small holes for the compass)

For technical drawings, computer-aided design (CAD) programs are used. This offers greater accuracy and ability to visualize a design, as well as ease in changing details without creating a whole new drawing.

PRODUCING AND INTERPRETING DRAWINGS

There are a variety of types of technical drawings, as different types are needed for different situations. It is important to be able to create and understand these various types. Some of the common types include:

- **Multiview drawing** (this uses orthogonal projection to show a design from different 2D perspectives).
- **Sectional view** (this "cuts" into the image to show an interior part of the design).
- **Pictorial representation** (a 3D image of the design).
- **Detail drawing** (a small part of the overall design that is drawn separately in a larger scale to show detail).
- **Assembly drawing** (an image that shows all the design components in their final, connected form to show how the finished product will look).
  Working Drawings, Presentation Drawings, and Models

Drawings and models are created for a variety of needs, such as residential, community, and business, and can differ according to their purpose. A **working drawing**, sometimes called a blueprint, has necessary information for construction such as dimensions and needed materials. **Presentation drawings** are made for the client rather than the contractor and are meant to show general design, such as a house floor plan. A **model** is a 3D representation of a design that can give an overall view of a structure as well as allowing a viewer to zoom in for detail. Models are especially helpful in large commercial structures with many components.

62

SCALES AND DIMENSIONING IN TECHNICAL DRAWINGS

Drawings are created to a specific **scale**. This can vary, depending on the size of the building and of the drawing. It is important to be able to both accurately calculate and notate the desired scale and to be able to interpret the listed scale on a drawing so that materials can be ordered and assembled accurately. Scales are written with the drawing measurement followed by the actual measurement. For example:

- A 1:10 scale means that the actual building is ten times the size of the drawing, or the measurements on the drawing are 1/10 of the actual measurements.
- A 1:48 scale means that the actual building is 48 times the size of the drawing. This scale is common for architectural drawings: one foot of a building is pictured as ¼ inch on a drawing.

For hand drawing, engineering scales can be used: similar to rulers but often triangular or beveled rather than flat.

Another component of technical drawings is **dimensioning**. Certain measurements are included directly on the drawings, such as lengths, widths, and angles on a blueprint.

SOFTWARE FOR TECHNICAL DRAWING

While hand drawing is still used, particularly for early sketches, there are many available types of **software** that can be used for drawing. These are often called **CAD (computer-aided design) programs**. These range from simple 2D capabilities that give a basic outline to complex 3D software that outlines every tiny component of a building. Most CAD programs include a **library** of symbols to specify various electrical, HVAC, and other components of a building. Walls can quickly be built and shifted by typing dimensions and angles rather than dragging a mouse to draw. **Scales** can be preset. One can navigate from one **view** to another: working on a 2D view of a single room, then switching to view a 3D model of the entire building.

Graphic Design and Photography

PRINCIPLES OF GRAPHIC DESIGN

There are many principles of graphic design to create images that catch a viewer's attention:

- **Perspective** – one key element of graphic design is perspective, which adds depth and directs the viewer's eye to the focal point.
- **Shading** – this involves adjusting the level of darkness to aid in depth perception.
- **Balance** – the various elements in an image have a visual "weight" (how greatly they attract the eye) and if too much weight is on one side or element of the image it can feel unbalanced. A well-designed image should be balanced in one of several ways:
  - **Symmetrical balance** – an image is symmetrically balanced when it has even visual weight on both left and right (vertical symmetry), or both top and bottom (horizontal symmetry).
  - **Asymmetrical balance** – sometimes the elements are not distributed evenly, but are still balanced. For instance, a large element in the upper left corner may be balanced by a smaller but significant element in the lower right corner. Asymmetrical balance often utilizes contrast in color (dark vs. light) and scale.
  - **Radial balance** – some images such as a sun or mandala have radial balance: the weight spreads out from a central point.
- **Proportion** – the human eye is drawn to things that are well proportioned and disturbed by things that are out of proportion. When proportion is used well, a design is said to be harmonious. This does not mean that everything must be the same size. Sometimes one element is intentionally given a different proportion to emphasize it, like moving one figure to the foreground by making it larger than the rest.
- **Harmony** – this refers to the arrangement of colors, shapes, etc., in a visually pleasing manner. It combines the principles above to create an overall effect that the viewer is drawn to.

ELEMENTS OF GRAPHIC DESIGN

Graphic design has several basic **elements** that should be considered:

- **Line** – lines can be used to direct the eye of the viewer, add weight to balance an image, or adjust the mood (heavy, dark lines can give an oppressive sense while light, soft lines can convey lightness or happiness).
- **Form** – a form is a shape in an image. These forms can be geometric or organic. A **geometric** form is typically a recognizable shape such as square, triangle, or circle. An **organic** form may be something like a flower, tree, or abstract doodle. The shapes that are selected can suggest various ideas like stability, freedom, power, or joy.
- **Space** – it is very important to make careful use of space in graphic design. An image should never be cluttered or visually overwhelming. The designer can communicate through space, such as placing two elements close together, surrounded by space, to show their link, or separating them to show distance.

- **Color** – color schemes should be thoughtfully selected. Different colors—and particularly different color combinations—convey different emotions or ideas. Colors chosen from opposite sides of the color wheel can show energy, vibrancy, or chaos, while analogous colors (next to each other on the wheel) convey calmness, simplicity, and sometimes dullness. Many designers prefer **split-complementary color schemes**: a main color plus the two closest to its opposite on the wheel. This provides a sense of contrast without being quite as stark or jarring as true opposites. A study of **color theory** can help in planning.
- **Type** – if any verbiage is incorporated in the design, the font and size must be chosen to fit with the overall scheme. Fonts can be bold, serious, lighthearted, fun, angry, or nearly any emotion. The size should be readable but not overwhelming. If the words are the focal point of the design, they may be larger than if they are more of a caption.

APPLICATIONS OF GRAPHIC DESIGN

Nearly every field utilizes graphic design, whether in a company website, safety posters on the wall, or other uses. Graphic design is especially useful, though, in some professions:

- **Architecture** – architecture uses principles of graphic design in planning buildings and other projects. Balance, color, and other principles are all important. Graphic design can also be used to create projected images of a finished product for clients.
- **Engineering** – several branches of engineering use graphic design, particularly software engineering. Graphics engineers design images and visual effects for websites, video games, etc.
- **Marketing** – naturally, graphic design is very important in marketing, which studies a target audience and prepares materials specifically designed to attract that audience.

DESKTOP PUBLISHING EQUIPMENT

Desktop publishing requires specific equipment:

- **Computer** – a computer should have sufficient speed and memory to handle the software.
- **Software** – there are multiple options for desktop publishing software at a variety of price points, depending on the customer's needs.
- **Input devices** – these include keyboard and mouse, and possibly other attachments such as a scanner, camera, or extra monitor.
- **Output devices** – this is typically a printer. For good quality, a high resolution printer is recommended.

DESKTOP PUBLISHING SOFTWARE

When selecting desktop publishing software, there are several factors to consider:

- **Operating system** – the operating system of the computer that will be used must be compatible with the chosen software.
- **Other software** – if a designer plans to incorporate files from other software, or export with other software, the desktop publishing software must be compatible.

- **Features** – each software will have slightly (or vastly) different features, so if any particular feature is important, it should be researched before choosing a software. Some common features that most programs include are:
  - o **Layout tools** – these are for positioning and aligning objects. Rulers and grids can be used to make sure objects are in line, and objects can be grouped so that they can be moved together.
  - o **Text tools** – Text boxes can be created and adjusted. Style sheets can be created to make all similar text elements (headers, captions, etc.) align.
  - o **Graphic tools** – along with adjusting size, angle, and cropping, graphic tools allow the user to add effects or filters to images.

SKILLS FOR DESKTOP PUBLISHING

Many desktop publishing programs are designed to be user friendly and require little experience for basic use. To truly utilize the features, though, there are several skills that are helpful:

- First, simply knowing the available **tools** is invaluable. A program may have hundreds of tools from adjusting text to coloring images, so taking time to learn how to use them will greatly enhance the ability to create a quality product.
- A knowledge of how to create **harmonious visual effects** is very useful. Publishing is more than getting all the information on the page. It needs to be attractive, whether that means neat and organized or artistically chaotic. Knowledge of color, perspective, and other graphic design principles is helpful.
- Along with creating an aesthetically pleasing design, a necessary skill is creating a layout. It needs to not only look nice but communicate clearly. Objects must be a good size, font must be readable, and all information should be easy to access. The user can drag objects and use gridlines to create a clean, attention-catching layout.
- **Word processing** skills will be used in desktop publishing. Being able to align text, use fonts well for clarity and emphasis, and use the spelling and grammar checks will help create clear and error-free documents.
- **Illustrations** are a valuable tool in desktop publishing, but the user must know how to import and insert them in the document without losing resolution. It is also important to be aware of copyright rules, either using public domain images or paying for the rights to use other images.

PHOTOGRAPHIC COMPOSITION

If someone is taking his or her own pictures for a project (or editing another's pictures for publishing), knowledge of photography basics is necessary. There are several principles of composition that are important:

- **Lighting** – this sets the tone for the picture. Lighting can make the atmosphere feel cheerful, somber, hot, scary, etc. Light can be either natural or artificial:
  - For **natural** light, some times of day are better than others, depending on the goal. Early morning is often soft light for fresh, peaceful photos. Later afternoon, just before sunset, is another good time when the sun is angled instead of overhead, giving a soft, warm glow.
  - If pictures are being taken with **artificial light**, the lights should be placed carefully to avoid harshness (unless that is the goal). **Front light** is placed directly in front of the subject, decreasing shadows. It provides very even lighting, so the subject may not stand out from the background. **Backlight** comes from behind. It darkens the subject, sometimes creating a silhouette effect or long shadows. It can be good for artistic effect but will not help the viewer see features of the subject well. **Soft light** is diffused, like natural light on a cloudy day. Shadows and contrast are decreased. **Hard light** is bright, direct light that provides high contrast and intensity.
- **Perspective** – this refers to how objects in an image are related spatially. By taking a picture from a different angle, objects can be made to look larger or smaller, closer together or farther apart. For instance, a picture taken from the bottom of a tree, angled up to the leaves, will give it an effect of tallness that is different from a picture taken from a distance, aimed horizontally. A photographer should know the angles to use or how to position subjects to create the desired perspective.
- **Focus** – focus is used to draw a viewer's attention. Some photos, like landscape scenes, are uniformly focused so the viewer can clearly see everything. A portrait may blur out the background to draw the eye to the subject. Some pictures blur very heavily, especially when the subject is a close-up of a small object like a flower or insect. This brings the subject into sharp contrast, making it easier to see and more vivid.

PHOTOGRAPHY EQUIPMENT

A photographer uses multiple tools and equipment:

- **Camera** – there are a myriad of options and an enormous price range, so it's important to know what specific needs a user has before purchasing. Some settings that should be understood:
  - **ISO** – this describes how sensitive a camera is to light. The higher the ISO is, the brighter the image will be, so a high ISO allows for better pictures in low light.
  - **Aperture** – this refers to the diameter of the camera's lens opening. A wider aperture lets in more light, which blurs everything but what the camera is focused on. A narrow aperture allows the camera to focus on a broader depth.

- o **Shutter speed** – this refers to how long the camera spends absorbing light. A higher shutter speed lets in less light but captures a shorter time period, so these shots will be less blurry if there is any movement. A lower shutter speed lets in more light so is preferred if there is no danger of sudden movement.
- o **Focal Length** – this refers to how far the camera lens is zoomed in. The longer the focal length is, the more zoomed in it is. A long focal length can be handy, but it is harder it is to keep steady. If a camera is not steady or has too slow of a shutter speed to match the focal length, the blurrier the picture will be. With longer focal lengths, a tripod is recommended.

- **Lenses** – different lenses have different focal lengths that are ideal for different types of photos (landscape, portrait, macro, etc.). A photographer may have a variety of lenses or may choose the one he or she is most likely to need.
- **Reflectors** – to adjust lighting and eliminate shadows (especially on faces), a reflector can be invaluable. These are especially useful in bright, harsh light.
- **Filters** – depending on the subject and location, various filters may be useful. These can help with reflections, unbalanced lighting, etc.
- **Tripod** – tripods are useful for keeping a camera steady, as well as using the camera's timer.
- **Flash** – many cameras come with a built-in flash, but a professional photographer will usually purchase a separate one that is more effective. A flash can not only help in dimly lit photo shoots, but can help get rid of shadows in bright, sunny conditions.
- **Batteries** – cameras can go through batteries quickly, so it is a good idea to have several backups.
- **Memory cards** – these store pictures as they are taken. When purchasing memory cards, it is important to choose ones with plenty of storage (at least 64 GB is recommended) and good read/write speed.
- **External hard drive** – to avoid the risk of losing photos, it is crucial to back them up. A hard drive with plenty of storage (at least 2 TB) and speed (for transferring) is recommended.

PHOTOGRAPHY EDITING TECHNIQUES

After pictures are taken, there is still much work to be done. Some editing techniques include:

- **Cropping and straightening** – a good first step is to make layout adjustments through cropping and straightening. If the picture contains a distracting element near an edge, or the subject needs to be more centered or simply zoomed in, cropping is an easy and effective way to make these changes. Sometimes the camera is tilted slightly, and the picture may need to be realigned to ensure that the horizon is straight.
- **Cleaning** – if dust gets onto the camera lens, this can result in fuzzy spots on the picture. Using the spot-removing tool in the editing software can remove these blemishes.
- **Exposure** – a photo may need to be brightened or darkened slightly by adjusting the exposure.
- **Contrast** – similar to exposure, this refers to brightness and darkness, but how different elements in the picture relate to each other rather than the overall look. Contrast can be heightened to make a dark object darker and a light object lighter, so the elements stand out more, or contrast can be lowered to make them blend together better.
- **Sharpness** – many editing programs have tools that allow the user to adjust the sharpness, or clarity, of a photo. This makes the edges of the photo's elements stand out more.

- **White balance** – this is used to adjust the overall color tone of a photo. The picture can be made warmer or cooler, or given more of a blue or red tint, etc.
- **Color** – after adjusting the white balance, a photo can be edited to stand out more by adjusting the color. There are two ways to do this. Adjusting the **vibrancy** makes the duller colors in the photo more vibrant while maintaining the colors that are already bright. Adjusting the **saturation** affects all colors in the frame.

PHOTOGRAPHY FINISHING AND PUBLISHING

After photos are edited, they still need to be finalized. Professional pictures are often in **raw image format (RAW)**, which means that they have not been compressed or processed yet. This is necessary to maintain excellent resolution, but the files are very large and not good for distribution. They will need to be converted to a format such as **JPEG** before sending or printing them. However, it is important to save copies of the original files as well in case any other editing needs to be done, since editing the JPG files will result in lower quality photos (and many edits are not possible with JPGs anyway).

IMAGE TRANSFER AND REPRODUCTION

Once a photo is edited in its RAW state, it can be converted to a format for sharing and printing. While **JPEG** is the most common format, other types may be more useful for different purposes.

- A **Joint Photographic Experts Group (JPEG)** file is ideal for sharing because the file size is small and the format is widely compatible. The image quality is not as good as some others due to compression, but for sharing or printing multiple photos, or illustrating a website, it is a good choice.
- A **Portable Network Graphics (PNG)** file is often used for website images because it preserves the image's quality. It has a larger file size so is not as good for sending through email, etc., but will give sharp, vibrant images for online viewing. If a website has multiple images, it may be slow to load, so it's best not to use PNG for more than a few photos that need excellent quality.
- **Tagged Image File Format (TIFF)**, like PNG, is good at preserving quality but also tends to have large file sizes. This can be helpful for printing high-quality pictures (quality is especially important for large prints).

When pictures are ready to print, there are several options. Photos can be printed on a variety of media: paper, canvas, metal, wood, and more. When using paper, there are two general options:

- **Glossy** – this paper is very smooth, giving the image extra clarity. It also tends to be more vibrant, catching the eye. But it can cause reflection, making the image more difficult to see in certain lights or under glass in a frame.
- **Matte** – the surface of this paper is course, which causes light to be scattered instead of reflecting it. This makes the image easier to see, especially in artificial lighting or behind glass. Large prints or fine art are typically printed on matte paper.

IMAGE CARRIER PREPARATION, TRANSFER, AND REPRODUCTION

The final step in preparing a graphic design project is producing it. An office printer may be sufficient for some projects, but for mass-producing a quality design, it is necessary to go through the process of creating a plate and using it to transfer the design, whether it is on paper, plastic, fabric, or other media. The edited image must have a very high resolution, with good color separation so the image stands out clearly in the final product.

A plate, or **image carrier**, is used in lithography or screen printing. The carrier is treated with a light-sensitive coating. An image is then photomechanically transferred to the image carrier. This is done by directing light onto the carrier through a transparent image (such as a film negative) and then treating it to have printing and non-printing areas (this is typically done with soluble and insoluble coatings so the ink will be either attracted or repelled and only print in the desired areas).

The ink (which is composed of **carrier**, **pigment**, and **resin**) is applied to the plate. Sometimes this is done in multiple stages with different colors. It can then be transferred to the medium.

To **reproduce** in large quantities, there are several methods. Sometimes a reel of paper is rolled through the press machine for continuous printing. For screen printing, the screen may need to be re-coated between each application.

Audio and Video Production

VIDEO AND AUDIO PRODUCTION EQUIPMENT

To produce video or audio files, specialized equipment is needed. Some of this equipment includes:

- **Camera** – for video production, a good quality video camera is needed with high resolution.
- **Microphone** – for either video or audio, it is important to have good sound equipment. The type of production will determine whether a wireless digital mic, a plug-in USB mic, or a simple hand-held mic is best. Without good sound equipment the quality can be fuzzy and distracting with background noise or wind.
- **Mixer** – this is an invaluable tool for balancing sound—it can filter out background noise, enhance a voice that is too quiet. The mixer is used both during recording and after, during editing.
- **Amplifier** – this adjusts the amplitude, ensuring that the sound reaches throughout a room
- **Lighting** – several different types of lights are needed for the best quality:
  - **Key light** – this is used directly on the subject (typically the actor the camera is currently focusing on) to highlight.
  - **Fill light** – this softens shadows, balancing the key light.
  - **Backlight** – this gives depth, helping the subject to stand out from the background.

As the film or audio is being recorded, the information can be transmitted to a computer where a recording software combines video and audio and the file can later be edited.

SKILLS AND TECHNIQUES FOR VIDEO AND AUDIO RECORDING

To create a high-quality video or audio recording, one must understand not merely how to work the equipment but specialized techniques for using it. For instance, the three types of lights have been previously discussed, but each must be set up differently:

- The **key light** that focuses on the main subject is directed 45 degrees upward, off the camera axis.
- The **fill light** that provides a softening effect is directed vertically 30 degrees, opposite the key light.
- The **backlight** that separates foreground from background goes directly behind the subject, focused downward at 45 degrees.

A **sound mixer** must have a good grasp of which sounds to amplify and which to fade or mute. This may involve visiting the film location ahead of time to check for loud background noise, wind, etc. Depending on the size of the production team, the mixer may be directing sound assistants and boom operators. As the film is being recorded, the mixer makes adjustments, mixing in real time. After each take, he or she checks quality and decides if a retake is necessary.

POSTPRODUCTION SKILLS: VIDEO AND AUDIO FILES AND IMAGE AND SOUND INTEGRITY

Once a video or audio file is recorded, the work is far from over. The editing is a significant portion of the work, taking the raw footage and audio and transforming them into a seamless final product. This is typically done with a video or audio editing software that allows the video and audio files to be integrated and adjusted as needed. Sound can be amplified or dampened, background music can be added, scenes can be deleted or moved to a different place. Some techniques an editor may use include:

- Using a good, fast **computer** – it may be necessary to install a faster **storage drive (SSD)** or add **memory (RAM)**. A **video card and processor** may also be needed.
- Choosing a good **software** – there are many options, and no one is "best" for each task. It is wise to research to find what will best help with a particular project.
- Maintaining **quality** – this can be a challenge when working in multiple formats and compressing a file. One way to avoid quality loss is to make sure the format does not change throughout the editing process. In the editing software, the format should match the format that the footage was shot in. The master version should also be in this format and copies saved before making any lower-resolution files.
- **Cuts** – a video often cuts between scenes and times. Cuts allow the story to move, leaving out unnecessary details and going straight to action. They also allow for transition between points of view. There are several types of cuts, such as:
  - A **jump cut** shows an action and then immediately cuts to the result, like hitting a baseball and immediately showing it landing in a glove.
  - **Cutting on action** helps guide the viewer through a scene change, like showing a girl reaching for a doorknob and then shifting to show the door opening from the other side.
  - A **montage** is several quick cuts in a row that give a storyline without taking much time (often backstory or something that happens between important events).
  - A **match cut** is used to show passage of time by artistically moving from one scene to another. For instance, one scene may show a person blowing out a candle and the screen goes black, then slowly lightens in a dim scene that is another time and place.
- **Color correction** – even with good lighting equipment, a producer may want to adjust coloring in the editing stage. It is important to have consistency, and if two scenes were filmed at different times of day, one may be brighter than the other. Color correcting can fix this. **Color grading** is changing the color to look different than other scenes, such as showing that an event happened in the past by giving it a washed-out or sepia look.
- **File compression** – the finished file needs to be an appropriate size so that it can be downloaded. This may vary depending on where it is being exported (YouTube, Facebook, email, etc.). The resolution, bit rate, and supported frame rates can be adjusted to meet requirements. There are several video converter software options for compressing files.

Electronic Communication

SCIENTIFIC AND TECHNOLOGICAL CONCEPTS OF ELECTRONIC COMMUNICATION

Electronic communication includes communication through phone (audio calls, video calls, text messaging), Internet (email, instant messaging, websites), radio, and television. All modes of communication rely on three key features:

- A **transmitter** that sends a signal.
- A communication **medium** that carries the message.
- A **receiver** that receives the message in a form that can be understood.

The message must be **converted** into an electronic form to send. For instance, a phone takes the input through the microphone and converts it into an electronic audio signal. When typing an email, the words are converted to binary code to transmit.

The communication medium can include fiber optic cable, wiring, and even space (such as using the electromagnetic spectrum to send radio signals). The message must be in the correct electronic form to pass through the medium.

Many transmitters are also receivers so that communication can be two-way. These are known as **transceivers**, such as phones.

MATERIALS AND COMPONENTS FOR ELECTRONIC COMMUNICATION SYSTEMS

Various equipment and parts are needed to set up electronic communication. Some of the common materials and components include:

- **Transmitter, receiver,** and **transceiver**
  - the **transmitter** is composed of circuits and other electronic components that convert the message into a form that can be sent electronically.
  - the **receiver** is also made of circuits and other electronic components that can receive the message and convert it back into the form that was sent (audio, typed words, etc.).
  - many devices combine the transmitter and receiver into one device called the **transceiver**.
- **Satellite dish** – this is an antenna that can both transmit and receive electronic information by radio waves.
- **Uplink** – this is the link from a station on the ground to a satellite.
- **Downlink** – this is the link from a satellite to a receiver on the ground.

ELECTRONIC COMMUNICATION PROCESSES

Electronic signals can be analog or digital. **Analog** signals are continuous, like a sine wave. Examples include landline signals or photocopiers. **Digital** signals are in specific increments instead, typically using binary code or two-state code. These are more common today and include computers and cell phones.

These signals can be sent in several different ways, depending on the type of signal and the communication medium:

- The **electromagnetic spectrum** transmits radio waves for television and radio. Radio waves travel easily through air with no need for wires or cables.
- **Fiber optics** work by sending data as pulses of light through glass or plastic fiber. This is often used for Internet and phone services.
- **Satellite** communication uses satellites in space. A transmitter (satellite dish) on the ground sends a signal to the satellite through an uplink. At the satellite, the signal is changed to a different frequency and amplified. The signal is then transmitted back to Earth to a receiver (satellite dish).
- **Laser communication** uses free space to send messages via infrared laser light or LED via a modem module, optical module, and controller electronics module that connects the other two.

PRESENTATION SOFTWARE

Presentation software is software used to present information in meetings and classes in business, organizational, and academic settings. The most popular presentation application is Microsoft PowerPoint; others include Google Slides (freely available online), Prezi, and Keynote (available for the Mac).

While they have differences, most of these applications have some standard features. For the most part, they work by allowing the user to create separate "slides"; for the full presentation, the slides are shown in sequence. Individual slides may be given animation and interactivity. Most applications include pre-made templates so that users don't have to design the layout and graphics of the slides themselves, though advanced users can customize the layouts.

Creating a presentation is a matter of adding and editing slides. In PowerPoint, a new slide is added by clicking "New Slide" in the Home menu and selecting the type of slide you want, or by right-clicking in the pane on the left showing the slides and selecting "New Slide". The text on a slide can be edited by clicking in the text field you want to edit and typing. Images and charts can be added using the Insert menu. Slides can also be deleted and rearranged.

PRESENTATION HARDWARE

You can give a presentation to a small group of people using just your computer, or even your phone, but for a large group it's impractical to have them all crowd around your screen. It's useful to have a way to project the presentation onto a wall or large screen so that everyone can see it.

Formerly, presentations were done using overhead projectors or slide projectors that could project printed slides or transparencies. Now, presentations are usually done on the computer, so the computer must be connected to some **presentation hardware** that can project the information from the computer screen to a larger display. There are **digital projectors** that can do this, descendants of the old-fashioned overhead projector that work with computer displays instead of printed transparencies. These often come with remote controls so that the presenter doesn't have to stay by the computer to give the presentation. Computers can also be connected directly to large televisions or other displays. One increasingly popular piece of presentation hardware, especially in academic settings, is the **interactive digital whiteboard**, or **smartboard**. Smartboards work much like other digital displays, but have additional functionality to allow the user to draw on the screen.

EMAIL

It's possible to receive and send e-mail either directly in the web browser (the URL depending on your e-mail provider), or using an external e-mail application such as Microsoft Outlook or Mozilla Thunderbird. In either case, by default, the webpage or application presents you with a list of recent messages in descending chronological order, usually showing the name of the sender, the subject, and the beginning of the message. You can click on the message to read the whole thing. You can see older messages by clicking on an arrow button. You can also search for specific messages; most e-mail sites and applications provide means of searching for message text or searching by date, sender, or other criteria.

To send a message, you can click on a button for that purpose (in Gmail it's an oval button in the top left that says "Compose"); most mail applications also have a menu option for that purpose. Type the e-mail address of the person you want to send it to (you can include multiple recipients), the subject, and the message text. You can also reply to an open message by clicking a Reply button or using a menu option.

BLOGGING

A **blog**, short for "web log," is a website where one or more people post short essays about their activities, current events, or other subjects. On the front page of the blog, the most recent posts are usually shown in descending chronological order; older posts are typically accessible through an archive or through links in a sidebar. Many blogs allow readers to post comments on blog entries. The people who maintain a blog and write the posts are called **bloggers**.

Many blogs are just chronicles of the life of the blogger, and may be of little interest to anyone outside the blogger's family and acquaintances. Other blogs are meant purely for entertainment, created to bring in views and get the bloggers money from advertisements. There are some blogs, however, that cover technical and scientific subjects and that are written by working and knowledgeable professionals and academics; these blogs can be good and reliable resources, and include much useful information.

While it's possible for a programmer to create a blog site from scratch, software and websites exist that allow people to create blogs with little or no technical skill. Some of the most popular blogging platforms include WordPress, Blogger, and Tumblr.

TOOLS FOR COLLABORATION

A **collaboration application** is an application designed to allow multiple users to work together on documents or other tasks, while not having to be physically near each other. Collaboration software collectively is sometimes called **groupware**. The implementation details vary widely by application, but there are certain features that define collaboration applications. Collaboration software allows multiple users to remotely edit the same documents, either incorporating all their edits in real-time or maintaining different versions that include each users' edits. Users are often able to comment on each other's edits, and roll back to previous versions of documents. Collaboration applications also typically include messaging systems that allow users to communicate with each other. They may also include management tools to allow users to better organize their shared documents and make plans for their collaboration.

Some popular collaboration applications include Slack, Asana, and Microsoft SharePoint. There are many other software packages and applications that facilitate collaboration and have many of the same features as collaboration software but are not necessarily formally considered groupware. This is true of the Google online productivity applications (Google Docs, Google Sheets, and Google

Slides), and of wiki software like MediaWiki, the framework behind Wikipedia and other similar sites.

Computer Technology

CAREERS

Software developer (also known as an analyst developer, developer, and programmer) examines requirements for new or modified computer applications and translates them into program specifications. Responsibilities include designing programs, testing programs, writing programs, and using programs to solve problems. Developers often must know multiple programming languages.

Business systems analyst (also known as a business systems planner and solutions architect) identify the business and information needs within an organization, and then enhance productivity and efficiency by helping develop new IT solutions.

Database programmer (also known as a database coordinator and database administrator) is responsible for database design, implementation, maintenance, and security. Specifically, the database programmer develops the database strategy and identifies means of improving performance and capacity.

Information systems analyst (also known as an information systems designer) determines whether or not the computer system is fulfilling the organization's need in the most efficient manner possible. This position requires comprehensive knowledge of telecommunications technology, software applications, and business operations and processes.

Chief Information Officer, or **CIO**, leads an organization's IT group. The CIO determines how information technology can benefit the organization competitively, and reports directly to the CEO. In this position, leadership skills, business knowledge, and the ability to create and impart vision are more important than technical skills. CIOs may have an IT degree, but many simply work their way up the company ladder.

Computer engineers design, install, and perform maintenance on computer and computer equipment. They use product control techniques to enhance total system performance, and may design the complex hardware equipment that is necessary for system operation. In most cases, the position requires an electronics degree, mechanical engineering degree, or electrical engineering degree. Trade certifications are beneficial when the focus is repair work.

Web developers create, test, and maintain Web pages and links. This includes updating content (video, audio, animation, etc.), creating interactive components (search engines, chat rooms, etc.), ensuring continuous operation, creating appropriate documentation (maintenance, installation, troubleshooting, etc.), and compiling statistics. This position may require an IT or similar degree, and knowledge of HTML, programming languages, databases, and various software applications.

HARDWARE, SOFTWARE, AND PERIPHERALS

Hardware refers to physical, tangible technological devices. Hardware includes the computer itself and its core components, such as the power supply and the **central processing unit** (CPU) that carries out the basic instructions. Additional pieces of hardware that are connected to the main processor are called **peripherals**. Peripheral **input devices**, used to get information into the computer, include keyboards, mice, microphones, and tablets. **Output devices**, used to display or transfer information from the computer, include monitors, printers, and speakers. Another important kind of peripheral is a **storage device**, used to store data external to the computer itself. Storage devices include disk drives, CD drives, and USB flash drives.

In contrast to hardware, **software** exists not in tangible form, but as data in computer storage; it consists of the applications and operating systems that run on the computer. Among the many types of software are word processors such as Microsoft Word and WordPerfect; spreadsheet software such as Microsoft Excel and OpenOffice Calc; web browsers such as Google Chrome and Mozilla Firefox; and computer games, from the solitaire games that often come pre-installed on computers to high-end action games with sophisticated 3-D graphics.

OPERATING SYSTEMS

An **operating system** is the set of software programs that handle the basic functions of the computer system such as file and memory management, interfacing with peripherals, and the execution of other applications. Typically, the operating system is set up to run automatically when the computer starts. The user can then use the functions of the operating system to launch other programs and to switch between applications and transfer data between them as necessary.

The most widely used operating system on personal computers today is **Microsoft Windows**, which comes pre-installed by many computer manufacturers. Microsoft Windows has gone through many versions, each with a similar basic look and feel but refinements in presentation and functionality; the latest version of Windows for personal computers is Windows 10, released in 2015. Apple computers use a different operating system, **macOS**, which has likewise gone through many iterations. After Microsoft Windows and macOS, the next most popular operating system is **Linux**, which unlike Microsoft Windows and macOS is free and open-source, meaning that the source code is freely available to anyone who wants it. Despite their differences, all of these operating systems have enough similarities that someone comfortable with one system generally can adapt to another.

COMPUTER MEMORY

Memory refers to the part of the core computer hardware that is used to store data that is needed immediately, including executable programs. This is different from storage space on peripherals such as disk drives; this "external memory" is referred to as **secondary storage**, in contrast with **primary storage** or "main memory" within the computer itself. Secondary storage has a higher capacity than primary storage, but is much slower to access.

There are two main types of memory. **Volatile** memory, also known as **RAM** (an acronym for "Random Access Memory"), can be both read from and written to, but requires a constant flow of power; any data in volatile memory is lost when the computer is shut off. **Non-volatile** memory, also known as **ROM** (for "Read Only Memory"), retains information even without power, but cannot be easily written to; it is used to store the main start-up functionality of the operating system.

In general, the more RAM a computer has, the less data it has to store to temporary disk files ("**virtual memory**"), and the faster it will run. Having too many programs or documents open at once can use a lot of memory and slow down the computer.

TROUBLESHOOTING

Troubleshooting refers to systematically determining the cause of a problem with a piece of hardware or software and resolving the issue. When something isn't working the way it should be, it's generally a good idea to try the simplest solutions first; sometimes just restarting a program or rebooting the computer is enough to set things right. When it isn't, other methods are necessary. Going through a process step by step and carefully noting the results at each step can pin down exactly where the problem is occurring, and help narrow down its cause. Most programs have documentation accessible through the Help menu, in text or PDF files in the program directory, or (now rarely) in paper booklets that come with the program; this documentation often includes troubleshooting tips.

If all this fails, help can often be found online. The website of the hardware or software manufacturer often has a troubleshooting guide or a list of common issues and their solutions. A web search, using terms as specific as possible (including the text of any error messages you receive), often turns up helpful information. If all else fails, most manufacturers have technical support departments you can contact for further aid.

SELECTION AND MAINTENANCE OF SOFTWARE

A user should **select** software programs to use or purchase based on the **tasks they need performed** and the **program's proficiency** at carrying out that task. Additionally, the user's computer must have the requisite processing capacity to run the programs. When software fails to run on a computer, it usually falls under one of the following categories:

- The computer cannot properly install the software. Troubleshooting solutions: Ensure that the files on the drive are capable of reading the software CD. Ensure the computer is capable of running the software. Ensure the correct verification number is being entered.
- An error occurs during the software's installation. Troubleshooting solutions: Ensure the computer meets software requirements. Try installing the software when the computer is in safe mode. Examine the CD for scratches or dirt.
- The program cannot load or an error occurs during program load. Troubleshooting solutions: Check software documentation for possible tips on solving the problem. Check for the existence of patches or updates from the developer. Close all other programs. Reboot computer at least once after program has been installed.

SELECTION AND MAINTENANCE OF HARDWARE

Before purchasing new hardware, the user should make certain it is **compatible with his computer** and that it fits their needs. For instance, if they require full color copies and fax ability, they may need to purchase a top-of-the-line printer. However, if they are only printing text documents without graphics, they may opt for a less-expensive model. Some peripheral devices can be fairly easy to install, such as printers, fax machines, speakers, scanners, and similar equipment. However, installation may be more difficult for hardware that actually goes inside the computer, such as processors, expansion cards, motherboards, etc. Before opening a computer, the user should disconnect all cables connected to the back of the machine in order to avoid electrocution and ground their self in order to avoid the dangers associated with electrostatic discharge, or ESD. Like most electronic devices, computers make extensive use of semiconducting materials, such as silicon, which are less conductive than conductor materials but more conductive than insulators.

OPENING AND CLOSING FILES

To **open** a file means to read it from a hard drive or other storage medium; to **close** a file means to remove it from active memory. (Be sure to save the file first—a file that has not been saved is usually lost for good when it's closed.) Although programs may implement this functionality different ways, there are two methods that have become standard and are used in most modern applications. First, a file can be saved through the **menu** at the top of the program. Usually "Open" and "Close" are under the "File" menu; select "File" from the main menu, and then "Open" or "Close" from the dropdown. If opening the file, you may be prompted for the name and location. Second, most programs implement **keyboard shortcuts**, or **hotkeys**—sequences of keypresses for common functions such as opening and closing files. To open a file, the usual shortcut is Ctrl-O in

Windows (hold down the Ctrl key and then press O), or Command-O in macOS. To close a file, the shortcut is Ctrl-W in Windows, or Command-W in macOS.

Creating a new file is similar: select "New" under the file menu, or use the shortcut Ctrl-N or Command-N.

METHODS OF SAVING FILES

To **save** a file means to store it to a hard drive or other storage medium so that it will not be lost when the computer is shut off and can be read back into memory in the future. A file can usually be saved through the File menu, or through the shortcut Ctrl-S on Windows, or Command-S in macOS. If the file has not been saved before, you will be prompted to choose a filename and save location; otherwise the program will usually use the same filename and location as before.

Most applications also have a "Save As" command, often also under the File menu and often accessible through the shortcut F12 on Windows or Shift-Command-S in macOS. This allows the user to save a copy of the file under a different name or in a different format; if you choose this command you will be prompted for a new filename and location even if the file has been previously saved.

A file set to Read Only cannot be modified or saved over, though it can be opened and saved under a different name. This status is generally set not in the application, but through the operating system.

COPYING, MOVING, AND RENAMING FILES

Copying, **moving**, and **renaming** files are typically done not through an application but through the operating system. Graphical operating systems like Windows and macOS work similarly. To move a file, **drag** it into its new location—position the mouse cursor over it, click the mouse, and while holding down the mouse button move the cursor into the folder you want to move the file into, then release. Copying a file is similar, but hold down the Ctrl key while dragging it in Windows, or the Option key in macOS. Alternatively, you can select the files and press Ctrl-X or Command-X (for Cut) if you want to move them, or Ctrl-C or Command-C (for Copy) if you want to copy them, then navigate to the new directory and press Ctrl-V/Command-V (for Paste).

To rename a file, you can either select it and then click again on its name (leaving enough of a pause to not register a double-click), or right-click on it and select "Rename" from the pop-up menu. In either case, the filename will be highlighted, and you can type a new name. In macOS, you can also select the file and hit the Return key.

FINDING FILES AND APPLICATIONS

If you don't remember where a file is, both Windows and macOS provide ways to locate it. In **Explorer** (the graphical interface for Windows where your files and folders are shown), there is a search box in the upper right. Typing text into a search box will locate files that contain that text; if you know the name of the file, you can type "name:" followed by the filename. In **Finder** (the macOS counterpart to Explorer), you can press Command-Space to open Spotlight, the macOS search utility. Type some text in the file, or if you want to search by filename, click the + button to add a search criterion, and select "Name" from the first popup menu that comes up.

To **execute** an application means to make it start; this is also referred to as **running** or **launching** the application. You can execute an application in Explorer or Finder by just double-clicking on it, or by right-clicking it and selecting "Open". (These same methods also can be used to open documents using default applications.) You can also access many applications through the **Start menu** (Explorer) or the **Go menu** (Finder) accessible from an icon at the corner of the screen.

FILE TYPES AND EXTENSIONS

A **file extension** is a sequence of characters at the end of the filename, following a period, that defines the type of file it is—for example, in the filename "notes.txt", the file extension is "txt". File extensions are not necessarily shown by default in the operating system; you can show them in Windows by clicking the "File name extensions" checkbox in the View menu in Explorer, or in macOS by clicking the "Show all filename extensions" checkbox in the Advanced tab in the Preferences menu in Finder.

Following are a few common file extensions:

- avi, mov, mpg, mp4 – Video files (of various formats)
- doc, docx – Microsoft Word file
- gif, jpeg, jpg, png, tiff – Image files (of various formats)
- htm, html – HTML file (a file describing a webpage and readable by a web browser)
- mp3, ogg, wav – Sound files (of various formats)
- pdf – PDF file (viewable in Adobe Acrobat)
- ppt, pptx – Power Point file
- rar, zip – A compressed file (files can be compressed to take up less space, but must be uncompressed to be used)
- rtf – Rich Text format (readable by most word processors)
- txt – Plain text files
- xls, xlsx – Microsoft Excel file

FORMATTING IN A WORD PROCESSOR

To **format** a document means to change its layout and appearance, such as the size and color of the text and the width of the paragraphs. Word processors have many complex formatting features; those described here are only some of the most commonly used. The techniques described here work in Microsoft Word, the most widely used word processor, but most other word processors work similarly, though not identically.

To change the appearance of text, you can highlight the text and then use the buttons and dropdowns in the Font section of the Home menu to change the text's size and font (typeface), bold or italicize the text, etc. You can also click the arrow in the corner of this section to bring out a Font menu. Some common keyboard shortcuts are Ctrl-I or Command-I to italicize text and Ctrl-B or Command-B to bold it.

The controls for changing the appearance of paragraphs, including indentation, line spacing, and use of numbered or bulleted lists, are in the Paragraph section of the Home menu; the Paragraph menu can be accessed by clicking the arrow in the corner of this section.

More advanced formatting features include the use of tables, columns, and styles.

EDITING AND PROOFING DOCUMENTS

To **edit** a document means to change its text and other content (as opposed to formatting, which is changing its layout and appearance). The techniques described here work in Microsoft Word, the most widely used word processor, but most other word processors work similarly, though not identically.

To insert text in a document, you can just position the cursor where you want it and start typing. You can delete text using the Delete and Backspace keys; you can delete a lot of text at once by selecting it first. To move or copy text to a different part of the document, you can select it and then hit Ctrl/Command-X (Cut, to move it) or Ctrl/Command-C (Copy, to copy it) and then position the cursor in the new location and hit Ctrl/Command-V (Paste). You can search for specific text in the document using "Find" under the Editing section of the Home menu (shortcut Ctrl/Command-F).

Most word processors come with automatic spelling and grammar check functionality; it's very fallible and not as good as a skilled human proofreader, but better than nothing. To turn this on in Microsoft Word, you can click "Check Document" in the Proofing section of the Review menu.

USING GRAPHICS IN A WORD PROCESSOR

Modern word processors allow the user to insert graphical elements into documents to include pictorial information or increase their visual appeal. The techniques described here work in Microsoft Word, the most widely used word processor, but most other word processors work similarly, though not identically.

To insert an image saved in an external file, go to the Insert menu and click Pictures in the Illustrations section. You will be prompted to select the file you want to insert. Once the image is in your document, you can click and drag it to move it to a different location, or select it and then move the **control points** at the corners and sides to change its size. Right-clicking on the image brings up a pop-up menu that allows you to change some characteristics of the image such as the border and the way the text wraps around it; these features can also be accessed through the Format menu.

Word also allows you to draw graphical elements directly in the word processor, though its functionality is limited compared to that of dedicated graphics programs. This feature can be accessed through the Shapes or SmartArt selections in the Insert menu.

USING SPREADSHEETS

A **spreadsheet** is an application that allows text and data to be stored in rows and columns that can be rearranged and used in calculations. The techniques described here work in Microsoft Excel, the most widely used spreadsheet application, but most other spreadsheet applications work similarly, though not identically.

To sort the data in a spreadsheet, first select the cells you wish to sort. (A **cell** in a spreadsheet is a single space in the grid, the intersection of a row and a column.) Data outside the selected cells will be left in its original position. Now, select Sort from the Data menu. A popup window will come up that will allow you to select the criteria you're using for the sort. In the "Sort by" dropdown menu, select the column you want to sort by. If you have labels at the top of the data that should not be sorted, click the "My data has headers" checkbox. In the "Order" dropdown, you can choose whether you want the data to be sorted in ascending or descending order.

You can sort by more than one column; to add an additional column, click the "Add Level" button.

USING FORMULAS IN A SPREADSHEET

A **formula** in a spreadsheet is a cell entry that depends on a calculation. Formulas are what give spreadsheets their power and flexibility, and make them more than just static collections of data. The techniques described here work in Microsoft Excel, but most other spreadsheet applications work similarly, though not identically.

To enter a formula in a cell, click on the cell and type the formula, preceded by an equal sign. Most formulas have **arguments**, lists of values or references that the formula should use, which are

82

enclosed in parentheses and separated by commas. Many arguments comprise **ranges** of cells, which can be entered by writing the first and last cell separated by a colon. For example, "=SUM(A1:A5)" sums the values of the cells from A1 to A5. Ranges can also be chosen by selecting the desired cells.

Listed below are a few common formulas:

- AVERAGE – Takes the average of the arguments
- COUNT – Counts cells in the range that have a nonzero numerical value
- COUNTA – Counts cells in the range that are not blank
- COUNTIF – Counts cells in the range that meet some condition
- IF – Yields different results depending on some criterion
- PRODUCT – Multiplies the arguments
- SUM – Sums the arguments

DISPLAYING INFORMATION

It's often useful to display the information in a spreadsheet in a chart or graph. Most spreadsheet programs can produce various kinds of charts, including bar graphs, line graphs, histograms, pie charts, and more. The techniques described here work in Microsoft Excel, but most other spreadsheet applications work similarly, though not identically.

To create a chart, first select the data that you want to include. Go to the Insert menu, and select the desired type of chart from the Charts section. A chart will automatically be created that includes the desired data. This chart will use default settings, and may not look exactly how you want it to, but it can be changed and customized. Many options for customizing the chart are available in the Design and Format menus; individual parts of the chart can also be altered by right-clicking on the element in question and making a selection from the pop-up menu that comes up, or by clicking on the element and editing it or making a selection on the pane that comes up on the right.

COMPUTER NETWORK ARCHITECTURE

- **Local Area Network (LAN)** - covers a local area, such as the inside of a home or a public business. Wi-Fi can be a type of LAN.
- **Metropolitan Area Network (MAN)** - connects multiple LANs.
- **Wide Area Network (WAN)** - covers a wide outdoor area and usually serves to connect office buildings or provide public Internet access.
- **Personal Area Network (PAN)** - includes Wi-Fi networks, Fixed Wireless Data networks, and other small area networks. Bluetooth is a type of PAN technology.
- **Basic Input/Output System (BIOS)** - is a chip that is built directly into the computer. It is known as boot firmware because it is the first program run when the computer is turned on. The main function of BIOS is loading and starting the operating system. In doing so, it initializes all computer hardware; locates software stored on peripheral devices; and, then loads and executes the software. This process is known as booting.

INTERNET TERMINOLOGY

The listed words have the following definitions:

- **Browser** – A program used to access the internet
- **Cloud** – A location, or collection of locations, where files are stored online but made accessible to local computers
- **Cookie** – A piece of information stored on a local computer to allow a website to "remember" information about the user (such as whether the user is logged in)
- **Domain** – A specific "region" on the internet, defining a particular site or group of sites, such as "mometrix.com". Domain names always end with a **top-level domain**, some of the most common of which are ".com", ".gov", ".edu", and ".org"
- **Download** – To copy a file from the internet to a local computer
- **Forum** – Also known as a **message board**, a place online where users can post comments and read the posts by other users
- **FTP** – An acronym for "File Transfer Protocol", a procedure for uploading and downloading files
- **Home page** – The "front page" or "landing page" of a website, the first page that most users see when they visit it
- **IP address** – A code corresponding to a particular "location" on the internet. An IP address consists of four numbers separated by periods, such as 64.233.191.0.
- **Registrar** – A company that keeps track of domains and their ownership
- **Search engine** – A website designed to allow users to search the web for other sites. The most popular search engine is Google; others include Bing and Yahoo Search.
- **Upload** – To copy a file from a local computer to the internet
- **Username** – The nickname by which a user is identified on a particular website
- **URL** – The "address" of a webpage or online resource, such as "https://www.mometrix.com/about.htm". A URL begins with a domain name.
- **Webhost**, or just **host** – The company that owns and administers the physical computer where the data on a website is stored
- **Website**, or just **site** – A linked collection of webpages under the same domain
- **Wiki** – A collaborative site like Wikipedia that allows users to create and edit pages and link them to each other using special markup codes

COMPONENTS OF PROGRAMMING

Source code is the human-readable language in which a computer program is written. Many programs are then translated into **object code**, machine-readable code much less accessible to humans; this process is known as **compiling** the code, and the programs that perform the process are called **compilers**. In other cases, the source code is not compiled, but is executed directly, or **interpreted**, by a program called an **interpreter**.

Even if you never do any programming yourself, it's useful to recognize the names and uses of some programming languages. Some common compiled languages are:

- **C** – A "low-level" language (that is, one that is fairly close in format to the ultimate machine code) on which many more modern languages are based
- **C++** – An offshoot of C with features to make it more user-friendly and efficient
- **Java** – A language often used for web applications, though now waning in popularity

Some common interpreted languages are:

- **JavaScript** – A language used on many web pages to provide interactivity
- **PHP** – A language often used as the "back end" of websites; most modern websites that do any sort of database manipulation or user account control are written in PHP
- **Python** – A relatively new but increasingly popular general-purpose language

NAVIGATING THE INTERNET

Along with e-mail, the web is one of the primary ways by which users interact with the internet. The most widely used browser is Google Chrome; other popular browsers include Mozilla Firefox, Internet Explorer (which comes preinstalled on Windows systems), and Safari (which comes preinstalled on macOS systems). Though they have their differences, all these browsers have the same basic functionality.

One important feature of the browser is the **address bar**—a space in the top center where you can type in the URL of a webpage to go to directly. Once you're at a specific webpage, you can click on certain text or images called **links** on that site to go to other connected pages. Text links usually look different from the surrounding text—by default they are blue and underlined, but individual sites can display them differently.

Two other important navigation features are the back button and the refresh button, both in the upper left of the browser. The back button (keyboard shortcut Alt-Backspace in Windows, Command-[in macOS) returns to the previous page. The refresh button (Ctrl-R or F5 in Windows, Command-R in macOS) reloads the current page, useful for pages that may change over time.

BOOKMARKS

Bookmarks are a feature of most web browsers that allow the user to store the URLs of frequently visited pages to avoid the need to remember the URL or type it in each time the user wants to visit the page. Various browsers may implement bookmarks in slightly different ways, but in Google

Chrome you can bookmark a page by opening the browser menu (by clicking on the three dots in the upper right) and selecting Bookmarks, then Bookmark this page, or you can use the shortcut Ctrl-D in Windows, Command-D in macOS. You can also bookmark a page by clicking the star at the right end of the address bar.

To open a bookmarked page, you can click on it in the Bookmarks bar under the address bar. If the Bookmarks bar isn't showing, you can show it by opening the browser menu and selecting Bookmarks, then Show bookmarks bar. You can also access your bookmarks by opening the browser menu and selecting Bookmarks, then Bookmarks Manager.

If you no longer want a page bookmarked, you can delete a bookmark through the Bookmarks manager, or by navigating to the page, clicking on the star in the address bar, and selecting "Remove".

USING TABS

Tabs are a feature of most web browsers that allow the user to have more than one webpage open at once, and to navigate quickly between open pages. The "tabs" are small trapezoidal or rectangular projections above the currently visible page that each includes the title of the page the tab corresponds to (if there's room—the more pages you have open the smaller the tabs are). It's also common, however, to refer to the other pages themselves as "tabs". The instructions here work for Google Chrome; tabs may be implemented slightly differently in other browsers.

To navigate to a different open page, just click on the corresponding tab. You can also go to the next tab using the keyboard shortcut Ctrl-PgDn on a PC or Command-Option-Right Arrow on a macOS, or the previous tab with Ctrl-PgUp/Command-Option-Left Arrow.

You can open a new tab by selecting "New tab" from the browser menu, or using the shortcut Ctrl-T/Command-T. You can also open a linked page in a new tab by holding down Ctrl/Command when clicking on the link. To close an open page, click the X in the corresponding tab, or use the keyboard shortcut Ctrl-W/Command-W.

USING A SEARCH ENGINE

The simplest way to look for information on the internet is by using a **search engine**—a website such as Google or Bing designed to allow users to search the web. Type the text you want to search for into the text field and click the search button, and the search engine will list pages including your text.

Be as specific as possible; if you want information on jaguars, the animal, you can include "animal" or "cat" in your search to exclude pages about the car model. In many engines, you can also include "-car" to exclude pages about cars; the minus sign means to return pages *not* including the term in question. You can search for an entire phrase by enclosing it in quotation marks.

Once you've found one webpage or website relevant to the information you're trying to find, you can often from there find more relevant pages by following appropriate links. There are also reference websites that include information on large numbers of topics; Wikipedia is the best known. These sites can be useful jumping-off points, but should not be relied on as sole sources of information.

RELIABLE SOURCES AND THE INTERNET

The internet is full of information, but not all of it is true. It's important to know how to evaluate information you found online and judge its reliability.

The fact that a claim is repeated on a lot of websites does *not* mean that it's reliable, since sites often copy from each other, especially from reference sites like Wikipedia. Since anyone can edit Wikipedia, errors and misinformation can creep in; these errors may be corrected on Wikipedia itself, but often not before they've spread around the web.

One important factor is the trustworthiness of the source. Information from an academic site or that of a major, respected agency or organization is more likely to be true than information from a social media site or a random blog.

If in doubt, it's also useful to check the sources—does the page state where its information came from? If it cites actual published books and papers, that may give more confidence in its reliability—though if you still have doubt, it may be useful to check those sources yourself; writers can cite sources that don't support their claims, either to be willfully deceitful or because they misunderstood the sources themselves.

COMPUTER SYSTEM REQUIREMENTS

To install and successfully use various applications, the technology education teacher must understand computer system requirements for each application. Many applications need significant storage space or processor speed. Requirements to consider include:

- **Operating System (OS)** – The operating system will vary, depending on whether the computers are PC or Mac, but it is important to check that the operating system of the computers is compatible with the software before purchasing it. For example, if an application requires Windows 10 but the computers are equipped with Windows 8, it will be necessary to either update the OS or choose a different software.
- **RAM (System Memory)** – It is important to check the amount of RAM that a program requires before installing.
- **Free Storage Space** – Along with system memory, a program will require a certain amount of storage space on the computer, so check the available amount before purchasing and installing software.
- **CPU Speed** – Different software applications need different CPU speeds. Certain applications like video editing in particular need higher speeds.
- **Audio Hardware** – Certain applications, especially music and video software, require specific audio hardware to use.

COMPUTER SOFTWARE APPLICATIONS

The technology educator must be familiar with multiple software applications. Some examples of these applications include:

- **Productivity** – Productivity software refers to applications that produce documents, graphs, and a variety of other materials. This includes word processing software, software that produces spreadsheets, and even music- and video-producing software. The Microsoft Office suite includes a multitude of productivity applications, though there are many other options as well.
- **Graphic design** – There are many graphic design programs (Adobe Photoshop or Illustrator are among the most well known, but schools may use a variety of applications). These allow users to design digital art and layouts for print materials.
- **Modeling** – Modeling software allows users to create 3D designs. This can range from a simple object, to a highly detailed building, to an entire world for a simulation.
- **Multimedia** – Media software applications are often used for creating and publishing material to the Internet. Music, videos, and games can be created—or just a creative school presentation for class.
- **Authoring** – An authoring system, such as an HTML editor, enables the user to create digital content without the challenge of creating complex programs. These may be website authoring tools that allow for quick and easy website creation, tools that convert documents and other content to Internet-capable content, and multimedia authoring tools as discussed above.

SECURITY ISSUES IN TECHNOLOGY EDUCATION

The technology educator must be aware of potential issues in regard to security. Schools have firewalls that protect students from accessing certain sites and protect the computers from viruses. But it is also important to protect student privacy. Personal data is constantly being collected in databases and information systems, allowing educators and administrators to monitor learning and adapt programs based on student performance, but they must be aware of legal guidelines to ensure they do not violate laws.

PASSWORD SECURITY

The purpose of a password is to secure an account so that people other than the user cannot illegitimately access it. As such, it's important that the password be one that is difficult to guess, or to find by any procedural technique. The most common—and therefore worst—passwords include "123456", "Password", "qwerty", and "111111". While these are particularly poor choices, that doesn't mean that passwords not on this list are secure.

Dictionary words, even relatively obscure words, make very poor passwords; it's trivial to write a login script that tries every word in the dictionary. Adding a few numbers on the end, or changing one or two letters into similar symbols, is of little help, since it's not hard to procedurally account for these variations—"g!raffe12" isn't much better a password than just "giraffe". The most secure passwords combine letters, numbers, and symbols in ways that bear no obvious relation to dictionary words, names, or other easily guessable sequences.

It's also a good practice to use different passwords for different sites, so someone who discovers one password won't be able to get into all your accounts. Programs called **password managers** can help you keep track of multiple passwords securely.

INFORMATION OWNERSHIP AND LICENSURE

Many people have the misconception that anything freely available online must be freely available to copy and reuse, that because something is posted online it must be in the public domain. That isn't the case; copyrights apply to online material just the same as they do to printed matter. Just as the fact that you can freely borrow a book from the library doesn't mean it's legal to duplicate it and sell copies, you can't necessarily legally reuse and resell any text or images you find online either.

Some online resources *are* released under licenses that allow other people to reuse their content, under certain conditions. For example, Wikipedia's content is released under a "Creative Commons Attribution-Share-Alike" license, which means that anyone is free to copy and redistribute it, provided that credit is given to Wikipedia, and that any modified versions are released under the same license. Other sites, however, do not necessarily have such licensing, and may not permit any reuse or republication of their content. If there's any doubt about the copyright status of a particular image or piece of text, you can contact the site owner and ask for permission to use it.

VIRUSES, MALWARE, AND PHISHING

A **virus** is an unwanted computer program that produces copies of itself and damages other files. **Malware** is a more general term that includes not only viruses, but also other kinds of undesirable software, such as **adware** that shows unwanted advertisements. Malware is a common hazard of the internet, but there are ways to minimize the danger.

One important precaution is to have an antivirus program installed, and run frequent virus scans. Windows comes with an antivirus program, but there are others commercially available. Even if you're using an anti-virus program, however, there are certain high-risk activities that should be avoided. Don't open unfamiliar files you receive by e-mail, or execute applications downloaded from sites you don't know to be trustworthy.

Phishing refers to tricking users into revealing account and password information. For instance, you could receive an e-mail warning about an issue with a bank account, and be prompted to enter your banking information on a linked page—but the page isn't really associated with the bank at all.

Check URLs carefully before entering sensitive information, and if there's any doubt contact the company directly to make sure that such a message is legitimate.

INTERNET PRIVACY

Internet privacy refers to the protection of personal information on the internet, including not only sensitive financial information but also demographic information and more. In the modern internet, many websites are constantly collecting data about their users, which they may not only use for their own purposes but also sell to advertisers who can use the information to better target their ads. The search engine Google, for example, keeps records of users' searches, and uses those records to infer the users' interests and other characteristics.

There are ways to minimize this data collection—using a feature called private browsing, disabling cookies in the browser—but they also limit the functionality of websites, and many users, if they're aware that their information is being collected, accept that as the cost of browsing the web and don't worry much about it. The extent to which you want to prevent the collection of your personal data is up to you.

However, even if you're not bothered by corporations collecting your data, having too much personal information readily available to the public may be another matter. It's rarely a good idea, for instance, to have your home address on the internet where anyone can see it.

Transportation and Energy

Energy and Power

CONCEPTS AND PRINCIPLES OF ENERGY AND POWER

Energy is simply the capacity for performing work. There are many types of energy, such as kinetic, potential, electrical, thermal, and more, but each of these types is associated with motion (or potential motion). Energy can be transferred between objects and transformed from one type of energy to another but can never be created or destroyed. This concept is known as **conservation of energy** (also called the first law of thermodynamics). Similarly, the **work-energy principle** explains that the sum of the work done on an object by all forces acting on it is equal to the change in the object's kinetic energy.

Another term that is often associated with energy is **force**. It is similar to energy but not quite the same. A force is a specific action that has an effect (typically moving or attempting to move something), while energy is simply the ability to do work and is a more abstract concept. Force is used in calculating the **mechanical advantage**, which measures a machine's performance by dividing the output force (force produced by the machine) by the input force (force applied to the machine).

While energy is capacity for work, **power** is the rate at which energy is used. In other words, power is the amount of work done, divided by the time it took to complete. Power can also be calculated as the force multiplied by the velocity, assuming both force and velocity are constant.

FLUID DYNAMICS

Pressure is force divided by the area that it is acting on. This is described in **Pascal's principle**, which states that in a contained liquid, if the pressure is changed on any part of the liquid, this pressure change is transmitted uniformly throughout the liquid rather than simply acting on that one portion.

Bernoulli's principle also describes pressure in fluid. It states that when liquid is flowing horizontally, the faster it flows, the less pressure it will have. In other words, as the kinetic energy (the speed) increases, the potential energy (the pressure) decreases to maintain conservation of energy.

TYPES OF ENERGY

There are a number of different types of **energy**, as work can be performed in many different ways. Some of the main types include:

- **Electrical energy** – This energy travels through **electrons**, carrying charge. It is a type of kinetic energy.
- **Chemical energy** – This is a type of potential energy, stored in chemical compound bonds. The energy is released during reactions, such as the energy in fossil fuel being converted into electrical energy through combustion. These reactions often produce heat and are called **exothermic reactions**.
- **Thermal energy** – Thermal energy is created as atomic particles vibrate, bumping against each other and producing heat. It is considered a type of kinetic energy.

- **Mechanical energy** – This energy can be either kinetic or potential or a combination: it is the sum of an object's kinetic and potential energy. So an object at rest has only potential energy, but an object in motion can have kinetic or both. For example, a pendulum swinging back and forth has a constant flux of potential and kinetic—when it reaches its maximum height and pauses momentarily, its potential energy is at its height while its kinetic energy is negligible. As it swings and gains momentum, the potential energy drops as the kinetic energy grows.
- **Nuclear energy** – This is created by splitting atoms to release the energy from the atom's nucleus. It is typically used to generate electricity.

ENERGY CONVERSION

Energy is commonly converted from one form to another. By the law of conservation of energy, no energy is "lost" or decreased or increased during transformation. However, according to the **second law of thermodynamics**, not all of the energy is converted purely into useful work. Some is converted into less useful forms, described as **entropy**.

The kinetic energy of wind or water can be converted into electrical energy with **wind turbines** or **hydroelectric dams**. Much of our daily life is built around energy transformation. For instance, a **gas turbine** converts the chemical potential energy of gasoline into kinetic electrical energy. A **steam turbine** also uses the chemical energy of fuel, using the heat produced by combustion to create steam. The thermal energy of the steam is then converted to electrical energy. A vehicle is powered by an **internal combustion engine** that converts the chemical energy of gasoline into thermal energy by combustion, and then into mechanical energy to propel it. A **photovoltaic cell** transforms solar energy into electricity by converting the heat energy to chemical energy and then to electrical energy.

APPLYING ENERGY, FORCE, WORK AND POWER TO TECHNOLOGY

Energy, power, work, and force are all important to understand for solving technological problems. **Energy** is required for any object to move or function. For technology, this typically involves energy conversion from stored energy (such as solar or chemical) to electrical or mechanical energy. These conversions cause machines to move or electronic devices to be powered. Energy is measured in units such as **joules**, **kilowatt-hours**, and **horsepower**.

To apply this energy, we need **force**. Force is the actual use of the energy, like pushing on a piston in an engine. Force is measured in **Newtons** (a Newton describes the amount of force needed to accelerate a 1-kilogram mass by 1 m/s^2).

Work describes what is actually accomplished through energy and force. It may be as simple as moving an object one inch, or by using sunlight that has been converted to electrical energy to light a lamp and power a computer. Work is typically measured in **joules**, or sometimes **foot-pounds**.

Power refers to how much energy is used in a given amount of time. It can be measured in **watts**. Measuring power can show the efficiency of a machine, and the cost required to maintain it.

SOLVING ENERGY, POWER, AND TRANSPORTATION PROBLEMS

Scientific principles are used frequently to solve problems relating to energy, power, and transportation. For example, **transportation engineering** is a field of study that applies scientific principles and technology to transportation. Artificial intelligence, more energy-efficient vehicles, and improved electronic equipment all depend on understanding and applying the basic principles of energy and power to create vehicles that operate more smoothly, safely, and effectively.

The field of **renewable energy** is growing quickly, and also requires thorough understanding and application of scientific principles. The three laws of thermodynamics describe energy:

- The first law, also known as conservation of energy, states that the universe has a constant total sum of energy that cannot be increased or decreased.
- The second law states that while energy is always the same amount, it becomes increasingly disorderly. Converting between forms of energy results in **waste heat** rather than complete transfer. The **efficiency** of mechanical systems can be calculated to see how much energy is wasted and whether efficiency should be improved.
- The third law states that no molecule can move below a temperature called **absolute zero**. This is used in calculations of entropy and efficiency of various substances.

POTENTIAL ENERGY

It is not easy to conceive of energy, in part because it comes in so many different forms. Wherever work is done, there is energy. Indeed, physics defines **energy** as the ability to do work. The unit of energy is the **joule (J)**. Perhaps the most difficult form of energy to understand is **potential energy (PE)**, the stored capacity for work in a physical body. For instance, when a brick is raised in the air, it acquires the potential energy to be pulled down by the gravitational force of the Earth. This particular form of potential energy is known as **gravitational potential energy**, and can be calculated by multiplying the object's mass by the force of gravity and the height to which the object has been raised. An object raised above the ground is storing energy to be used in a fall.

KINETIC ENERGY

When an object is in motion, it has **kinetic energy (KE)**. Kinetic energy is calculated by halving the mass of the object and multiplying it by the square of the object's velocity: $KE = \frac{1}{2}mv^2$. A heavy object will have more kinetic energy than a light one, and a fast object will have more kinetic energy than a slow one. Actually, the velocity of the object has much more effect on kinetic energy than the mass, as indicated by the fact that it is squared in the equation. A relatively small change in velocity can have a very large impact on the measure of kinetic energy.

WORK

In physical science, **work** is defined as the energy required to exert a given force over a given distance. In fact, work is calculated by **multiplying force by distance**. The unit for work is the joule (J), also known as the **newton-meter (N·m)** because it combines the units for force and distance. One joule of work is performed when one newton of force is exerted over one meter. Note that unless there is motion, no work is performed. Pushing hard against a brick wall may feel like work, but it is not defined as such in physical science. Also, work requires that the force and distance be in the same direction. If the direction of the force is only part of the direction of the distance, then work can only be calculated for the component of distance moving in the same direction of the force. For instance, if you push a toy sailboat straight ahead but the wind carries it to the right at the same time, your work can only be figured for the distance the sailboat moves forward.

POWER

Power is the measure of the amount of work performed in a certain interval. Another way of describing power is as the amount of energy changed in a given period. The basic equation for power is **work divided by time**. The unit of power is the joule per second, otherwise known as the watt (W). When one joule of work is performed in one second, one watt of power has been used. If, for example, a force of 10 N is required to move a book 1 meter, and the motion is accomplished in 2 seconds, the power is calculated $10N \times 1m \div 2s = 5W$. Note that power is inversely proportional to time; the faster work is done, the more power is used.

92

WORK AND POWER

When work is performed on an object, the kinetic energy of the object increases. Indeed, the change in the kinetic energy is equal to the amount of work performed. This is known as the **work-energy theorem**, and is expressed by the equation **Work = ΔKE**, where Δ (delta) means "the change in". This theorem can also be applied to decreases in kinetic energy: a heavy object moving quickly (that is, an object with a high level of kinetic energy) will require more work to be stopped. In addition, the work-energy theorem describes situations involving potential energy: when an object is lifted off the ground, the amount of work required to lift it is equal to the increase in its potential energy. Conversely, the gravitational force required to bring the object back to the ground is equal to the decrease, or negative change, in the object's potential energy.

THERMAL ENERGY

Thermal energy is the degree of motion of the atoms and molecules that make up a substance. Thermal energy is also referred to as **heat**, because the motion of atoms and molecules is related to the heat of the substance. Let's consider water as an example. As its thermal energy increases it moves from a solid (ice), to a liquid (water), and then to a gas (steam). Each change in state is accompanied by more movement by each individual water molecule. Likewise, your palms will produce more thermal energy (that is, they will get warmer) if you clap a few times. This is because the impact of the clapping actually causes the atoms in your skin to vibrate more.

INTERNAL COMBUSTION MOTORS

An **internal combustion motor** converts chemical energy into mechanical energy through burning. Motors are referred to as internal combustion when the burning takes place on the **inside**. The fuel combusts in small cylinders inside the motor. Each cylinder contains a piston, which is driven up and down by the tiny combustions of fuel. These up-and-down movements turn a crankshaft, which in a car is used to rotate the wheels. Some internal combustion motors have carburetors, which vaporize gasoline before it enters the cylinders, while others have fuel injectors, which inject gasoline vapor into the cylinder after it has been filled with compressed air. One of the problems with internal combustion motors is that they lose much of their energy in the form of heat.

ELECTRICAL MOTORS

Electric motors convert magnetic force into kinetic energy. In a **direct current (DC)** motor, a wire coil is placed in between two pieces of charged metal. A current running through the coil gives it a magnetic charge and causes it to rotate. The end of the coil can be attached to a shaft and used to do work. For instance, the coil could be connected to the axis of a fan blade, so that when it spins the blades rotate as well. There are a couple of devices used to refine the operation of an electric motor. A **commutator** reverses the charge of the wire every time it makes a half-rotation. This ensures the continuous spinning of the wire, since every time the positive side of the coil approaches the negative piece of metal, its charge is reversed and it must continue spinning to reach the positively charged metal.

CAMS, GEARS, AND LINKAGES

- **Cams**: an elliptical wheel that, when connected to a driveshaft, powers some mechanical motion; in an automobile engine, for instance, the up-and-down motion of the pistons rotates the cams, causing the wheels to move forward
- **Gears**: interlocking toothed wheels, one of which is connected to a shaft; when the shaft is twisted, the drive wheel spins in one direction and causes the other wheel to be spun in the opposite direction; if the other wheel is smaller than the drive wheel, it spins more quickly but produces less force; if the other wheel is larger than the drive wheel, it moves more slowly but produces a greater force
- **Linkages**: a system of connected bars held together by springs or hinges; the piston, rod, and crank in a car engine comprise a four-bar linkage

PNEUMATICS AND HYDRAULICS

Pneumatic systems operate with the aid of compressed air. Pneumatic systems are known for being safe, because compressed air is not flammable. **Hydraulic systems**, on the other hand, rely on the pressure exerted by liquid in a tube. In an automotive brake system, for instance, pulling the handle presses fluid against a lever that in turn forces the brake pad against the tire rim. Hydraulic systems work because most liquids cannot be compressed. Hydraulic systems are known for being efficient, and for being able to generate more force than pneumatics.

PULLEYS AND TRANSMISSIONS

- **Pulley**: a simple machine composed of at least one wheel with a rope extended around the rim, such that the wheel spins when the rope is pulled; the use of pulley systems can create great mechanical advantage (energy output is much greater than energy input); for instance, a two-pulley system is capable of halving the energy required to lift an object off of the ground
- **Transmission**: the component of a machine that directs the energy created to the intended task; for instance, an automotive transmission takes the spinning of the crankshaft and coverts it into the mechanical work of turning the axle

BASIC MOTOR MAINTENANCE AND REPAIR

The better part of motor maintenance is **regular cleaning and oiling**. Mechanics are able to keep engines running for decades so long as they are periodically lubricated and tested. **Lubrication** minimizes the friction in the engine, and keeps heat and abrasion from destroying the components. Most mechanics recommend **replacing certain parts** (as for instance the drive belts in an automotive engine) every so often in order to prevent more serious and expensive problems. In recent years, many car and other engines have been outfitted with computer systems to monitor performance. Mechanics must be able to evaluate data as well as perform the necessary repairs.

Energy Consumption and Conservation

CAREERS

Energy and power technology are continuously expanding **careers**. There are always jobs available for individuals who want to maintain and repair power station equipment, like substations, relays, and transformers. Power dispatchers monitor electricity dispersal to guard against overloads and insufficiencies. A nuclear plant operator tests and calibrates equipment and ensures that safety guidelines are being followed. There are also many jobs, like electrical lineman, that involve installation and maintenance of equipment used to deliver electricity. Increasingly, there are abundant and lucrative career opportunities in green energy technology. All of these jobs require **specialized education and training**, but they can never be outsourced and will continue to offer excellent pay and intellectual stimulation.

RENEWABLE AND NONRENEWABLE ENERGY RESOURCES

Scientists distinguish between **renewable energy resources**, which can be replaced in a relatively short time, and **nonrenewable energy resources**, which cannot. Fossil fuels are considered nonrenewable energy resources because they take so long to form. Indeed, the rate of consumption of fossil fuels vastly outstrips the rate of new fossil fuel formation. This is one of the reasons scientists are desperately searching for alternative forms of energy. The most common forms of renewable energy are nuclear, hydroelectric, solar, wind, and geothermal. All of these energy sources can be replaced in short order. However, it should be noted that renewable sources of energy are not necessarily good for the environment. Nuclear energy has been responsible for many devastating natural disasters, and hydroelectric power systems manipulate the water system in potentially damaging ways.

FOSSIL FUEL

Fossil fuels, so named because they are made of the **decomposed bodies** of prehistoric creatures, are a mixture of **carbon and hydrogen molecules**. Nevertheless, these fuels come in a number of different forms. **Coal** is a solid fossil fuel, made up primarily of carbon. It has to be extracted from the ground through mining. **Natural gas**, on the other hand, is a gas or liquid that has to be extracted from porous rocks. The main ingredient in natural gas is methane. **Oil** is a liquid fossil fuel that is found on or beneath the ground, either in large pools or soaked into porous rock. Oil is useless as fuel unless it is purified. Through the purification process, oil can be turned into kerosene, gasoline, and diesel fuel, among other products.

POWER FROM FOSSIL FUELS

The overwhelming majority of the Earth's energy is produced by burning fossil fuels. According to recent statistics, all but 16% of the energy consumed on Earth is produced by coal (22%), oil (37%), and natural gas (25%). Most fossil fuel-based power plants work according to a similar system. Fossil fuels are burned, and the resulting heat boils water and created steam. This steam is kept under high pressure and directed against the blades of a turbine. The whirling axis of the turbine is connected to a generator, where the kinetic motion of the blades is converted into electricity. The electricity generated is sent out from the power plant through a series of wires.

SOLAR AND WIND POWER

Although the sun provides more than enough energy to power the entire world, scientists have struggled to develop systems capable of harnessing this power. It was not until the 1990s that scientists established the first set of **solar panels** that stored energy as heat. This facility is in the Mojave Desert of California. At present, the **solar cell** is the most common way to convert the rays of the sun into electricity. Sunlight hits an outer layer of phosphorus and silicon, exciting electrons and generating current in a circuit. The current terminates in a layer of boron and silicon atoms. **Wind power** is also derived from the sun, specifically from the variations in temperature that create areas of low and high pressure, thus producing the shifts in air known as wind. The windmills of today are similar to those used hundreds of years ago: these days, the spinning blades power an electrical generator rather than a grinding wheel.

HYDROELECTRIC AND GEOTHERMAL ENERGY

Hydroelectric energy is generated from the flow of rapid rivers and streams. In a typical arrangement, a hydroelectric power plant is adjacent to a dam, which holds back a flowing body of water. Water from the resulting reservoir is directed through a series of channels (called penstocks) and used to spin large turbines. The rotation of the turbines powers an electrical generator. **Geothermal energy**, meanwhile, is obtained using the heat of the Earth. Specifically, geothermal power plants are based on extremely hot pools of subterranean water. A deep well is drilled into the pool, and the rising steam is used to spin turbines. Unfortunately, geothermal energy production is only practicable in areas where volcanic magma is close the surface, as for instance in New Zealand and California.

NUCLEAR ENERGY

In nuclear power plants, scientists cause atoms to undergo **nuclear fission (separation)**. The resulting chain reactions produce a great deal of energy, in the form of heat. This heat is applied to large pools of water, inside the familiar nuclear reactors. The steam rising off the water powers turbines, which are attached to electrical generators. The process of nuclear fission and nuclear energy creation is quite clean, but it requires the use of radioactive materials which are difficult to dispose of. Scientists are optimistic that nuclear fusion will become a viable way of creating nuclear energy in the future. For the time being, however, concerns over the safety and environmental hazard of nuclear power generation limit its use.

FUEL CELLS

The most efficient way to convert chemical energy to electricity is with a **fuel cell**. In a hydrogen-oxygen fuel cell, there are separate reservoirs for the two gases. The hydrogen is oxidized and emits a number of electrons, which act as an electrical current flowing to the oxygen chamber. The oxygen is then reduced (that is, it gives up electrons), and the extra negative particles are carried back to the hydrogen chamber to begin the process anew. This flow of electrons throughout the fuel cell produces **electricity and steam**. Fuel cells have been used to power space shuttles and buildings, but engineers are still trying to develop small-scale models appropriate for cars. At present, the amount of hydrogen gas needed to power an automobile has too much volume to be functional.

ENERGY LOSS DURING CONVERSION

Whenever energy is converted from one form to another, some of it is lost. Indeed, some **fossil fuel power plants lose** 2/3 of the energy they produce. The ways in which energy can be lost are several: burning fuels heat not only the water but the surrounding air and the water container; some steam escapes before it can power the turbines; the turbines are subject to friction forces; and some electricity escapes the generator cables. With the inevitability of energy loss in mind, scientists have set about developing ways to **minimize inefficiencies**. For instance, many countries use the water heated during electricity generation to warm homes in the winter or to use as bath water. This does not diminish energy loss, but rather gets more use out of the energy retained.

ENERGY CONSERVATION

One of the most amazing insights of physics is that the amount of energy in the universe never changes. This is known as the **law of conservation of energy**: energy cannot be created or destroyed; it can only be converted and transferred. When a brick falls to the ground, the kinetic energy of motion is transferred into the sound of the impact and the tiny amount of heat generated by the friction. When you eat a carrot, the chemical energy created by the sun is turned into cellular and muscular energy in your body, which in turn are expressed as **motion**. The overall amount of energy remains constant in every physical system. One of the challenges of technology is to ensure that as much energy as possible is applied to the intended task.

ENERGY EFFICIENCY

Efficiency is the degree to which a device uses the input energy to accomplish its intended task. Automobiles are relatively inefficient machines, because they use only about 20% of the energy from gasoline combustion to propel the car forward. The rest of the energy is lost through friction, wind resistance, heat loss, etc. Efficiency is equal to the **amount of work done divided by the amount of energy consumed**. It is usually expressed as a percentage; if 50 joules of work produce only 40 joules of energy towards our purpose, we are operating at only 80% efficiency. It is almost impossible to create a system that is totally efficient; friction forces and heat loss are constantly draining energy.

Electronics

ELECTRICAL CHARGE

An **electrical charge** is created when electrons are gained or lost. For instance, when you scuff your rubber-soled shoes on a carpet, you are transferring electrons from the carpet to your shoes. Then, when you touch the refrigerator, the charge you picked up from the carpet is transferred to the metal, giving you a little shock. The basic rule of electrical charge is that like charges repel and opposite charges attract. There are only two kinds of charge, **positive and negative**. Since electrons are negative, the object that gains electrons becomes negative and the object that loses electrons becomes positive. Note that no electrons are created or destroyed in the charging process. The resulting positive charge is equal to the negative charge, a phenomenon known as the conservation of charge.

COULOMB'S LAW

Coulomb's law describes the force relationship between two charged particles. The formula for Coulomb's law is $F = k(q_1q_2/d^2)$, where F is force, k is a constant, q_1 is the charge of one particle, q_2 is the charge of the other particle, and d is the distance between the two particles. The distance between the particles is an inverse square of the force relationship, meaning that as the distance expands, the force between the particles decreases markedly. The proportionality constant k is similar to the force of gravity, insofar as it is consistent for all charged particles. One difference is that k can be either **attractive or repulsive**, while the force of gravity is always attractive. The unit of charge is the **coulomb (C)**.

ELECTRICAL CURRENT

In a piece of metal, the electrons on the very outside of the atom are only loosely held together. Indeed, they can flow freely throughout the metal, enabling the conduction of heat and electrical energy. The flow of electrons is known as **electrical current**. The flow of electrons through a charged material is analogous to the flow of water. An electrical current only exists when there is a net flow of electrons in one direction. The random flow of electrons in all directions is typical of uncharged materials. Electrical current is measured in **amperes (A)**. One ampere is equal to the rate of flow of one coulomb of charge per second.

DIRECT AND ALTERNATING CURRENT

Direct current (dc) flows in one direction, while alternating current (ac) flows in one direction and then the other. The classic example of **direct current** is a battery system, in which the terminals of the battery always have the same charge, and the flow of electric current is from one to the other continuously. In a system with **alternating current**, on the other hand, the charges on the terminals of the generator (whether a battery or some other power source) are constantly switching back and forth. The electrons in an alternating system never really go anywhere; they simply quiver back and forth in place as the direction of the current shifts. Interestingly, even in a direct current system, electrons move at a speed of less than one centimeter per second.

VOLTAGE

An electric current can only exist when there are more electrons in one area than another. The current is the result of electrons moving into areas of lower pressure, just as wind is the result of air moving from areas of high pressure to areas of low pressure. In an electrical system, pressure is known as voltage. The **voltage** of a system is directly proportional to the electric potential energy of the system, a relationship that can be calculated as **voltage = potential energy/charge**. In other words, a higher voltage translates into a higher electrical potential energy. In order for voltage to exist, there must be a difference in pressure on opposing ends of the circuit. A battery is simply a device for creating this difference: one end of the battery generates high pressure, while the other generates low pressure. This ensures steady voltage.

ELECTRICAL RESISTANCE

The amount of electrical current in a circuit is dependent on the voltage and the resistance. **Resistance** is measured in **ohms (Ω)**. The amount of resistance is influenced in part by the length and width of the wire. There is greater resistance in a longer and narrower wire. Like most features of electrical current, this is analogous to the flow of water: a long and narrow pipe will slow down water much more than a short, road pipe. The most important determinant of resistance, however, is the **material** through which the current must travel. Some metals, like copper, have almost no resistance, while rubber and other materials have an extremely high resistance. One way to decrease the resistance of a substance is to lower its temperature. When a material offers virtually no resistance, it is designated as a superconductor.

OHM'S LAW

The unit of electrical resistance, the ohm, is named for Georg Simon Ohm, a German scientist who explored electrical current, voltage, and resistance. He found that in a given circuit the current is directly proportional to the voltage and inversely proportional to the resistance. This relationship is known as **Ohm's law**, and as a formula is expressed **current = voltage/resistance**. It is common, however, to see Ohm's law written $I = V/R$, where I is current. In terms of units, the law is expressed amperes = volts/ohms. According to Ohm's law, the level of current will rise when the voltage rises, and by the same proportion. So, if current is doubled, voltage will be doubled as well. However, when current is doubled, resistance is halved.

ELECTRIC POWER

Electrical current is capable of doing work. The amount of work that a given current can do in an interval is called **electric power**. Electric power only exists when the current is converted into a different form of energy, as, for instance, when it is used to spin the blades of a fan or to light a bulb. Electric power, then, is the amount of transformed energy divided by the time elapsed. It is typically calculated by multiplying current by voltage. The unit of electric power is the **watt (W)**. Many electrical devices and appliances list their power. For instance, power and voltage are printed on light bulbs. A light bulb with 60W of power and 120 V of voltage will require a current of 0.5 A.

SERIES AND PARALLEL CIRCUITS

In order to flow, electrons require a circuit, a complete and unbroken pathway. When a circuit contains more than one device powered by electrical energy, it is either arranged as a series circuit or a parallel circuit. In a **series circuit**, all of the devices are connected along the same pathway. For instance, in a simple series circuit a wire extends from a battery terminal to first one light bulb, then another light bulb, and finally to the other battery terminal. The path of the wire resembles a ring. The main problem with a series circuit is that the failure of one device breaks the entire circuit. In a **parallel circuit**, on the other hand, the wire extends out in branches to each device. Each device, then, has its own electron path.

CURRENT IN A SERIES CIRCUIT

In a series circuit, the electric current only follows **one path**. For this reason, the current in a series circuit is the same in every part. The resistance in a series circuit is the sum of the resistances of all the devices. Assuming that there is no resistance in the wire, the total resistance can be derived by adding up the individual resistances of the devices. The current in a series circuit can be calculated by dividing the voltage of the source by the total resistance. Each device in a series circuit gets the same amount of voltage. Finally, the drop in voltage across each of the devices in a series circuit is in proportion to the resistance of the device. In other words, more energy is expended when the current must pass through a device with higher resistance.

CURRENT IN A PARALLEL CIRCUIT

In a parallel circuit, each electric device is **connected by a branch** to the main part of the circuit. So, if one of the branches is broken, the rest of the circuit does not cease to work. In a parallel circuit, the flow of electricity, and therefore the voltage, is the same across every device. However, the total current in the circuit is divided up among the various branches, and so the more devices in the system, the lower the current in each branch. The quantity of current in each branch is inversely proportional to the resistance of the branch. Also, the current in the circuit is equal to the sum of the currents in all parallel branches. If more parallel branches are added, however, the resistance is lowered. In other words, the total resistance of the entire circuit is less than the resistance in any of the individual branches.

ELECTRONIC COMPONENTS

- **Terminal**: the point in a circuit where the current is either initiated or broken; for example, a battery has two terminals
- **Resistor**: controls the level of current in a circuit by providing resistance; in other words, voltage decreases as current passes through a circuit; most resistors work by converting electrical current into heat, which escapes into the air and is thus taken out of the system
- **Diode**: restricts the flow of current in one direction only; used to convert alternating current to direct current and to amplify the current in one direction; composed of two parts (anode and cathode)
- **Amplifier**: any device, such as a transistor or an electron tube, that increase the amplitude of an electrical current; in other words, an amplifier receives an input signal and produces a larger signal with an identical wave form
- **Capacitor**: (also known as a condenser) stores electrical charge temporarily; typically composed of two metal plates separated by a thin insulator (often air); used for controlling and moderating current
- **Transducer**: converts energy into a different form; for instance, a microphone converts sound energy into electricity, a photoelectric cell converts light energy into electricity, and a loudspeaker converts electricity into sound
- **Detector**: identifies and possibly responds to certain electrical signals
- **Transistor**: can function in a circuit as a detector, switch, or amplifier

ELECTRONIC DEVICES

- **Transformer**: shifts electric energy from one circuit to another, often with a change in current or voltage; for example, a small transformer is used to diminish the current flowing through a doorbell, in order to reduce the risk of serious shock
- **Switch**: alternately completes, diverts, or breaks a circuit
- **Relay**: a type of switch that, when activated by a small current, initiates a larger current; when the small current reaches the relay, a gate is closed, thus completing the circuit for the larger current; relays are used in television and telephone transmission, in which a small input signal initiates the broadcast of a much larger signal

Vehicles and Vehicular Subsystems

TRANSPORTATION

- **Transportation planners** address transportation issues at both the local and regional levels. They **research** different modes of transportation (automobiles, bicycles, ride-sharing, etc.), **forecast** the impact of those modes using computer modeling, and promote alternative transportation modes. Transportation planning usually requires a two-year degree in transportation technology.
- **Transit operations analysts** examine mass transit operations, such as trains and buses, and determine how they can better serve the community through either new technologies or revised procedures. This career normally requires a two-year degree in transportation technology.
- **Civil Engineering Technicians** assist in the planning, design and construction of transportation structures such as highways, subways, railways, tunnels and airports. They **analyze** highway survey data and traffic signal timing, conduct repair work on damaged structures, and collaborate with CAD technicians to create maps and building specifications. Civil Engineering Technicians usually require a two-year degree in civil engineering and can work in a variety of organizations, both public and private.

RAIL, AIR AND ROAD

- **Rail transportation** is the use of a **railway**, which is simply either a set of two steel rails running parallel and connected by ties; a monorail, which is a single rail; or a maglev, which is magnetic suspension. A train runs along the railway, and can be powered in a variety of ways including steam, diesel, electricity, gas turbines, gravity, cables, and others.
- **Air transportation** is the use of **aircraft** (such as airplanes, helicopters and gyroplanes) to reach a destination. Aircraft will not operate properly without air flow to provide lift and an area reserved for landing. The air transportation industry makes use of airports for loading, maintenance, and refueling. Air transportation is one of the fastest modes of transportation.
- **Road transportation** is the use of **prepared pathways** (paved, smoothed, etc.) to travel between multiple places. A prominent example is a highway. Roads are most commonly used by automobiles, such as cars, buses and trucks. Bicycles and pedestrians also make use of the road system. Although automobiles are very adaptable, they have poor energy efficiency and create pollution.

MARINE, SPACE, AND INTERMODAL

- **Marine transportation** is the use of **boats, ships, barges and other buoyant transports** that utilize water. Marine craft use a variety of propulsion methods such as wind power, steam power, petroleum engines and nuclear energy. Marine transport is highly efficient and cost effective, but tends to be slow. Its primary commercial use is transportation of non-perishable goods.
- **Space transport** is the use of **spacecraft** to travel into space. Examples include space shuttles, satellites, and rockets. It is the rarest form of transportation.
- **Intermodal transportation** is the use of **multiple transportation systems** to reach a destination. For instance, if a person orders a piece of furniture online, it may be transported on an airplane and a truck before it reaches its destination.

PROBLEMS ASSOCIATED WITH TRANSPORTATION SYSTEMS

Transportation systems have greatly enhanced mankind's ability to travel and opened up new possibilities for both work and recreation. However, advances in transportation have not come without problems. For instance, as the population within cities increases, the number of cars and motorists increases as well. This creates problems such as **traffic congestion** and **air pollution**, especially within heavily urbanized areas. A possible solution is better public transportation systems, such as monorails, buses and subway systems. Another solution is to build residences nearer to places of work so that people have the option of walking or biking to their jobs. Another problem with transportation systems is **urban sprawl**, which occurs when people live outside the city and then commute in for work. Urban sprawl not only increases air pollution, it requires removal of natural habitats, further displacing animal populations and limiting their food supply.

INTERNAL COMBUSTION ENGINE AND EXTERNAL COMBUSTION ENGINE

An **internal combustion engine**, or **ICE**, generates propulsive force through the combustion of fuel—usually gasoline or a similar energy-dense liquid—and air within a combustion chamber. This action produces **high pressure gas** that is directed over a piston, turbine, nozzle, or similar engine component. ICEs serve as the primary means of power generation in all types of automobiles, aircraft, and water transports. Common types of ICEs include two-stroke engines, four-stroke engines, diesel engines, wankel engines, jet engines and gas turbines.

An **external combustion engine**, or **ECE**, generates propulsive force by using an **external heat source** to heat and cause expansion in a fluid. The heat source acts through a heat exchanger or engine wall. The fluid is then cooled and reused. Common types of ECEs include steam engines and Stirling engines.

TRANSPORTATION INDUSTRIES

- The **automotive industry** performs functions related to the **design, creation, manufacturing and marketing** of automobiles. Many automobile manufacturers in the United States are part of a trade group known as The Alliance of Automobile Manufacturers, which represents their common interests and works to fulfill social transportation needs.
- The **automotive repair and service industry** handles **repairs and servicing** of automobiles after they have been purchased by the consumer. The National Institute for Automotive Service Excellence, or ASE, provides training and certification to service technicians and professionals in the United States.
- The **airline industry** transports passengers and cargo via **air transportation**. There are commercial airlines in most of the civilized world. To become a commercial aircraft service in the United States, an aircraft operator must be granted an air operator's certificate (AOC) by the National Aviation Authority, or NAA.
- The **shipping industry** transports passengers and cargo via water transportation. It serves commercial, recreational and military purposes, and is less expensive than air travel.

FOSSIL FUELS, STEAM, ELECTRICITY AND GRAVITY

- **Fossil fuels** are created from decomposition of dead animals and plants over a period of time. Fossil fuels such as petroleum are especially important in transportation because they provide a variety of fuels, such as gasoline, diesel fuel, oil, and jet fuel. Fossil fuels are considered non-renewable resources because their current rate of usage exceeds their rate of renewal.
- **Steam** is created by boiling water, and then harnessed to power steam engines, which propel transports such as locomotives, tractors, and ships. Fossil fuels, solar energy, nuclear energy, and geothermal energy often provide the heat necessary to create steam.
- **Electricity** is often used to power trains and street cars via electric lines. It can also increase the efficiency or serve as the sole power source of a car engine.
- **Gravity** is used to power rail systems.

BUOYANCY AND GRAVITATIONAL ACCELERATION

Buoyancy is a force that causes objects to **float** in a fluid, such as air or water. Buoyancy is generated because there is more pressure at the bottom of a column of fluid than the top; consequently, objects that are less dense than the fluid rise to the top while denser objects sink. In air transportation, buoyancy is a key consideration in lighter-than-air modes of transport, such as hot air balloons and blimps. The gas within the balloon or blimp will only be pushed up (i.e. float) if it less dense than the surrounding air. In marine transportation, ships hulls must be designed such that they are less dense than the surrounding water; otherwise, they will not float.

Gravitational acceleration is a downward force exerted on an object by gravity. It is used as the primary means of propulsion for certain types of rail systems. In the absence of friction, all objects fall at the same rate. In the presence of air friction, buoyancy will cause denser objects to fall faster.

MOMENTUM, INERTIA, AND WEIGHT

- **Momentum** equals an object's **mass multiplied by its velocity (p = mv)** and indicates both the direction and magnitude of an object. When objects collide, they transfer their momentum to each other. Momentum helps engineers predict and determine the outcome of a collision between two objects.
- **Inertia** is an object's innate resistance to changes in its state of motion or rest. Put simply, a stationary object will remain stationary and a moving object will remain moving unless they are acted upon by outside forces. More massive objects possess more inertia than less massive ones. Inertia helps designers to understand the level of force necessary to propel a particular mode of transport.
- **Weight** is a force that gravity applies on an object. An object will not fly unless its thrust-to-weight ratio is greater than the pull of gravity. An object's weight will vary according to the strength of the gravitational field in which it is situated.

PROPULSION, ENERGY STORAGE AND GUIDANCE

Propulsion is achieved through the following means:

- **Air transportation** – generates thrust by pushing airflow over a wing.
- **Marine transportation** – relies on propellers driven by some type of internal combustion or steam engine. Some ships still rely on oars or sails.
- **Space transportation** – uses a rocket engine to expel hot gas.
- **Road and rail transportation** – relies on wheels driven by some type of power force (e.g., combustion engines, electric motors, animal muscle).

Energy storage is the process of using devices or media to store energy for use at a later time. For instance, batteries and fuel cells can store electrical energy for use in electric motors. Petroleum and other fossil fuels store energy for use in internal combustion engines.

Guidance is the process of controlling the movement, speed and navigation of craft. In air transportation, guidance is achieved through manipulating ailerons, rudders, fuel pumps, and similar devices. In marine transportation, it is achieved by adjusting sails or manipulating rudders. In road transportation, it is normally achieved through a steering mechanism.

DISPATCH AND VEHICLE TRACKING

Dispatch is a vehicle assignment procedure used by companies that operate fleets of vehicles. A dispatcher **receives call information** from customers, and then **assigns a vehicle** to the customer based on the order in which the call was received and the proximity of the driver to the customer's location. **Computer assisted dispatch** increases the efficiency of the dispatch procedure by using various software applications and devices, such as GPS. In some systems, each truck may record information through an onboard GPS system. This information is downloaded once the truck returns to its base. In other systems, the truck may be able to communicate and relay its position in real time to the base. The latter system is more expensive but enhances efficiency.

Vehicle tracking is a system capable of determining the location, speed, and direction of a fleet vehicle. The system can be based on GPS or satellite tracking technology.

THRUST, LIFT, AND DRAG

- **Thrust** is a reaction force that occurs when mass expelled or accelerated in one direction causes a proportional force in the opposite direction. In air transportation, thrust is generated by pushing airflow over a wing, usually by means of a spinning propeller, a fan pulling air through a jet engine, or a rocket engine expelling hot gas. In marine transportation, propellers generate thrust by accelerating water in one direction.
- **Drag** is a force created by a fluid (such as air or water) passing over an object. Drag exerts a force that runs parallel to and opposes the movement of an oncoming object.
- **Lift** is a surface force created by a fluid (such as air or water) passing over an object. Lift exerts a force that goes perpendicular to the direction of an oncoming object. In air transportation, airfoils must generate sufficient thrust and lift to overcome drag; otherwise, the object will not fly. Lift is not limited to upward movement. By adjusting the shape of a wing, aircraft can generate the lift required to climb, descend or bank.

FLEET MANAGEMENT, DRIVER TRAINING, FLEET EXPENDITURE MANAGEMENT, ROUTING AND SCHEDULING

- **Fleet management** seeks to decrease the risks, improve the productivity and lower the operating costs of a company's fleet of vehicles. Fleet management encompasses many different functions, such as vehicle tracking, diagnostics, maintenance, fuel usage, and health and safety.
- **Driver training** should include courses on performing basic vehicle maintenance, improving driver skills, and following certain procedures when the driver is involved in an accident.
- **Fleet expenditure management** should include a system for account management, handling tax invoices electronically, and fuel management.
- **Routing** involves selecting the paths and roadways a group of vehicles will use to reach their destinations. Selections will be made based on the roads which provide the most efficient and effective means of access.
- **Scheduling** is the process of assigning customers to routes. The goal is to optimize the efficiency with which drivers can service customers.

PNEUMATICS AND HYDRAULICS

Pneumatics is a type of fluid power that creates mechanical movement through the use of **pressurized gas**, such as **compressed air**. In transportation, pneumatics has a variety of applications:

- **Air brakes** on buses, trucks, and trains.
- **Air engines**, pneumatic motors, and compressed air engines in locomotives, automobiles, and commercial airlines which use compressed air to start their main engines.
- **Pneumatic tires**, which are filled with compressed air.

Hydraulics is a type of fluid power that creates mechanical movement through the use of **incompressible liquids**. These liquids are pressurized and then used to transmit power throughout the system. In transportation, hydraulic principles are often incorporated into brakes. Hydraulic systems use far higher pressures than pneumatic systems, can generate much greater forces and can bear much greater loads, and consist of the following components: hydraulic pumps, control valves, actuators, accumulators, filters, and hydraulic fluids.

TRANSMISSION AND GEAR

A **transmission**, also known as a **gearbox**, uses gear ratios to convert between speed and torque. In an automobile, the transmission receives output from the internal combustion engine via the **crankshaft**, and then transmits power to differentials (drive wheels) via the **drive shaft**. Transmissions are necessary because the engine operates at a much higher **RPM (revolutions per minute)** than the wheels rotate. The transmission converts speed into torque at lower velocities and then torque into speed at higher velocities, such as highway driving. Transmissions can also increase fuel efficiency.

A **gear** is a circular rotating component with cogs cut into it around the edges. These cogs mesh with the cogs of another gear, and thereby **transmit torque** (i.e. rotational force) between the gears. A transmission is simply two or more meshed gears working together. The gear ratio is the relative number of cogs between two meshed gears. When a smaller cog is turning a larger cog, the larger cog possesses more torque.

PISTONS AND CRANK SHAFT

A **piston** converts pressure into rotational force. It is a reciprocating component inside an internal combustion engine as well as other types of reciprocating engines. The piston is contained within a cylinder. When gas expands inside the cylinder, the piston is driven down and up in a continuous reciprocating motion, which is transmitted to the crankshaft through piston rods or connecting rods.

A **crankshaft** converts linear motion of the pistons into rotational motion that passes through the transmission and eventually turns the wheels. The crankshaft is connected to the pistons via a series of rods. Each rod is connected to a crank pin—a section of the crankshaft with an axis that does not line up exactly with the main axis of the crankshaft. By pushing down on these pins, the linear force is converted into rotational force.

BELT AND PULLEY SYSTEM

A **belt and pulley system** consists of multiple pulleys connected to a belt. A **pulley** is a wheel that is part of an axle or shaft, and is also known as a drum or a sheave. In some cases, the belt may fit into a groove running around the circumference of the wheel. When the **belt** is pulled, it transmits torque and speed over the axles to which it is connected. A belt and pulley system can perform speed and torque conversions if the pulleys differ in size. The ratio between the sizes determines the nature of the conversion. There are three types of pulley systems: **A fixed or class 1 system** has a fixed axle and a mechanical advantage of 1, meaning the force is not multiplied. **A movable or class 2 system** has a free axle that can move in space, and applies a mechanical advantage of 2, meaning the force is doubled on the object attached to the pulley. **A compound pulley** incorporates class 1 and class 2 systems. A block and tackle is a type of compound pulley in which each axle has several pulleys.

WEAK COMPRESSION WITHIN AN INTERNAL COMBUSTION ENGINE

Weak compression within an internal combustion engine can have a variety of causes, and there are simple methods for determining these causes:

- If a compression test shows that one cylinder has low compression, put a small amount of oil into the cylinder. Test its compression again. If the compression reads normally, then the engine simply has worn piston rings. If the compression does not increase, the engine may have leaky valves or a blown head gasket. If compression increases but does not return to normal, the engine may have worn piston rings and leaky valves.
- When two neighboring cylinders have low compression, the engine likely has a leaking head gasket. Adjust the head bolts so they match engine specifications. Retest the compression. If the compression does not return to normal, remove the head gasket and examine the engine blocks for cracks. If no cracks are discovered, replace the head gasket.

TESTING COMPRESSION

A **compression test** checks the compression within each cylinder of an internal combustion engine. The test requires a compression gauge, and follows these basic steps:

- Ensure the battery is completely charged and the automobile's tuning is good. Take the car on a 20 minute drive so that all engine components have reached full operating temperature.
- Determine appropriate engine compression and operating parameters by consulting a shop manual.
- Ensure that the engine is turned off. Remove all spark plugs and disconnect the ignition coil. This prevents the engine from starting. Block open the throttle and choke.
- Crank the engine as you test the compression. Insert the compression gauge into each engine cylinder, and record the reading. Reset gauge back to 0 before moving on to the next cylinder.
- Determine if there are any pressure differences between cylinders, and compare all cylinders against operating specifications. If the differences are too great, the engine may have a problem.

VACUUM TEST

A **vacuum test** is performed with a **pressure gauge**, which is also known as a **vacuum gauge**. It measures the difference between the air pressure inside and outside of the intake manifold. A vacuum test can find intake manifold gasket leaks, ignition issues, blocked exhaust systems, burned valves, weak springs, and other problems. It follows these basic steps:

- Ensure that the battery is completely charged and that the automobile's tuning is good. Take the car on a 20 minute drive so all engine components have reached full operating temperature.
- Attach the vacuum gauge. On a car, fasten the vacuum gauge where the vacuum tubing leads to the windshield wiper motor. If necessary, detach the vacuum booster pump on the windshield wiper. This may interfere with the accuracy of the readings. Ensure that all connections are airtight.
- Turn on the engine and allow it to idle. A healthy, well-tuned engine will idle at a reading between 18 and 22 inches at sea level. Large fluctuations in the reading or a lower reading than expected indicate an engine problem.

WEAK OR FLUCTUATING VACUUM READINGS

If a vacuum test on an internal combustion engine produces **large fluctuations in readings**, it indicates a problem with **some (but not all) of the cylinders**. Possible problems include the following:

- Intake manifold leak in one cylinder.
- Wear in the intake valve guides.
- Defective piston or piston rings.
- Faulty throttle shaft.

If a vacuum test produces **low but constant readings**, it indicates a problem with **all cylinders**. Possible problems include the following:

- Poor value timing.
- Faulty vacuum lines.
- Faulty carburetor throttle shaft.
- Damaged flange gasket.

By revving the engine to 2000 RPM and repeating the vacuum test, a tester can check for additional problems, such as ignition, timing, sticking valves, manifold leaks, and an incorrect mixture.

CREATING AUTOMOBILE ENGINES, SHIPS' HULLS AND AIRPLANES

Engine blocks for automobiles are typically made of cast iron; however, the reciprocating pistons within the engine generally consist of aluminum. As the engine warms up, the aluminum cylinders will begin expanding into their cast cylinder bores. The bores must be large enough to accommodate the pistons when the engine is hot; consequently, the bores will be very loose when the engine is cold. Compression tests should only be conducted when the engine is hot.

Modern ships' hulls are made of steel with various structural members, such as bulkheads, girders, and stringers. Hulls must be watertight and mostly hollow so that the ship has enough buoyancy to float.

Commercial airplanes are built using aluminum alloys and composite materials. Titanium is used in constructing both the jet's engine as well as other structural members.

Biotechnology and Environmental Quality

Biotechnology in Business, Industry, and Society

CAREERS

The field of **biotechnology** is broad and lucrative. In addition, research continues to develop new areas for study, so the job supply is ever increasing. Perhaps the most basic job in biotechnology is the lab technician. **Lab techs** are employed by police departments, research facilities, and medical institutions. A **quality control analyst** is a special employee who continuously monitors lab performance to ensure that standards are being met. A **bioinformatician** uses computer science skills to convert the data gathered through research to actionable information. A **biomedical engineer** builds the equipment and develops the materials that make biotechnological research possible. Finally, a **validation technician** ensures that research adheres to the law and to the rules established by regulatory agencies and professional organizations. These professionals also work to improve productivity and efficiency within the lab.

ANTHROPOMETRICS AND ERGONOMICS

Anthropometrics is a systematic approach to **measuring the human body**. It originated after the Second World War, as designers began to notice that many machines and pieces of furniture were inappropriately configured for human bodies. It became clear that designing better-sized machines could improve productivity as well as comfort. At around the same time, the field of ergonomics was exploring how better design could reduce injury in the workplace. Ergonomically inclined designers used the data generated through anthropometrics to create equipment that was easier to use and less taxing on the body. An emphasis on ergonomics was enshrined in United States law by the Occupational Health and Safety Act, which established some conditions for workplace furniture and equipment.

JOINT REPLACEMENTS AND PROSTHETICS

Advances in medical technology have made **joint and limb replacement surgery** an increasingly viable option for victims of pain or dysfunction. The most common joints to be replaced are the **knees and hips**. Typically, a hip replacement will entail replacing both the hip socket and the top of the femur; this leg bone will be cut off at the top so that the replacement bone and socket can be attached. An **artificial limb**, known as a **prosthesis**, must be precisely measured so that it will not throw off the balance of the body. Laser measurement techniques have made it possible to calculate the appropriate length for a prosthesis within thousandths of an inch. There are prosthetics available for every limb of the body, though the most common are arms and legs below the knee. There are now electronic prostheses that respond to nerve impulses and actually perform the movements of the limb they have replaced. For instance, there are amazing prosthetic arms capable of grasping and lifting objects in response to the myoelectric impulses transmitted by the muscles of the upper arm to which it is attached.

ARTIFICIAL ORGANS

Biomedical research has produced **artificial replacements for virtually every organ** of the human body. There are electronic devices that stimulate certain parts of the brain, providing relief from depression and epilepsy. There are artificial ears that actually enable the recipient to hear. Artificial eyes are still improving, but already they have restored sight to many blind people. The most popular artificial organ is the replacement kidney. It functions like a dialysis unit, passing blood through a solution that extracts waste matter and restores electrolytes. Artificial bladders are

108

unique in that they have been grown from living tissue in the laboratory. Artificial pancreases incorporate living tissue into a donor pancreas, which minimizes the risk of rejection by the recipient's body. **Stem cell research** has enabled doctors to grow replacement organs with cells from the recipient's own body. Perhaps the most difficult organ to replicate has been the heart. As of yet, there is not an artificial heart capable of sustaining life for more than a year and a half, though even this is quite a feat.

COMMON DEVICES FOR MONITORING HEALTH

A **blood glucose meter** helps people with diabetes keep track of their blood sugar levels. These devices are portable and easy to use. The most common version uses a small tack to draw a tiny blood sample, though there are also devices that measure blood sugar in the urine. A **sphygmomanometer** measures blood pressure. Inexpensive versions of this device are now available for personal use. In addition, there are now **personal cholesterol monitors** that let people keep track of their levels of triglycerides, cholesterol (including HDL), glucose, and ketones. These devices are valuable for people with heart problems. **Digital thermometers** are ubiquitous and can provide a much more accurate measure of body temperature than **mercury thermometers**. Finally, there are a wide array of electronic asthma devices, including **nebulizers** (inhaler), **spirometers** (measures lung capacity), and **peak flow meters**.

ORTHOTICS

Orthotics is the branch of medicine related to creating devices that improve physical performance and reduce pain. An **orthosis**, commonly called a **brace**, may control movement, limit the range of motion, provide support, or reduce the ability to bear weight on a certain part of the body. A common example of an orthosis is a back brace, which may be specially designed to treat a problem like lordosis or may simply diffuse the weight borne by the spine. The introduction of computer measurement has made it possible to create personalized braces quite inexpensively. Also, the development of extremely hard and durable plastics has enabled the production of lightweight, long-lasting braces. These devices have helped remediate pain and speed rehabilitation for millions of people.

REPRODUCING DNA IN A LABORATORY THROUGH POLYMERASE CHAIN REACTION

Scientists have developed a technique, called **polymerase chain reaction**, for reproducing segments of DNA. Living cells are not required for this process. In a matter of hours, it is possible to create 100 billion molecules that are exactly the same as a given DNA molecule. This process can be used in DNA fingerprinting, molecular biology, and biomedical technology. The process is complex, but it basically entails separating the two strands of the DNA double helix, isolating a section of the DNA to be replicated, and then using an enzyme to catalyze the formation of new bonds in that section. The result is that the amount of DNA in the specimen is doubled. Every time the process is repeated, the amount of DNA is doubled, so the total amount of DNA quickly gets very large.

DNA TECHNOLOGY IN CRIMINAL SCIENCE

The development of effective DNA identification procedures has revolutionized the branch of criminal science known as **forensics**. If doctors and law enforcement officers are able to recover some fresh tissue, blood, or semen after a violent crime, they can identify the perpetrator beyond a shadow of doubt. To begin with, laboratory technicians will use **antibodies** to identify the surface cells of the sample, which will indicate the particular type of tissue or fluid. Then, the DNA will be isolated and special enzymes will be applied to it. These enzymes cut the DNA into fragments. The fragments are different for every person, though identical twins will have the same fragmentation patterns. By analyzing the pattern of fragments, forensic scientists can make conclusive matches between samples taken from a crime scene and samples taken from suspects.

IMPROVING AIR QUALITY

Scientists have developed a number of ways to use **microorganisms** in the **improvement of air quality**. For instance, **biofiltering** is a technique in which microbes are placed on a support medium, like a sheet of plastic, and then bathed with aqueous nutrients. The microbes extract contaminants from a gas. In some instances, biofilters have removed 90 percent of the contamination. A similar method, **bioscrubbing**, entails the introduction of a microbe-filled liquid to the contaminated gas. This technique has also proved successful, though it can be difficult to enact on a small scale. Some labs have found it difficult to manage the pH of the resulting gas, while others have complained that the bioscrubber has an unpleasant smell. For these reasons, biotechnological efforts at air quality improvement have not been readily adopted by industry.

RESOLVING OIL SPILLS

There are several methods for cleaning up oil spills. One is **bioremediation**, in which microbes that "eat" oil are introduced in large quantities to the spill site. Another common approach for spills in water is to **burn the surface oil** carefully off. In some cases, oily water will be sucked up into a centrifuge, where it can be spun rapidly until the oil separates from the water. **Oil may be skimmed off the water surface**. Another approach is to **add dry hydrophobic solidifiers**, which mix with the oil and form a solid that can be more easily removed. Finally, scientists have developed **dispersant (or detergent) chemicals** that adhere to oil globules, neutralize them, and allow them to wash away naturally without damaging the environment.

DESALINIZATION

When the salt content of soil becomes too high, a process known as **salinization**, it can prevent plant growth. Excessive salinization can effectively turn arable land into a desert. Areas that are frequently irrigated are susceptible to this problem, because even fresh water contains a tiny amount of salt. Irrigation washes away soluble nutrients and leaves behind a salt precipitate. This phenomenon suggests the need for a technique of soil **desalinization**. At the same time, converting salt water from the ocean into drinking water requires desalinization. Thus, scientists have spent a great deal of time trying to develop an efficient means of removing salt from soil and water. The easiest way to remove salt from water is to heat the water within a glass or plastic enclosure, so that the salt adheres to the outside and can be scraped away. However, this typically requires a great deal of heating fuel.

BIOREMEDIATION

In **bioremediation**, microbes convert hazardous waste into other, less harmful materials. This process can be executed at the site of waste production or disposal. The most successful cases of bioremediation involve the use of microbes that already exist in the hazardous substance. For instance, many polychlorinated biphenyls and pesticides contain natural microbes that can be used in bioremediation. In addition, many laboratories are at work on genetically modified microbes that perform the same task. Some microbes are even capable of removing the toxins from heavy metals. Bioremediation is lauded by environmentalists and the general public, but it is unfortunately also very expensive, and therefore not used as often as it could be. Most companies determine that it is more cost-effective to bury their hazardous waste. Nevertheless, bioremediation has generated hope for future improvements in hazardous waste disposal.

REMOVAL OF HAZARDOUS WASTE

Scientists are constantly working on techniques for accelerating the **removal of hazardous waste** from the environment. One such technique is **biostimulation**, in which nitrogen-rich compounds are added to microbes in the hopes of speeding up natural bioremediation. Contaminated water sources have been improved rapidly by **infusions of methane**, which promotes the growth of local bacteria that clean the water. Another method of improving bioremediation is to increase the accessibility, or bioavailability, of **insoluble toxins** to remediating plants and microbes. Scientists must be careful when increasing bioavailability, because a toxic substance that is more accessible to microbes is also more accessible to other organisms. It is important to combine these efforts with measures to prevent the toxins from entering the soil. The bioavailability of some hazardous wastes has been increased by heating, moistening, and treating with surfactants.

WOOD PELLETS AND METHANE PRODUCTION

The invention and popularization of **wood pellets** have created a new way for people to obtain energy from the combustion of wood. Flammable wood is compressed into tiny pellets, which are burned in a special stove. These stoves are equipped with electronic sensors that automatically load more pellets when necessary to maintain a target temperature. These wood pellet stoves are extremely efficient and require very little care during their operation. Another source of energy from biogas is through the **production of methane**. When sewage undergoes anaerobic digestion, it produces a biogas that is mostly methane. The remaining components of the biogas can be used as fertilizer. Many rural and poor areas have developed systems for converting waste into fuel and fertilizer. In a typical setup, waste matter is placed in a well, where it is mixed with an equal amount of water and allowed to sit until the digestion process is complete. The methane can then be used for heating and cooking, while the fertilizer is great for agriculture.

ETHANOL AND BIODIESEL

Ethanol is a popular alternative fuel created by fermenting starches or sugars, most commonly corn or sugar cane. The resulting alcohol is distilled so that it can be used to power vehicles. At present, the cost of producing ethanol makes it much more expensive than gasoline, so ethanol is typically mixed with regular gas to make "gasohol." In countries like Brazil, there is a thriving ethanol industry. Ethanol makes fuel burn cleaner. In the United States, it is especially popular in the Midwest, because it provides an outlet for excess corn. Another alternative fuel, **biodiesel**, is made from vegetable oil. In most cases, biodiesel consists of 20% natural oil and 80% regular diesel fuel. Many biodiesel manufacturers obtain their oil from the deep fryers of local restaurants. Like ethanol, biodiesel is better for the environment than regular gasoline. However, it is also costly to manufacture, and only works in diesel engines.

APPLICATIONS OF BIOENGINEERING TO MEDICINE

One of the earliest examples of bioengineering in medicine is **amniocentesis**, a technique for identifying chromosomal abnormalities in fetuses. In recent years, DNA probes have made it possible to isolate individual sequences of DNA and thereby learn about mutations in the genes. This would enable doctors to identify problems with fetuses conceived through in vitro fertilization. Some of the most common medical products of bioengineering are based on recombinant DNA technology, which encourages the creation of specific proteins. The most popular recombinant DNA products are insulin, interferons, and erythropoietins. **Interferons** fight specific diseases, while **erythropoietins** encourage the production of red blood cells. **Recombinant DNA** is most often produced in bacterial cells, though yeast and mammalian cells are also used for certain applications. Scientists are very optimistic about the possibility of creating recombinant DNA in egg whites. Similar technology has been used to create transgenic varieties of corn, potatoes, and tobacco.

DIALYSIS

Dialysis is a medical procedure for **failing kidneys**. When a person's kidneys stop working, a dangerous level of toxins can build up in the body. One way to resolve this is to process the blood outside of the body. In dialysis, the blood is taken out of the body and passed through a special machine that filters out the toxins. A dialysis machine has a selectively permeable membrane that functions like the nephrons at the end of tubules inside the kidneys. This membrane allows urea and salts to pass out of the blood, while glucose passes in the other direction and reenters the stream. The blood then leaves the machine and is fed back into the person's body. Dialysis is an effective technique, but it takes several hours and must be performed three times a week. For this reason, many people with failing kidneys prefer to receive a kidney transplant if possible.

LASER SURGERY

In **laser surgery**, a concentrated beam of light severs tissue precisely and cleanly. Lasers may be used to perform the cuts normally made with a scalpel or to vaporize extremely moist flesh. Perhaps the most widely known form of laser surgery is the **LASIK eye procedure**, in which a laser cuts the cornea and corrects near- or far-sightedness. One advantage of laser surgery is that no physical contact is required, so there is very little risk of infection. Also, computer-guided lasers are able to make much more precise and even cuts than even the finest human hand. The scars from laser surgeries heal more quickly and with considerably less pain. Indeed, lasers have even been used at low intensity levels to encourage wound healing.

PACEMAKERS AND DEFIBRILLATORS

An **artificial pacemaker** is an electronic device that **provides the rhythmic electrical impulses** necessary for proper heart function. When a person's natural pacemaker is degraded or destroyed, doctors can implant a tiny electrode attached to a small generator to replicate its function. A temporary pacemaker may be affixed to the outside of the chest, while a permanent one may be attached to the heart itself. A somewhat similar device is the electronic defibrillator, which delivers a sharp electrical shock to the heart in the event of arrhythmia and cardiac arrest. A typical defibrillator consists of two pads attached by wires to a generator. The pads are placed on the chest and the generator sends a series of increasingly powerful charges to the heart, with the intention of restoring a normal natural rhythm.

YEAST

Yeast is a microscopic fungus that brewers and bakers have used for millennia in food production. Yeast, when deprived of oxygen, will ferment sugar and other substances. **Fermentation** creates adenosine triphosphate without requiring oxygen. When yeast ferments something, ethyl alcohol and carbon dioxide are produced. In the brewing process, the fermentation caused by yeast makes beer bubbly and intoxicating. In bread, the release of carbon dioxide causes the dough to expand during the baking process. The heat of baking evaporates the ethyl alcohol created by fermentation, which is why bread is not alcoholic. In both brewing and baking, yeast ferments because it is mixed with other substances such that it is no longer exposed to oxygen. Yeast will not ferment if it is simply placed on top of bread dough, however.

INDUSTRIAL USE OF BIOREAGENTS

A **bioreagent** is a chemical that is extracted from a living cell and used as a reagent during some production process. Bioreagents are currently used in the **production of pharmaceuticals, food, chemicals, and textiles**. For instance, pharmaceutical steroids are made from plant steroids using bioreagents. Other cellular enzymes are used in the production of high-fructose corn syrup, a popular sweetener in processed foods. To find the right bioreagent for a particular process, a company first has to find a cell that is already performing the desired task. Then, the company must examine the amino acid sequences of each enzyme in the cell until it can be determined which enzyme is responsible. Another method for finding the right bioreagent is to isolate the mRNA in a cell that is performing the desired process and see into which enzymes that mRNA translates. A final method is to assemble collections of inactive cells, add promising enzymes, and see which cells begin to behave in the desired manner.

HYDROPONICS

Hydroponics is a system for growing plants by placing their roots in an **inorganic salt solution** rather than soil. This technique was pioneered in the eighteenth century and was the first to suggest that plants could survive on sunlight and inorganic substances alone. It has since been refined so that plants can be grown with a precise admixture of nutrients. However, hydroponic cultivation is expensive and time-consuming, so it is not viable on a large scale. Some scientists believe that this technique will be especially useful if people ever need to grow plants in space. One spin-off of hydroponic technology has been hydroponic culturing, which identifies the relative importance of various nutrients. In a **hydroponic culture**, different mineral solutions are applied to the roots of plants: some plants receive a solution in which one mineral is missing, while the other plants receive the full range of minerals. The relative growth of the plants is then observed to indicate the importance of each mineral. For instance, if the leaves of a plant become discolored or are smaller than usual, it would indicate that the omitted mineral is essential to that plant's health.

GENETICALLY MODIFIED CROPS

Genetically modified (GM) crops contain foreign genes, known as transgenes, that give them special properties. Crops have been modified to be hardier, more productive, and even to contain certain pharmaceutical substances. At present, the most popular genetic modifications are for resistance to insects, pathogens, and herbicides. The vast majority of research on genetic modification has been on corn, soybeans, cotton, and other mass-produced plants. The development of recombinant DNA technology has exponentially increased the number of possible modifications. There is a great deal of resistance to GM crops, though it is mainly in developed nations where the need for reliable food sources is less desperate. In impoverished countries, there is great hope that genetic modification can create **more nutritious and durable foods**.

IMPACT OF GENETICALLY MODIFIED CROPS

Genetically modified crops promise to **improve productivity and nutrition**, but many people remain skeptical of their overall impact on the environment. For instance, crops that are modified to tolerate herbicides may eventually spur the development of "super weeds" that are impervious to any herbicide. However, in the short term these crops will reduce the use of herbicides that may be destructive to the environment. Crops that improve resistance to insects may increase agricultural yields and decrease the need for harmful insecticides, but at the same time they may encourage insects to mutate such that they become resistant to common insecticides. For example, many organic farmers rely on the soil bacterium Bt as an insecticide; scientists fear that GM crops will render Bt useless. There are pros and cons with all GM crops. Those that are grown to be more nutritious will benefit poor people but may lead to excessive influence for multinational corporations in poor countries. Extremely hardy GM crops may prove to be too durable, to the extent that they drive native species off land that could not be cultivated before.

BIOENGINEERING OF LIVESTOCK

Most people know about genetically modified plants, but few are aware of the similar efforts to develop "enhanced" livestock. One example of **bioengineered livestock** is the **transgenic salmon**, in which a growth hormone gene is spliced to a promoter, which encourages transcription of the growth hormone gene. The result is a fish that grows throughout the year and thus reaches a harvestable size much faster. Another example of bioengineered livestock is the **Enviropig**, which was created in the lab of a Canadian university. The Enviropig has a phytase gene that diminishes the amount of phosphorous in the pig's excrement, thereby reducing the environmental impact of pig farming. Biotechnology has also been used to identify popular and lucrative breeds, like the **Angus cow**. Bioengineering has often been controversial, as in the case of **bovine growth hormones**, which increase the growth and milk production of cows but also necessitate the use of more antibiotics on the farm. Many people are concerned that feeding more antibiotics to food animals will decrease the effectiveness of these drugs for people.

AQUACULTURE

Aquaculture is any cultivation of marine life in an artificial setting. Aquaculture may include fish, shellfish, and even aquatic plants. This practice has become extremely popular in the past few decades, as the market for certain species has increased while natural supplies have shrunk. Critics of aquaculture claim that it causes the rapid expansion of some populations, which puts stress on other parts of the marine ecosystem. Also, aquaculture is commonly practiced in estuaries and lagoons, which have more stagnant water and are therefore more likely to be polluted. There is a growing movement to promote aquaculture in curated environments several miles out at sea. This is called open-ocean aquaculture. Another potential improvement to aquaculture as it is currently practiced would be a greater focus on herbivorous species, which do not wreak such havoc on the ecosystem when they are encouraged to propagate.

Bio-Related Technology

SCIENTIFIC PRINCIPLES OF BIO-RELATED TECHNOLOGIES

Bio-related technologies include a variety of methods of producing items or providing services using properties of living things, in fields ranging from healthcare to agriculture to waste management. This can include using living cells or bacteria directly, such as genetically modified food, or simply using principles of living organisms to improve processes. There are several branches of biotechnology:

- **Medical biotechnology** focuses mainly on illness prevention and cures. Bacteria, plant and animal cells, and DNA are studied and information about their functions and makeup is used to create vaccines and drugs. For instance, plants may be genetically modified to produce needed antibodies for certain diseases. These plants can then be harvested to create antibiotics.
- **Environmental biotechnology** improves waste management and combats pollution. Studying how certain bacteria digest and break down certain objects can help researchers find new ways of safely disposing of waste without damaging the planet. Further, some bacteria can be used directly, either introducing them to a site or encouraging their growth if they already exist there.
- **Industrial biotechnology** uses microorganisms, or the principles seen in these microorganisms, to improve efficiency and production. These can be used to create renewable raw materials that decrease the need for traditional fuels and chemicals that can be harmful to the environment. Microorganisms can also be used to make replacements for plastic and other textiles, creating less waste.
- **Agricultural biotechnology** aims to develop new and more efficient methods of growing crops. Many of these efforts are devoted to genetically modifying food to create greater production and to make plants more resilient to weather conditions or pests. Similarly, agricultural biotechnology can be used in livestock to develop hardier, larger, or higher-producing animals by isolating the genetic markers for desirable traits and breeding animals that exhibit those markers.

PRINCIPLES AND METHODS OF ENVIRONMENTAL ENGINEERING

Environmental engineering focuses its efforts in several fields such as recycling, healthcare, and water management. Each of these fields (and many others) face environmental challenges such as waste disposal and pollution. Environmental engineers evaluate the impact of human development on the earth and seek ways to alleviate or reverse this impact. **Pollution** is a large area of impact, affecting the earth's air, water, and soil. Environmental engineers study how air is affected by transportation and manufacturing and propose solutions or precautions. They study how water is affected by water treatment, by waste disposal, and by diverting water sources for irrigation or residential use, and seek new methods that will be less harmful, such as developing bacteria to treat wastewater without chemicals that can harm the organisms that live in it.

When new human developments are proposed, such as roads or pipelines, environmental engineers project the expected impact to the ecosystem from these developments and recommend any needed **mitigation measures** to offset the impact. Environmental engineers also help to track pollutants, tracing them to find their source so it can be dealt with. They work with manufacturers and other businesses to help them reduce pollution. Environmental engineers must be knowledgeable in many areas such as chemistry, geology, geography, and biology, as well as knowing local, state, and national laws that apply to their field.

RENEWABLE AND NONRENEWABLE RESOURCES

Significant strides have been made toward renewable energy in the past few decades. Several different biofuels are available to replace fossil fuels and other nonrenewable resources. These include plant-based fuels such as ethanol, as well as solar and wind power. However, some biotechnology focuses on converting some nonrenewable resources such as coal into cleaner energy by filtering out the harmful elements. The challenge to many renewable resources is cost: implementing new methods often has a significant startup cost and often ongoing costs of maintenance as well. As future developments are made, improved technology may bring these costs down and make biotechnological advances more practical for widespread use.

TOOLS, EQUIPMENT, AND MATERIALS FOR BIO-RELATED TECHNOLOGIES

Those who work in a biotechnological field will need specialized tools for their job. Since there are a variety of bio-related tech jobs, the needed tools can vary greatly.

An **environmental engineer** may use the following equipment and materials:

- Devices to monitor and test quality of water, air, and soil (these can include PH meters, ozone monitors, and nitrogen and carbon analyzers)
- Radiation detectors
- Tools and containers for taking soil and groundwater samples
- GPS equipment for land surveying
- Software programs for analyzing data
- Lab equipment such as autoclaves, centrifuges, gas/ion chromatographs, and multiple other instruments for evaluating samples

Pedagogical Content Knowledge

RESOURCES AVAILABLE FOR PROFESSIONAL DEVELOPMENT AND LEARNING

- **Professional literature** - books and publications are examples of literature that can help a classroom teacher.
- **Colleagues** - a fellow member of a profession, staff, or academic faculty; an associate
- **Professional Associations** - an association of practitioners of a given profession, for example NEA, NSTA, etc.
- **Professional development activities** – sometimes put on by a local or state school board to teach educators the newest trends in education.

CODE OF ETHICS

Ethical codes are specialized and specific rules of ethics. Such codes exist in most professions to **guide interactions** between specialists with advanced knowledge, e.g., doctors, lawyers and engineers, and the general public. They are often not part of any more general theory of ethics but accepted as pragmatic necessities. Ethical codes are distinct from moral codes that apply to the education and religion of a whole larger society. Not only are they more specialized, but they are more internally consistent, and typically can be applied without a great deal of interpretation by an ordinary practitioner of the specialty.

STUDENT DIVERSITY

Cultural identities are strongly embraced by adolescents but they also want to be recognized and treated as unique individuals. Teachers walk a fine line between respecting cultural differences and avoiding overly emphasizing them or disregarding them altogether. Responding to discriminatory comments immediately, using a wide variety of examples, quoting scholars from many cultures and identifying universal problems needing complex solutions can indirectly communicate appreciation of and respect for all cultures. Teachers must take care never to imply any kind of stereotype or make comments that might indicate a cultural bias. They must refrain from asking a student to respond as a member of a particular culture, class or country. Teachers should learn as much as they can about every racial, ethnic and cultural group represented in their classroom. It is also important that teachers respect students' commitments and obligations away from school, their family responsibilities and job pressures.

CULTURAL INFLUENCES

Study after study has shown that a student's culture has a **direct impact on learning**. Since educational standards are based on white, middle class cultural identification, students who do not fall into that demographic face challenges every day. It's not that these students are incapable of learning; they simply judge that which is important and how they express that importance differently. Sometimes it is **difficult for them to understand and relate** to curriculum content, teaching methods and social skills required because their culture does things differently, emphasizes different choices and rewards different behavior. Adolescents identify with their culture; they become what they know. If teachers ignore cultural differences, it causes communication issues, inhibits learning and increases the potential for behavior problems. As long as a child has no physical or mental health issues, he is capable of learning. He simply needs that the information presented and examples used to be relevant to his life experiences; otherwise, it does not seem to make sense to him.

SOCIAL ENVIRONMENT

The **social environment** is the set of people and institutions with which one associates and communicates. It has both a **direct and indirect influence on behavior** by the individuals within the group. It is sometimes defined by specific characteristics such as race, gender, age, culture or behavioral patterns. When defined by **behavioral patterns** it can lead to unproven assumptions about entire groups of people. In America's diverse society, it is essential that teachers recognize that **various social groups exist** within a classroom and thus determine the best strategies not only to facilitate the learning of "book" facts, but also to encourage understanding and acceptance between the groups. The learning theory called **social cognitivism** believes that people learn by observing others, whether they are aware of the process or not. Creating opportunities for students to interact with diverse social groups in a neutral, non-threatening situation can bring about positive interpersonal growth that could have long-term societal impact outside of the educational environment.

COGNITIVE LEARNING

Cognitive approaches to learning focus on emphasizing ways to enhance students' intrinsic nature to make sense of the world around them. Students do this by learning and organizing information, problem-solving and finally developing the concepts and language in order to convey what they see. It refers to the way that students process information. The style in which one learns is described as a **dimension of one's personality**. Attitudes, values, and social interactions are all dimensions of these influences. Once a teacher has an idea of the cognitive learning styles of his students, he can better gauge how to direct the information at them. He may find that one of his classes does much better with small group work, whereas another group works more effectively individually. There will always be a wide range of ability in any class, and getting to know the students' styles is always going to be effective.

LEARNING STYLES

The different learning styles that affect how students learn and perform are:

- **Visual learners**—These students learn best by **seeing** written directions and benefit from having notes written down on a whiteboard or overhead. They are able to extract information from written text well and benefit from having main points summarized on the board during class discussions.
- **Oral learners**—These students perform better when information can be **heard**; for instance, they may prefer to read aloud or listen to someone else read aloud. Discussions can be helpful in order to hear the information once, and then repeat it to someone else.
- **Kinesthetic learners**—These students benefit from **hands-on** experiences and learn best from participating in the classroom, such as conducting a science experiment.

CULTURAL DIFFERENCES

The **cultural differences** that might affect behavior include: eye contact, hand movements, silence, religious belief and loss of face. It is important to know the differences that some students may have with eye contact; for example, in some cultures, looking down is seen as a sign of disrespect, whereas with some students that is the way to show respect and that they are paying attention. Some students may laugh or smile out of nervousness when under pressure, falsely leading teachers to assume that they are being rude or misbehaving. Silence is one that varies between genders and cultures. Girls tend to be quieter, and students who are silent when called upon could actually be waiting for more direction instead of the impression that they are not paying attention. Religious beliefs come into effect when doing particular activities that certain religions would find inappropriate, therefore causing students to be reluctant to participate, not because they don't know what to do but because they cannot do the activity.

MAINSTREAMING

Traditional mainstreaming in public schools is defined as allowing students with physical disabilities to be placed in **certain regular education classes**. As practiced in the 1970s and early '80s, mainstreaming was an attempt to meet the LRE requirement by moving students from separate schools and classes into regular education classes for part or all of the school day. Often, students received most of their academic instruction in special classes and their time with nondisabled peers was spent in nonacademic activities such as lunch and recess, and in less rigid subjects such as physical education, art, and music. This seems to be an easy thing to do, but the fact is that in order for this to be effective and beneficial for all the students involved, there must be the correct support services in place. Otherwise, the classroom teacher may be spread too thin if she is expected to differentiate for the student with the disability on her own. Due to this, some schools will only mainstream children with mild to moderate disabilities, instead of all students with disabilities. If a school is fully committed to the idea of mainstreaming students with disabilities, it should be done with support in the regular classroom in order to make the transition run smoothly.

EFFECTS OF MAINSTREAMING

Mainstreaming, when done correctly, can have **many positive effects** on social performance. If the students in the regular classroom are educated about the students with disabilities that could be entering their classrooms, then the rate of success tends to be much higher. If no transition work is done, then isolation can be the result, which is the exact opposite of the goal of mainstreaming. For academic performance, as long as the right support systems are in place in the regular classroom (such as a paraeducator and any necessary adaptations to the assigned work), then the academic performance of students with disabilities can only improve. Mainstreaming is meant to increase awareness and to welcome diversity, and when done properly, a classroom is a great place in which for this change to occur.

The traditional idea of **mainstreaming** allows students with disabilities to participate in **some regular classrooms** whereas **inclusion** allows these same students the ability to participate in **all regular classrooms and activities**. Generally, inclusion is thought of as the better option to better avoid the segregation that can sometime occur between students with disabilities and without. If they are mainstreamed, they are only mainstreamed in certain classes, whereas with inclusion, more possibilities are open to them, and depending on what is outlined in their **IEP**, they may have one-on-one support in the classrooms they are in. It also gives them the opportunity to participate in the same activities that all students participate in to the greatest extent possible, thus following the order that all students with disabilities be educated in the least restrictive environment possible.

INCLUSION

Inclusion is the meaningful participation of students with disabilities in general education classrooms. To practice inclusion successfully the school principal and staff must understand the history, terms, and legal requirements involved as well as have the necessary levels of support and commitment. The word inclusion is not a precise term, and it is often confused with similar concepts such as **least restrictive environment (LRE)** and mainstreaming. Educating children in the least restrictive environment has been mandated since the 1970s, when it was a major provision of the Education for All Handicapped Children Act. The law states that to the maximum extent appropriate, children with disabilities are educated with children who are nondisabled; and that special classes, separate schooling, or other removal of children from the regular educational environment occurs only if the nature or severity of the disability is such that education in regular classes with the use of supplemental aids and services cannot be achieved satisfactorily.

PROS AND CONS OF INCLUSION

Inclusion is defined as the commitment to educate the child, to the highest possible effect, in a regular school and classroom. It outlines bringing the **support to the students in the classroom**, such as special supplies, or other teachers, rather than separating them in separate rooms or buildings altogether. People who support inclusion could argue that students with disabilities who are educated separately are being discriminated against and therefore it violates their rights. They also voice a need for reform in the special education programs, which they argue are costly for the often inadequate results that they produce, both academically and socially. However, some special educators and teachers have voiced their concerns that inclusion could result in insufficient services for students with disabilities. A regular classroom may not be the place for children with behavioral problems or anti-social disorders. There is also the concern that inclusion could replace special education altogether one day.

MOTIVATION

Some ways in which teachers can motivate their students to learn are as follows:

- Ensure that students know what they are doing and how to know when they have achieved a goal in order for them to build their self-esteem and self-awareness.
- Do everything possible to satisfy the basic needs of the students, such as esteem, safety and belongingness.
- Try to encourage students to take risks in order to grow by talking up the rewards.
- Direct learning experiences toward feelings of success, in order to direct students towards individual and group achievement.
- Encourage the development of self-confidence and self-direction in students who needed help working on these qualities.
- Make learning relevant for the students by focusing on social interaction, usefulness and activity.

CLASSROOM MANAGEMENT

Classroom management is defined as the set of rules or activities that the teacher sets for his classroom that outline **effective and efficient instruction**. This can range from establishing attendance and homework routines to dealing with inappropriate behavior. Some would argue that classroom management cannot be taught and that it is something that can only be learned through experience. Nonetheless, it doesn't do anyone any good to have a new teacher in a classroom with no idea of good ways to instill order in his classroom. Being organized is the first way to start off with a good classroom management program, as well as having an experienced teacher as a mentor, are usually good ways for a new teacher to overcome his fears about classroom management as he will have someone to whom to turn for help.

COMPONENTS OF CLASSROOM MANAGEMENT

In order to be successful, classroom management should consist of the following:

- **Positive classroom environment**: Developing a friendly rapport with students from the first day onwards so that students will feel eager to come to class is important. Criticism of work should be worded by what the student has done well, and then some suggestions as to how to improve it, focusing on the positive aspects first.
- **Clear standards of behavior for students**: Rules should be enforced consistently so that there is no surprise as to what students should expect for misbehaving. Dealing with inappropriate behaviors should be done so with a calm and clear demeanor.
- **Student engagement**: Having students engaged in the task will help with classroom management as there should be less inappropriate behaviors. Smooth transitions are also important so that there is no time in between activities for students to lose their concentration.

TIPS FOR CLASSROOM MANAGEMENT SUCCESS

Some tips for daily classroom management success are:

- Ensure that students know the routines
- Always over plan for lessons
- Label materials clearly so that they do not need much further explanation
- Make sure expectations are clearly set for your students
- Discussions, debates and consequences are more effective than nagging, lecturing and threatening
- Review rules for behavior and work periodically
- Welcome students at the door
- Make sure there is plenty of opportunity for student participation
- Learn about the students' interests
- Involve students who misbehave
- Assign work ahead of time and give clear deadlines
- Color code materials in order to help organization
- Use eye contact
- Use both verbal and non-verbal ways to correct behavior
- Use humor daily
- Give your students compliments when they deserve them.

CLASSROOM MANAGEMENT THEORY

The major developers in classroom management theories are:

- **B.F. Skinner**—He outlined behavior modification which originated from behavioral psychology. He thought that the best way to change students' behavior was to reward them for good behavior and remove rewards, or punish, inappropriate behavior.
- **Carl Rogers**—Socioemotional climate was given importance by Rogers because he thought that having positive interpersonal relationship between students and teachers would foster a positive classroom.

- **Richard and Patricia Schmuck**—They derived group process from social psychology and group dynamics research and put the emphasis on the teacher establishing and maintaining an effectively controlled classroom with cooperation being the key skills needed in order to have groups work effectively together.
- **Lee and Marlene Canter**—They viewed classroom management as establishing and enforcing classroom rules as a way of controlling student behavior, mainly by discipline.

DAILY PROCEDURES, ROUTINES AND RULES

The most important thing to remember when dealing with students is that **consistency is vital**. If one student sees you deal with something in a certain way, the next student will expect the same treatment. If she is treated differently, then she will see your rules as flexible, or that they don't even matter. It is better to be tough at the beginning of the school year, and as many teachers will tell you—"Don't smile until after Christmas"—you are ultimately there in the classroom to be a teacher, not a friend to the students, and **remaining firm with your rules and routines** will earn their respect as well as maintain an orderly classroom. Empty threats can be especially damaging. It is best to clearly outline the consequences for misbehavior, or inability to produce class work or homework as soon as possible and then follow through.

CONSEQUENCES

When deciding on **rewards and consequences**, it is useful to make sure that they are **relevant to the students and the situation**. It makes sense to punish a student who does not complete his homework by having them complete the homework in a detention after school, or having the student complete it by a certain date, otherwise the parents would be notified. It would not be appropriate, for example, to have the student stand in the hallway, when he could be in the class learning the material. When students see clear links between the consequences and their behavior, they will know their limits and be more inclined to behave appropriately or complete assignments on time.

POSITIVE GUIDANCE

When the differences between girls and boys were looked at in many gender studies, it was found that **boys tended to be more assertive and aggressive**, while the **girls tended to be passive**. The way the teachers were dealing with the boys tended to be more verbal, thus reinforcing that calling out would get more attention than the more desirable behavior of the girls who would raise their hands and pay attention. Praising and giving compliments encourages students to focus and stay on task if they want to receive praise and attention. Ignoring misbehavior can be effective, as long as it doesn't get out of hand, at ensuring that the misbehaving students know that negative behavior will get a negative reaction, or no reaction at all. Focusing on the problems in a classroom can inadvertently be rewarding to those who misbehave and cause the negative behavior to manifest itself further.

CLASSROOM RULES

Starting off the school year with a clearly defined set of classroom rules will let your students know their limitations from the beginning. Many teachers have their **students participate in the creation of the rules**. Starting off by brainstorming ideas for rules may have you discover that student-created rules may be more strict that you would create yourself. Most students want to learn in a **safe environment** and feel better when there are **defined boundaries**. It is useful to **create consequences** after each repetition of the undesirable; for example, after the first violation, the student's name goes on the board. After the second violation, the student stands in the hallway, and after the third violation there is a note home, detention or whatever the relevant consequence may be.

The rules should be **positive by nature**. Some students tend to see rules that are worded negatively as a challenge and will attempt to break the rule, for example, "Raise your hand before speaking," is worded positively, whereas: "Don't call out," is worded negatively. Rules should also be worded as simply as possible, but should be well-defined in a discussion before it is decided upon. For example, if "Be respectful to others" is one of your rules, make sure the students know what respecting someone looks like by providing examples. Keeping the list short is also important because students will be more likely to keep to them if there are just a few. And lastly, enforce the rules that are created. It does no good for the students to see a rule being broken by another student who does not receive the prescribed consequences.

DIRECT INSTRUCTION

Direct instruction is defined as the procedure that is **led by the teacher** and is **followed by the students**. Students are given **specific instructions** as to what they are supposed to do. The teacher will introduce the task, providing background information, give the students work to complete individually, and then provide immediate feedback. The two main forms are **lecturing and explaining**, but could also include a question-answer session or a class discussion. By having the teacher relaying all of the information to the students, and then having the students practice the skills they have just learned, it can be easy to judge how well the students are progressing with the work.

ADVANTAGES

Direct instruction can have its advantages. If, for example, the material is simple and there is only one right answer, such as facts, then direct instruction can be the quickest and easiest way to convey this material. The teacher has **control of the timing of the lesson** and can make sure that it moves at a pace that is accessible to everyone. Also, the teacher has control over what will be learned and how it will be taught, so she can make it relevant to the majority of the students and cater it to the needs of the students to some degree. It is also easier to measure if the curriculum is being taught using this model of instruction because the teacher will be able to progress along a certain line of thought of teaching.

DISADVANTAGES

Some of the disadvantages of direct instruction is that it is **based on old theories of learning** that believe that simple tasks must be learned before complex ones, and that the emphasis is on learning that can be quantified. This type of instruction can also minimize the prior experiences and knowledge of the individual students as the students are taught as a whole, not as individuals. Sometimes, students can lose sight of the overall task as they are caught up in the series of tasks that can make learning seem irrelevant to them. If students are not given many opportunities to do the work themselves, they can have a **low retention level** of what they have learned. Finally, students who learn in styles other than verbally **may struggle to keep up with the lesson** because various learning strategies are not catered to.

MADELINE HUNTER DIRECT INSTRUCTION MODEL
- **Anticipatory Set**: This should involve the bait for students to show interest in the lesson and for the teacher to focus their attention.
- **Objectives**: The objectives should be clear, so that the teacher knows what students will have achieved by the end of the lesson.
- **Teaching**: The teacher provides the information, and then shows examples of the material.
- **Guided practice**: Students demonstrate what they have learned through an activity supervised by the teacher.

123

- **Checking for Understanding**: The teacher may ask students questions to check understanding in order to proceed to the next level of learning.
- **Independent practice**: Once students have mastered the skills, more practice can be done for reinforcement.
- **Closure**: The teacher gives the lesson a conclusion and gives the students a chance to make sense of what they have learned.

ASSESSMENT STATION

An **assessment station** is a designated area, inside or outside of the classroom, used for the specific purpose of **evaluating students' progress performing a task**. Individuals or groups can be assigned to complete a task, use a piece of lab equipment or work with some technological device. The purpose is to assess the knowledge acquired, processes used, skills displayed, and general attitude about the task, and if working in a group, how each student interacts with the other members of the team.

The assessment station should **function the same way every time** it is used. This builds consistency and reduces the time needed for explanations and demonstrations before and during future assessments. Instructions should be clear, concise and specific and explain exactly how the area should be left for the next student. Activities performed in the assessment station should be simple, straightforward and relate to the material being studied.

USING AN ASSESSMENT STATION

Because the assessment station is an interactive tool, the area needs to be **equipped with the appropriate equipment** necessary to complete the task. If the activity is an experiment, the area needs to be ventilated and appropriate safety precautions taken, e.g., having water available and a fire extinguisher at hand. The students need to understand how to operate the instruments in a safe manner and therefore instructions should be provided both in writing and verbally. Questions should be asked and answered before any activity is started. If it is a group activity, each student needs to contribute to the assigned task.

The work submitted by each student is **evaluated using a rating/grading scale or a checklist**. For example, if the task required the use of a microscope, the checklist should have points related to its use. If it was a group project, cooperation, helpfulness and leadership skills should be noted.

INDIVIDUAL ASSESSMENTS

Individual assessments focus on the **progress** each student made during a defined period of time (e.g., every six weeks, at the end of the semester) rather than in a team collaboration. A variety of activities such as written assignments, oral presentations, and class participation should be incorporated into the assessment in order to obtain a broader, more realistic view of the student's understanding of the material. The assessment process should be fully explained so that the student knows what is expected. He is evaluated using one or all of the following standards:

- **self-referenced** —based on his previous level of progress
- **criterion-referenced** — a defined, school or district-wide standard
- **norm-referenced** — based on the progress of groups of students the same age or grade level

Using a combination of standards instead of relying on one method presents a clearer, more accurate picture of the student's growth.

GROUP ASSESSMENTS

Group assessments focus on how students **cooperate and collaborate** in completing a project assigned to the group rather than to a single student. The same activities used in individual assessments are used, such as written assignments, oral presentations, and group participation, but they are used to evaluate social and interactive skills as well as the work produced. The students' willingness to accept being evaluated for a group project is based on if and how long they have been exposed to this type of cooperative collaboration and if they feel the grading system is applied fairly. If this project is the first time students in a competitive environment are expected to work together, there may be some misunderstandings and objections about what is expected, how it works, and how each student will be evaluated. It is critical the teacher explains the evaluation process clearly, answers questions, addresses reservations, and closely monitors individual contributions as well as the progress of the project.

ADVANTAGES AND DISADVANTAGES OF ASSESSMENTS

Individual assessments are **easily understood** by students and parents and mesh with most school districts' systems. Because each student is **evaluated based on criteria established by state performance and/or content standards**, it is easy to measure the success of department curricula. Self-referenced standards provide feedback about the student's strengths and weaknesses. They can help **motivate** the student to work harder and take more responsibility for his learning. Students sometimes set personal goals and expectations. Individual assessments help them measure their success. These evaluations provide the teacher insight into any special help the student might need.

Individual assessment can create and encourage a **very competitive environment** in which some students are **unable to compete effectively**. It makes it **difficult to evaluate** students' ability to work with a team and judge their interaction with others both of which are important to the educational experience. They can also be also very time consuming for the teacher to complete fairly and accurately.

There are three ways to evaluate a group project: **group grade only, individual grade only, or a combination of both**. The reason for group projects is to teach cooperation in a team environment. Giving everyone the same grade can foster some degree of esprit de corps. It also frees the teacher from having to decide who was responsible for what part of the project. A group grade, however, can cause resentment, especially if students are not used to working in a group and are used to earning grades based on a competitive scale. Students understand individual grades, but in a group project environment the competitive scale diminishes the spirit of cooperation because everyone is working for himself rather than for the good of the team. Giving a group grade and an individual grade addresses both issues. Basing eighty percent of the grade on cooperation and collaboration and twenty percent on individual production recognizes the importance of working for the group and the necessity of individual contributions.

PERFORMANCE CONTRACTS

A **performance contract** is a written agreement between an individual student or a group of students and a teacher about a specific activity. The assignment can be a research paper, an oral presentation with props, or some other project. The contract clearly states the goal, explains the activity, establishes a timeline, and describes who will do what and how it will be done. Sometimes the agreement also details the criteria to be used to evaluate the finished product. This tool helps students **learn to plan a project** by breaking it into manageable parts and shows them how to utilize their time more efficiently. Not only can the completed project be graded, but the performance contract itself can be evaluated. The teacher should assess the student's participation

125

in setting up the contract, his willingness to compromise when necessary and his general attitude about the concept and the process.

Performance contracts can be a great learning experience for students by teaching them how to plan and prioritize and encouraging them to avoid procrastination. However, **some students may have trouble** understanding the concept, so it may be necessary to review the planning, organizing, and writing steps several times before they are able to grasp the idea. Using contracts can also help a struggling student in other areas of his life. These agreements can be developed to address attendance requirements and expected behavior standards or to plan weekly or monthly homework schedules.

If a teacher has never used performance contracts, he needs to understand that setting up the system and helping the students write their agreements is **very time consuming**, especially in the beginning. It can help, as a class project, to create a performance contract based on a completed project. This strategy sometimes reduces the learning curve for all the students.

In order for a performance contract to be a learning experience, the guidelines for writing one should be very general. The teacher can either give the student a written list of suggestions or, preferably, discuss them one-on-one. Some questions that might be used:

- What work items are you planning to include?
- Where you will find the necessary data: Personal reference books, the internet, the library? Do you have additional sources?
- How long will it take to outline a plan, research the topic, and finish the project?
- What criteria should be used to evaluate the finished product?

Questions that might be used to evaluate the completed contract:

- Is the contract realistic relative to required completion date?
- Are the contract questions appropriate to the project objectives?
- Were reliable and appropriate sources chosen?
- How comprehensive is the plan?
- Does the student understand his capabilities and recognize his limitations?

EXAMPLE OF A PERFORMANCE CONTRACT

Student's Name: _____

Teacher's Name: _____

Contract Dates: _____

Purpose of Contract: _____

I am planning a study of: _____

Reason for choosing this topic: _____

Main focus of the study: _____

Questions I want to answer (add as many lines as needed):

_____

Sources I plan to use (check at least 5):
Books ___; Interviews ___; Experiments ___; Magazines___; Encyclopedia___; Newspapers___; Museums___; Pictures, Films, Videos___; Other Sources/ My Research____
Explain:

| The finished product will be in the form of: | _____ |
| The learning skills I will use: | _____ |

The study will be completed by (different dates may be given for various segments):

_____

The study will be reviewed by:	_____
Evaluated by:	_____
The evaluator will be looking for:	_____
Student's Signature	_____
Teacher's Signature	_____

PORTFOLIO

A **portfolio** is a collection of the student's work assembled over a period of time (e.g., six week grading period, one semester, the entire year). Various items can be included: contracts, copies of completed activities such as papers; presentations and pictures of props; performance assessments made by the student, his peers, and the teacher; copies of class work and homework; classroom tests; and state-mandated exams. A portfolio is a **powerful aide** in assessing the student's progress and an excellent format to present to parents so they can review their child's progress. The decision on what to include should be a collaboration between the student and the teacher. What will be included: examples of best work, worst work, typical work, or perhaps some of each? Will the student keep a copy as a reference point? Decisions need to be made and rules established as early as possible in the process so that progress is accurately and fairly recorded.

CONSIDERATIONS FOR USING PORTFOLIOS

Once decisions have been made about what will be included, it is important to begin with **baseline data for comparison** as the portfolio grows. Selected material can be placed in a folder or large envelope with the student's name on the front. Each addition needs to be dated with an explanation attached stating why the item was included and what features should be noted. Teachers who use portfolios will often create assignments with the intention of including it in the package. As the contents grow, it may become necessary due to space limitations to review the items and remove some daily work, quizzes, or tests. Once the portfolio is complete, the teacher needs to have a **method to evaluate the contents and review the student's progress** in areas such as creativity, critical thinking, originality, research skills, perseverance, responsibility, and communication effectiveness. A checklist can be useful.

STUDENT FEEDBACK FORM

Use the following form when asking for student feedback on a group project:

Rating For Group Project

Student Name: _____

Date of Project _____ to _____

Circle the phrase that describes how you feel.
Choosing the members of your group:
I really like it.   **It's okay.**   **I don't like it.**
Having the teacher choose group members:
I really like it.   **It's okay.**   **I don't like it.**
The group deciding how you are going to complete the project?
I really like it.   **It's okay.**   **I don't like it.**

Comments:

_____

_____

_____

WORK PRODUCTS, RESPONSE GROUPS

Work Products are completed assignments that are evaluated on the basis of the topic chosen as well as creativity, originality, organization, understanding of the subject matter, social and academic progress, and success in meeting and/or exceeding predetermined criteria along with any other items deemed important by the individual teacher. Work products can take many different forms, including but not limited to research papers, poems, fiction and non-fiction stories, bulletin boards, video and audio tapes, computer and laboratory demonstrations, dramatic performances, debates and oral presentations, paintings, drawings and sculptures, and musical compositions and performances.

Response Groups are discussions about a particular subject. Frequently, the students themselves start them spontaneously in response to a shared experience. They want to talk about the event because it affected all of them in some way. Teachers can gain insight into the students' critical thinking skills, information and observations shared, willingness to participate in the discussion and behavior within the group.

SELF AND PEER-ASSESSMENT

Self-assessment allows the student to become involved in the evaluation process. He takes more responsibility for the learning process because he is expected to reflect upon his attitude about and attention to assigned activities and the product produced. To be truly effective, the **student should be involved** in developing the evaluation criteria. It gives him more control. Instead of the teacher having all of the power and being perceived as such, some power shifts to the student in allowing him to help determine the rating scale used, to participate in evaluating the finished product, and to provide direct input into the grade which he receives.

During **peer-assessments**, students learn by listening to other students critique their work and make suggestions on ways to improve it. The student doing the evaluation must think analytically about their peer's work product; in doing so, it should help him become more critical about his own work. Teachers need to moderate these discussions and stress consistency, being descriptive and not judgmental, realistic, positive, and reflective.

ANECDOTAL RECORD

An **anecdotal record** is a written description of observed behavior. They are usually kept in an alphabetized book, binder, or folder and should be organized so it is easy to find notes concerning a particular student. There are computer programs available that make retrieving the data simple.

To be effective, **observations** need to be made frequently and **incidents** need to be described completely and objectively; the teacher's analysis should be used as a guide for appropriate responses. Both successful situations and unsuccessful attempts need to be recorded in order to present an accurate picture of the student's progress.

The evaluation context is:

- **Formative**: recalling the incident may raise an alert that something that needs to be addressed.
- **Summative**: since observations are made over a period of time, they are an effective way to track student attitude, behavior, knowledge acquired, cognitive skills learned, etc.
- **Diagnostic**: consistent attention to performance may spotlight areas that need special attention.

METHODS OF DATA RECORDING

There are three ways to record data about individual student performance. Each provides important information and lends itself to evaluating different aspects of student growth.

- **Anecdotal Records** are observations of day-to-day activities, e.g., how the student interacts in a group, his ability to complete a hands-on assignment, his demeanor while taking tests, and his development of particular cognitive skills. All these offer opportunities for teacher comments.
- The criteria on **Observation Checklists** vary depending on what the teacher wants to evaluate. They can be used to measure the growth of knowledge, a change in attitude, or the understanding of new skills. Checklists can also be used to evaluate written assignments, oral presentations, class participation, completion of individual and/or group work, or any activity that requires assessment.
- **Rating Scales** are similar to observation checklists. The difference between the two is that checklists are used to determine the presence or absence of a skill, while rating scales measure the quality of the performance.

OBSERVATION CHECKLIST

An **observation checklist** is a list of specific skills, behaviors, attitudes, and processes that are relevant to a student's development and contribute to his ability to successfully complete learning activities. To be effective, these checklists need to be used frequently and be collected over a period of time. One or two observations can be misleading and will not provide an accurate measurement to reach a fair evaluation. Before a using a checklist, a teacher must decide upon its purpose, how and when it will be used, and what the criteria will be. During the observation period, all occurrences of each item shown on the list need to be recorded. It is helpful for later evaluation if

the teacher has a quick reference shorthand system to describe each appearance, e.g., ! equals excellent, @ equals adequate, ? equals iffy, X equals inappropriate. After the session, notes should be added to clarify or elaborate the shorthand ratings.

SAMPLE FORM FOR AN ANECDOTAL RECORD

Anecdotal record for a group discussion
Subject Under Discussion: _____
Students' Names:
Date and Time Period of Observations:
Characteristics to be evaluated:
Balance between talking and listening: _____
Respect for others: _____
Actively participating in discussion: _____
Stating own opinion: _____
Acted as scribe: _____
Effectiveness: _____
Acted as reporter: _____
Effectiveness: _____
Acted as participant: _____
Effectiveness: _____
Acted as time-keeper: _____
Effectiveness: _____

NOTE: form may be modified to fit the observer's particular requirements.

DEVELOPING AN OBSERVATION CHECKLIST

Developing an observation checklist takes time. It can be helpful to **write down** all the skills, behaviors, attitudes, and processes required to acquire mastery of the subject and that are appropriate for the particular age group. The language should be **simple and easy to understand**, so that the checklists can be used during student and parent conferences. Items needed for the specific task or activity to be evaluated can be chosen from the master list. There should be no more than twelve items on a checklist: any more than that becomes difficult to track, especially when observing several students at the same time. Individual checklists can be developed for specific functions, e.g., participation in a class discussion, proficiency at using a microscope, the mechanics of preparing a term paper. Whatever the rating scale, it must be used consistently, applied fairly, and easy to use during the observation period.

SAMPLE OBSERVATION CHECKLIST

Observation Checklist
Subject Being Discussed: _____
Date: _____ Class: _____
Time Elapsed: _____

	Student Names		
Spoke Clearly			
Listened to Other Opinions			
Waited for turn			
Comment was Relevant			
Challenged a Comment			
Stated Reasons for Challenge			
Noticed a Discrepancy			
Stated a Relationship Between Ideas			
Offered a Conclusion			
Inclusive Behavior Shown			

NOTE: can be modified according to teacher requirements.

ORAL PRESENTATIONS

Oral presentations offer a wealth of possibilities to evaluate student growth and development in several areas, including:

- Understanding of the subject
- Planning and organizing abilities
- Communication skills

This **flexible assessment tool** can be assigned to an individual student or as a group project. If given to a group, additional skills can be evaluated including response to other opinions, listening behaviors, active participation in discussions, and contributions to the work product. Teachers need to recognize that some students may have difficulty with or little or no experience conceptualizing, organizing, and delivering a presentation. To address these issues as well as any performance anxieties, it is necessary to establish a classroom atmosphere of acceptance so that students feel confident when giving a presentation. Allowing students some control over the choice of topic also helps alleviate some of the stress involved in standing up in front of the group.

RATING SCALE

A **rating scale** is used to evaluate a student against a predetermined continuum. It is particularly useful for rating an oral presentation such as a speech, debate or stage performance, and for students to use as a self-assessment tool. To increase the scale's reliability, when developing the criteria to be evaluated, the activity needs to be broken into specific, manageable parts. Each criterion may need its own rating system. Scale points need to be created.

- Will the evaluation be based upon the one to five number scale with five being the highest?
- Will the Very Good/Good/Average/Poor/Very Poor standard be used?
- Will another system be developed?

It is helpful for the teacher to decide at the beginning of the semester which units of study will be evaluated using this method and to develop the criteria and rating system ahead of time.

WRITTEN ASSIGNMENTS

Written assignments can take many forms, including essays, reports, term papers, short answers questions, journal and log entries, letters, articles, poetry, solutions to math puzzles, and research, to name a few. It is important that the teacher's expectations and the rating scale are explained with as much detail as possible, especially if students are unfamiliar with the process or are afraid of writing in general. The entire process should be **reviewed**: choosing a topic, planning, organizing, researching, outlining, writing a first draft, reviewing content, editing, writing a second draft, proofreading, asking someone to read the final draft, and meeting the deadline. Criteria need to be developed for each segment so that when the student and teacher meet for regular consultations during the process, there is a framework for discussion. If it is a group project, it is critical for the teacher to monitor the progress and make sure that every student is contributing to each phase of the process.

CLASSROOM ACTIVITIES

Students are expected to engage in and complete various activities as a normal part of daily classroom participation. Teachers not only rate work products but they can and should use these activities to gauge progress in other goals such as social development, communication skills, and cognitive growth.

- **Written Assignments**: The ability to plan, organize, and produce a coherent, well-written essay, report, or term paper is just as important as the content of the finished product.
- **Presentations**: Whether planned or spontaneous, oral presentations need to be organized, logical, and engage the attention of the audience.
- **Performance Assessment**: Evaluating a student's participation and performance is important for helping him develop social and communicational skills.
- **Homework**: Homework requires independent study, planning skills, and the ability to prioritize. The student is expected to remember to do the work and turn it in by the required deadline.

RATING SCALE FOR ORAL PRESENTATION

Rating Scale For An Oral Presentation

Student's Name: _____

Date & Class Period:

	5	4	3	2	1
Voice is well modulated.					
Presentation is well paced.					
Pauses and emphases are appropriate.					
Can be heard easily by everyone.					
Material is: Organized					
Logical					
Interesting					
Good preparation is evident.					
Information used is on topic.					
Language is appropriate.					
Creativity in preparation and presentation.					
Audience is involved.					

ORAL ASSESSMENTS

Oral assessments are used for two reasons: when written assessments are not feasible, and to evaluate a student's mastery of such topics as verbal language proficiency, debating skills, and the ability to think and respond quickly. These types of assessments can be stressful and some students may have trouble responding and become tongue-tied; and therefore, it is important to conduct the session in **private or in an atmosphere of acceptance**. As an interactive form of communication, the teacher needs to avoid filling in the blanks and providing body language clues that might influence the student's response. It is also important to avoid accentuating gender, race, or cultural differences in the content or delivery of the questions and/or tasks. The examination period should be long enough and the tasks required general enough in order to ensure that the student's knowledge and proficiency can be adequately presented and evaluated.

PERFORMANCE ASSESSMENTS

- **Performance assessments** are used to evaluate students' progress in specific tasks like demonstrating a skill, solving a complex problem with multiple parts, or participating in a general classroom discussion. The teacher is looking for what the student has learned and retained through what he does and not merely what he says. Information gathered through performance assessments is easy to communicate to students and parents because it describes observable, verifiable actions and offers concrete discussion points to use during conferences. There are four steps to successfully integrate performance assessments into a balanced, comprehensive view of student progress:What is to be observed and assessed.
- **Develop** the criteria to be used.
- **Decide** which recording method to use between anecdotal records, an observation checklist, or a rating scale.
- **Inform** the students that they are being evaluated, on what they are being evaluated, and the criteria being used.

PERFORMANCE TEST

A **performance test** is used to evaluate a particular skill that is one of the **primary objectives** of the class. Playing a musical instrument, using the backhand stroke in tennis, making a dress, doing a tune-up on a motor vehicle, and conducting a lab experiment are all skills that can be tested using this method. The teacher must ensure that the **same criteria** are used to evaluate each student and that every student has the same amount of time to demonstrate the skill. If it is an outdoor activity, climate conditions should be considered. Students need to be **informed ahead of time** on what they will be evaluated and when it will take place. In designing a performance task, teachers should be as specific as possible and consider the objective carefully. Students should be evaluated on both the **process and the results**. An observation checklist or rating scale is helpful in evaluating a performance test.

QUALITY TESTS AND QUIZZES

Tests need to ask the right questions to **accurately measure** students' knowledge. There are several things to consider:

- Does each item represent an **important idea or concept**? If students understand the main objectives, their knowledge should be evident in their responses.
- Is each item an **appropriate measure** of the desired objective? Consider information presented and teaching strategies used.
- Are items presented in **easily comprehensible language** with **clearly defined tasks**? Students should not have to decode words or wonder what the item is asking them to do.
- Is the **difficulty** of the item appropriate? It should not be too difficult or too easy to complete.
- Is each item **independent and free from overlap**? Completing one item should not lead to completing additional items.
- Is the **subject matter covered** adequately?
- Is the test **free of gender, class, and racial bias**? Choose examples that are either familiar or unfamiliar to everyone.

CHECKLIST FOR WRITTEN ASSIGNMENT

Checklist for written assignment

Student Name: _____
Class: _____
Title of Paper: _____

	Yes	No	Comments
Understood objectives & requirements			
Met the timeline due dates			
Understood criteria for evaluation			
Actively participated in consultations			
Responded appropriately to suggestions			
Used reliable research sources			
Developed & followed a workable outline			

134

Used examples of prior knowledge			
Used good analytical & reasoning skills			
Developed good questions & answered them			
Worked in a methodical manner			
Used good grammar, sentence structure, spelling			

NOTE: checklist may be modified to reflect teacher's particular requirements.

HOMEWORK

Homework should never be assigned as punishment or due to the teacher falling behind as a result of a poorly executed lesson plan or due to outside circumstances. It should be used if students are unable to complete a project during class, to gather information, to practice new skills, or to devise a solution to a complex problem based on a real life situation. Assigned tasks should be interesting and relevant to the students' daily experiences.

Guidelines for assigning homework:

- Provide clear, unambiguous, written instructions. What is expected and how the results will be evaluated.
- Answer questions and address concerns.
- Make sure the due date is reasonable.
- Consider other academic requirements students may have.
- Be sure resource material is adequate and readily available.
- Collect the assignment on the date specified, grade it, and return it promptly.
- Be consistent with assessment protocol and provide thoughtful, helpful comments.

TEST EFFECTIVENESS

Teachers should have confidence that a test **accurately measures students' knowledge**: therefore, it is important to **monitor its effectiveness** each time it is used. Before the test is given, **all items should be reviewed** to ensure that they still meet the criteria established for understanding the material and if one item does not meet the criteria, either rework it or remove it. If most students, including the better ones, miss the same question, perhaps it is too difficult or is not worded properly. If the item is salvageable, rework it, and if not, delete it. Asking for student feedback on one or two items is an effective way to determine if they are still appropriate or if they should be reworked or removed. Veteran teachers usually develop a "feel" for whether a test is an accurate reflection of what students know. If individual items or entire tests are reused, it is imperative to keep them in a secure place to minimize the possibility of cheating.

ROLE OF GOVERNMENT IN THE SCHOOL

One function of government is **education**, which is administered through the public-school system by the Federal Department of Education. The states, however, have primary responsibility for the **maintenance and operation** of public schools. The Federal Government does maintain a heavy interest, however, in education. The National Institute of Education was created to improve education in the United States.

Each state is required by its state constitution to provide a school system whereby children may receive an education, and state legislatures exercise power over schools in any manner consistent with the state's constitution. Many state legislatures delegate power over the school system to a state board of education.

EQUAL EDUCATION OPPORTUNITIES ACT OF 1974

There is a strong concern for **equality in education**. Within states this leads to efforts to assure that each child receives an adequate education, no matter where he or she is situated. The **Equal Education Opportunities Act of 1974** provides that no state shall deny equal educational opportunity to an individual on the basis of race, color, sex, or national origin.

TITLE 20- EQUAL ACCESS

Title 20 states that denial of equal access is prohibited. More precisely:

Restriction of limited open forum on basis of religious, political, philosophical, or other speech content is prohibited. It shall be unlawful for any public secondary school which receives Federal financial assistance and which has a limited open forum to deny equal access or a fair opportunity to, or discriminate against, any students who wish to conduct a meeting within that limited open forum on the basis of the religious, political, philosophical, or other content of the speech at such meetings.

CONFIDENTIALITY

Confidentiality provisions help protect families from embarrassing disclosures, discrimination against themselves or their children, differential treatment, and threats to family and job security. Confidentiality provisions also may encourage students or families to take advantage of services designed to help them.

Many of the legal protections to confidentiality are constitutionally based in the fundamental right "to be let alone". Right-to-privacy protections also are reflected in federal and state statutes, statutory privileges, agency regulations, ethical standards and professional practice standards.

FERPA

A 1974 federal law, the **Family Educational Rights and Privacy Act (FERPA)**, protects the **privacy interests of students** in elementary and secondary schools (and their parents) with regard to certain types of education records. FERPA requires that **prior consent be obtained** from the student (if 18 or older) or the student's parents before certain types of information can be released from school records. FERPA also gives parents and students **access to records**, along with the right to challenge the accuracy of those records and make necessary modifications. Changes to FERPA most recently were enacted as part of the Improving Schools Act of 1994, resulting in the issuance of final regulations of FERPA by the U.S. Department of Education. These amendments help promote information sharing by educators.

NYSTCE Practice Test

1. Analog NTSC video uses which kind of scanning?

   a. Aliasing
   b. Interlaced
   c. Progressive
   d. Vectorscope

2. A wooden jewelry box is handmade with dovetailed joints. Which kind of wood is most appropriate to use while making the box?

   a. Cedar
   b. Balsa
   c. Birch
   d. Pine

3. A VU meter is used to monitor the audio of a student television talk show. While announcers are speaking, the signal should be adjusted to which portion of the scale?

   a. Near the bottom
   b. To about one-third
   c. Just below the red area
   d. In the red area

4. Which of the following is used to measure the ratio of volts to amps?

   a. Degrees
   b. Joules
   c. Ohms
   d. Watts

5. Students are planning to assemble and operate a small gasoline engine. Which safety concern should have the highest priority?

   a. An open fuel tank could release sickening fumes.
   b. Fingers could be injured if caught in the gears.
   c. Spilled liquids may cause a short in the starter.
   d. The exhaust fumes require adequate ventilation.

6. Students using table-mounted power tools are required to tie back long hair. What is the primary danger if this rule is ignored?

   a. Corrosive fluids spilled on hair could cause permanent damage.
   b. Hair may become caught and pulled by the machinery.
   c. Long hair presents an unprofessional appearance.
   d. Vision may be obscured by hair falling across the eyes.

7. A block of modeling clay should be stored in a way that minimizes the evaporation of moisture. Which shape is best suited for this purpose?

   a. Cylinder
   b. Flattened
   c. Pyramid
   d. Sphere

8. A class activity involves flying model rockets. Which safety mishap is most likely to occur?

a. Exhaust fumes may cause fires.
b. Ignition may cause electrocution.
c. Noise may cause hearing loss.
d. The rocket body could explode.

9. Which product is likely to include a safety data sheet?

a. Computer
b. Lumber
c. Paint thinner
d. Razor blade

10. Which division of colors is most commonly used for video production?

a. Cyan, magenta, and green
b. Cyan, magenta, and yellow
c. Red, green, and blue
d. Red, yellow, and blue

11. The generation of hydroelectric energy depends primarily on which physical force?

a. Combustion
b. Gravity
c. Heat
d. Radiation

12. What is meant by the word fossil in the phrase fossil fuel?

a. It can be put into storage for a long time.
b. It is an outdated way of generating power.
c. It is the remains of ancient organisms.
d. It occurs in sediments containing fossils.

13. Why is "light sweet crude" the most economically valuable form of petroleum?

a. It is easily mined.
b. It can be refined efficiently.
c. It produces less pollution as fuel.
d. It yields a higher-energy fuel.

14. The length of a shipping container is 3 times the width, while the depth is 1.5 times the width. What is the depth if the length is 226 cm?

a. 113 cm
b. 169.5 cm
c. 452 cm
d. 508.5 cm

15. What causes the filament of an incandescent bulb to turn electrical current into light?

a. Combustion
b. Excitation
c. Oxidation
d. Resistance

16. **Electricity from an array of wind generators pumps water into a dam. As electricity is demanded by users, it is generated by hydroelectric power. Which statement describes the greatest limitation to this system?**
    a. Consumer demand is limited.
    b. Little electricity is generated.
    c. Much pollution is generated.
    d. The amount of water is limited.

17. **Which characteristic distinguishes the Engineering Method from the Scientific Method?**
    a. Creative input
    b. Evaluation of data
    c. Solving a problem
    d. Testing a hypothesis

18. **Which document is most important for retracing steps taken in previous work?**
    a. An engineer's logbook
    b. Expense account records
    c. A personnel roster
    d. Orders from customers

19. **Which design is best suited for a two-dimensional diagram?**
    a. Architectural plans
    b. Circuit board
    c. Combustion engine
    d. Microwave oven

20. **Most modern computers operate with which number system?**
    a. Base 2
    b. Base 10
    c. Base 12
    d. Base 60

21. **Classify each of the following as hardware or software: a monitor, a printer, a word processor application, and an operating system.**
    a. All four are hardware.
    b. All four are software.
    c. The monitor and the printer are hardware; the word processor and the operating system are software.
    d. The monitor and the word processor are hardware; the printer and the operating system are software.

22. **What is the conventional method for turning heat into electricity?**
    a. Steam turbine
    b. Thermal diode
    c. Radiation
    d. Transduction

23. Which factor would likely cause a braking system to overheat?

    a. Excess friction
    b. Excess slope
    c. Lack of electricity
    d. Lack of fuel

24. "Proper grounding" is a term used in which field of engineering?

    a. Aviation
    b. Construction
    c. Electric
    d. Plumbing

25. Who would be involved in building a bridge?

    a. Aerospace engineer
    b. Agricultural engineer
    c. Chemical engineer
    d. Civil engineer

26. Which department of an engineering firm would arrange the purchase of building materials?

    a. Design
    b. Marketing
    c. Operations
    d. Sales

27. The results of a stress test yield a bell curve. What is meant by the term standard deviation?

    a. Proportion of non-average data
    b. Range from least to greatest
    c. Most likely result
    d. Least likely result

28. The image below shows part of a spreadsheet. How would you write a formula to count the highlighted cells?

	A	B	C	D	E
1	PREFIX	ITEM CODE	PRICE	#AVAILABLE	
2	W	124124	$39.99	40	
3	G	432145	$19.20	300	
4	G	142413	$199.99	16	
5	W	555328	$29.99	240	
6	D	82356	$0.49	585	
7	G	91415	$1.99	422	
8	G	101256	$119.99	27	
9	W	4982	$49.99	48	
10					

    a. =COUNT(B2–B9)
    b. =COUNT(B2–9)
    c. =COUNT(B2:B9)
    d. =COUNT(B2:9)

29. **When should high-carbon steel be favored over stainless steel?**
    a. When it will come in contact with food
    b. When it's necessary to have something that's easy to weld
    c. When it's necessary to have something with good heat resistance
    d. When it's necessary to have something that maintains sharpness

30. **Mass is measured with which unit?**
    a. Grams
    b. Joules
    c. Ounces
    d. Newtons

31. **A radian is a length equal to which part of a circle?**
    a. Circumference
    b. Circumference ÷ pi
    c. Radius
    d. Radius x 2 x pi

32. **Which amount has five significant digits?**
    a. About 308.00
    b. About 30800
    c. Exactly 308.00
    d. Exactly 30800

33. **Which field is most concerned with lightweight materials?**
    a. Aerospace
    b. Agriculture
    c. Chemistry
    d. Construction

34. **Which technology-oriented profession involves the most hands-on labor?**
    a. Operations
    b. Engineering
    c. Management
    d. Sales

35. **When data from a conventional square grid is graphed on a logarithmic grid, which option describes what may happen?**
    a. Curves become lines.
    b. Exponents become powers of one.
    c. Lines become curves.
    d. Powers of one become exponents.

36. **Traffic barriers on public roads are ideally designed to do what?**
    a. Absorb impact
    b. Decrease traffic flow
    c. Direct traffic flow
    d. Resist impact

Copyright © Mometrix Media. You have been licensed one copy of this document for personal use only. Any other reproduction or redistribution is strictly prohibited. All rights reserved. This content is provided for test preparation purposes only and does not imply an endorsement by Mometrix of any particular political, scientific, or religious point of view.

37. Which department of an engineering firm is responsible for gauging customer needs?

   a. Accounting
   b. Management
   c. Marketing
   d. Sales

38. Which Internet resource is a good reference material for a student report?

   a. Discussion group post
   b. Manufacturer's website
   c. User-modifiable encyclopedia
   d. Video gaming sites

39. A chart of data from a student experiment displays an S-shaped curve. Which degree of equation could model the data on a graphing program?

   a. $y = x$
   b. $y = x^2$
   c. $y = x^3$
   d. $y = x^4$

40. Where does the physical reaction that propels a rocket or jet primarily take place?

   a. Where the exhaust hits the open air
   b. In the forward area of combustion
   c. In the nozzle where gases escape
   d. In the oxygen delivery system

41. Thin sheets of wood are layered with the grain alternating to form veneer-core plywood. What is the reason for alternating the grain?

   a. Creative design
   b. Low cost
   c. Prevent warping
   d. Rot resistance

42. The functioning of hydraulic systems depends on which principle?

   a. Liquids cannot be compressed.
   b. Liquids cannot be ionized.
   c. Liquids cannot be pressurized.
   d. Liquids cannot be vaporized.

43. Which statement describes the typical operation of an assembly line?

   a. Product moves between factories.
   b. Product moves between workers.
   c. Workers move between factories.
   d. Workers move between products.

44. The kerf produced by a saw is mainly determined by which factor?

   a. The angle of the cut
   b. The thickness of the saw
   c. The type of saw used
   d. The type of wood used

45. Which scale is most appropriate for printed architectural plans showing a house?

    a. 1:3
    b. 1:10
    c. 1:50
    d. 1:200

46. Which material is appropriate for casting?

    a. Cloth
    b. Resin
    c. Stone
    d. Wood

47. Why does a bar code scanner use multi-directional lasers?

    a. For identity protection
    b. To scan codes at different angles
    c. To scan in many directions
    d. For user safety

48. Which consumer appliance likely requires the highest outlet voltage?

    a. An air conditioner
    b. A computer
    c. A photocopier
    d. A vacuum cleaner

49. Which of the following options is a typical function for a capacitor?

    a. Alters voltage level
    b. Resists current
    c. Stores electrical charge
    d. Turns current into light

50. Which temperature is most commonly used for soldering?

    a. 180 degrees Celsius
    b. 320 degrees Celsius
    c. 400 degrees Celsius
    d. 550 degrees Celsius

51. Excess current in electronic components may cause what harmful factor?

    a. Cold
    b. Dryness
    c. Heat
    d. Moisture

52. Which condition is most important to help concrete harden properly?

    a. Cold
    b. Dryness
    c. Heat
    d. Moisture

53. Which saw is appropriate for cutting metal?

a. Chain saw
b. Cold saw
c. Hand saw
d. Rip saw

54. Which of the following options is a characteristic of flash drives?

a. Uses electricity to retain memory
b. Single writing session
c. Spinning disc
d. Solid state components

55. Pieces of wooden frame for the walls of a house are commonly cut to which degree of accuracy?

a. 0.005 inch
b. 0.01 inch
c. 1/32 inch
d. 1/4 inch

56. Which choice is a positive characteristic typical of concrete?

a. Good compressive strength
b. Good tensile strength
c. Resistance to cold
d. Resistance to heat

57. The word carbon in carbon steel refers to what?

a. Alloys
b. Finish
c. Magnetism
d. Reproduction

58. A miter joint is most often used for what kind of woodworking?

a. Finished furniture
b. The frame of a wall
c. Shipping crates
d. Warehouse pallets

59. What is the primary reason that engineers sign, stamp, or otherwise certify their work?

a. To encourage follow-up business
b. To protect intellectual property
c. To receive payments and royalties
d. To verify the origin and quality of work

60. Students present when arc-welding is conducted are required to look away, even if they are standing several meters distant. What is this safety practice intended to prevent?

a. Burns caused by sparks
b. Eye damage due to brightness
c. Inhalation of contaminants
d. Making the operator nervous

61. Which material is most effective for safety gloves used with power tools?

a. Cotton
b. Leather
c. Rubber
d. Vinyl

62. What most commonly provides the main structural support for the foundation of a ground-floor wall?

a. Concrete
b. Soil
c. Steel
d. Stone

63. Which option is the primary ingredient in drywall?

a. Ash
b. Cement
c. Gypsum
d. Paper

64. The walls of a basement are usually positioned to extend below what?

a. Airline
b. Frostline
c. Waterline
d. Windline

65. What is a practical purpose for the glass walls of skyscrapers?

a. Decoration
b. Insulation
c. Privacy
d. Support

66. Which option is the most common function of a multitester?

a. Heat
b. Light
c. Moisture
d. Resistance

67. What is an example of a substrate?

a. A Printed circuit board
b. An underground pipe
c. An underwater pump
d. A varnish or paint

68. What is a good reason to use a patent instead of a trade secret for intellectual property?

a. For licensing to other companies
b. For long-term exclusive use
c. If the invention is a process
d. If the technique is not novel

69. Which tool is a surveyor's compass that distinguishes between magnetic north and true north?

    a. Theodolite
    b. Transit
    c. Vernier
    d. Wye level

70. An industrial standard most likely comes from what source?

    a. A single company or firm
    b. A consumer protection group
    c. International legislation
    d. A professional organization

71. An older machine in the school workshop may be replaced for $1,000, or the school can continue to repair it for about $50 a year. The older machine will probably become obsolete in five years, while any replacement will become obsolete in ten years. Which option is the most economical solution?

    a. Buy a replacement immediately
    b. Keep the older machine for five years
    c. Keep the older machine for ten years
    d. Keep the older machine indefinitely

72. Which option best fits the most prevalent definition of biotechnology?

    a. An alteration of chromosomes
    b. Airplane bodies that mimic birds
    c. A new way of sealing wood
    d. Developing artificial limbs

73. Which classification includes plotter printers?

    a. Font
    b. Raster
    c. Typeface
    d. Vector

74. A jigsaw will be used to make a cut in the middle of a board, without touching the edges of the board. Which step should be taken before using the saw?

    a. Apply any varnish or paint to be used.
    b. Attach any accessories for the piece.
    c. Drill holes between the endpoints of the cut.
    d. Sand the surface of the wood.

75. Which activity requires a dust mask?

    a. Applying paint
    b. Cutting sheet metal
    c. Sanding wood
    d. Tanning leather

76. Which of the following options is a role of project management?

    a. Deciding who's right for a job
    b. Determining the pace of work
    c. Finding the best materials to use
    d. Interpreting customer wishes

77. In the modern practice of manufacturing, individual copies of a given component are virtually identical. How does this aid the assembly of components into a finished product?

    a. Individual parts are interchangeable
    b. Scale drawings can be made
    c. The finished products are identical
    d. Quality control is assured

78. When a teacher wishes to contact a student's parents, what is an advantage to using notifications on paper rather than electronic communications?

    a. A parent might not have access to electronic communications.
    b. Electronic data can be falsified more easily than paper.
    c. Handwritten notes are more personable and friendly.
    d. Paper documents are seen as more important and binding.

79. The storage of digital video on a computer takes up more memory than does storage of digital audio. Which ratio best approximates the difference of scale?

    a. 10:1
    b. 200:1
    c. 1,000:1
    d. 5,000:1

80. Which activity is most likely to be restricted by local safety ordinances?

    a. Applying chemical surface treatments
    b. Flying combustion-driven model rockets
    c. Radio or television transmissions
    d. Using outdoor power tools

81. Which of the following best describes why an engineering degree includes requirements for humanities courses?

    a. Better communication with clients
    b. Empathy for environmental regulations
    c. Improved grammar and spelling
    d. Understanding the history of an industry

82. Which subject of study best adheres to the general curriculum of technology education?

    a. Physics of astronomy
    b. Production of video games
    c. Soil erosion and retention
    d. Standardized assessments

83. Which of the following options is an example of industrial biotechnology?

a. Blood plasma substitutes
b. Enzymes used as catalysts
c. Improved seed crops
d. New cancer treatments

84. Which self-contained system is the most energy-efficient?

a. A diesel engine
b. A gasoline engine
c. An electric engine powered by a diesel generator
d. An electric engine powered by a gasoline generator

85. Which aspect of quality control determines the validity of quality standards?

a. Company quality
b. Failure testing
c. Statistical control
d. Total quality control

86. Which is a likely example of a marketing department's directives or information provided to an engineering department?

a. Availability of materials
b. Investment resources
c. Cost of the product
d. Relevant safety standards

87. The sizes of paper for printing are addressed by which standards organization?

a. American National Standards Institute
b. Institute of Electrical and Electronic Engineers
c. National Institute of Standards and Technology
d. Institute of Nuclear Materials Management

88. Your technology class requires students to provide combination locks for securely storing project materials. Which type of lock is most advisable?

a. Electronic keypad
b. Multiple dial
c. Push-button
d. Single dial

89. Lumber is often sold in a nominal size that is not exactly the same as the actual size. Which statement describes the actual dimensions in comparison to the nominal dimensions?

a. Length may be longer, and width and thickness may be longer
b. Length may be longer, while width and thickness may be shorter
c. Length may be shorter, and width and thickness may be shorter
d. Length may be shorter, while width and thickness may be longer

90. Which option is a common use for an oscilloscope?

   a. Determining mechanical rotations
   b. Displaying the wave patterns of a signal
   c. Finding small surface defects
   d. Viewing the interior of a machine

91. Powder painting is an industrial method that uses an electrostatic charge. What is the primary reason for using such a charge?

   a. Corrosion resistance
   b. Demagnetization
   c. Easy paint removal
   d. Improved adhesion

92. Some manufacturing processes are conducted in an atmosphere of nitrogen and argon. What is the primary reason for using this mixture instead of ordinary air?

   a. Avoiding oxidation
   b. Better calcification
   c. Moisturization
   d. Pressure regulation

93. In which of the following are fiber optics commonly used?

   a. Agriculture
   b. Communication
   c. Magnification
   d. Textiles

94. Plans for a vehicle are drawn to 1:192 scale. If one part of the vehicle measures 3/16 inch on the plans, what is the measurement of the actual part?

   a. 3 inches
   b. 6 inches
   c. 3 feet
   d. 6 feet

95. Chemical vapor deposition is a manufacturing process that produces thin films. Which industry most commonly uses this technique?

   a. Automotive
   b. Furniture
   c. Motion pictures
   d. Semiconductors

96. One gear in a machine has 25 teeth, and turns another gear with 36 teeth. Which option properly expresses the gear ratio?

   a. 0.69:1
   b. 0.83:1
   c. 1.2:1
   d. 1.44:1

97. Video may be recorded with a subject in front of a green-colored screen, which allows an additional video source to be added to the picture. Which statement describes the most relevant operating principle?

    a. The added video appears in a corner.
    b. The camera ignores the green screen.
    c. The focal length of the lens changes.
    d. The subject appears in a green light.

98. Many varieties of sandpaper are made to be used while moistened with water. What is the primary reason for this practice?

    a. Abrasion
    b. Cleaning
    c. Lubrication
    d. Sealing

99. Epoxy adhesives are supplied in two separate containers that are mixed together before application. What is the primary reason for this step?

    a. The compound contracts after mixing.
    b. The compound expands after mixing.
    c. The compound hardens after mixing.
    d. The compound softens after mixing.

100. Biotechnology has produced results such as improved varieties of vegetable crops. This is mainly accomplished by which method?

    a. Irradiation of harvested crops
    b. Monitoring pests by video
    c. Transferring genetic material
    d. Using specially enriched soils

Answer Key and Explanations

1. B: Analog NTSC (National Television Standards Commission) video scans in alternating, interlaced lines designed to handle moving images without a flickering effect. Computer CRT monitors often use progressive scanning of consecutive lines, while many modern flat-panel digital displays can display both formats. Failure to maintain the relationship of continuously flowing data can lead to aliasing, where a given frame's information becomes confused with that of another frame. Improper conversion between formats can produce aliasing. One must be aware of the formats used by each piece of equipment and adjust formats as necessary.

2. C: Birch is a hardwood suitable for intricate, durable joint-work. While many kinds of lumber may be machine-made into dovetailed joints, working by hand requires a durable wood that is less likely to chip. Balsa is technically a hardwood by botanical definition, but has the soft characteristics associated with softwoods. Cedar and pine are softwoods with softer, more easily breakable characteristics. Therefore, while cedar, birch, and pine could under the proper circumstances be used for intricate joint-work, only birch is well-suited for this application in handmade student work. Machine-worked pieces are more common in an industrial context.

3. B: Speaking voices adjusted about one-third of the way up the scale produce occasional peaks just below the undesirable red area. Therefore, this is the highest level that can be maintained. If the needle or digital indicator is near the bottom, the sound level will be too low, and if it is amplified by another component afterwards the amount of usable data will also be correspondingly too low. The sound levels generated by many forms of music do not have as much variation as the human voice, and so the highest possible level is just below the undesirable red area.

ideal level

4. C: Voltage divided by amperage is equal to ohms of resistance. Division is a kind of ratio, which can be stated or written in several ways. The measurement of watts contributes to the measurement of amps (or amperage), but in and of itself cannot be stated as part of this particular ratio. Joules are a measurement of energy, which may include electricity as well as all other forms of energy, but do not constitute a term of this ratio by itself. The degree is a term with a variety of uses and definitions, but is not a term of this ratio.

$\frac{V}{A} = \Omega$

5. D: Exhaust fumes are an ever-present concern, while the others are incidents that might or might not occur. A combustion engine of any kind produces fumes which can rapidly cause health damage, brain damage or death if allowed to fill an inadequately ventilated space. Therefore, activities of this kind are usually conducted near an open garage door or loading dock if not out-of-doors. A situation guaranteed to happen--the production of fumes--is of higher priority than incidental dangers.

Fumes trump other dangers in closed spaces

6. B: Long hair may fall into the machinery when an operator leans forward. This may cause the hair to be caught in gears or similar moving parts, causing the hair to be pulled and subsequently causing injury, either by pulling the hair from the scalp or by pulling the operator towards and into the machinery. The other listed options include obscuring of vision, something that could be a problem but which depends upon the individual. Health damage or property damage due to spills of corrosives are not limited to hair.

machinery

7. D: Of all three-dimensional shapes, a sphere has the lowest surface area, minimizing the escape of moisture. Moisture evaporates from the surface of an object, so the greater the surface area the greater the potential for loss or moisture. While storage in this ideal shape is not always possible, the question asks which option is theoretically most desirable. An analogy can be made to rounded

sphere

best for retaining moisture

151

blocks of cheese, having flattened tops and bottoms to allow easy stacking, while spheroid elements are incorporated where possible along the edges. If the block of clay is flattened, surface area is maximized and so drying would be accelerated.

8. A: Model rockets produce flammable exhaust, while the other incidents are very unlikely. Ignition is usually accomplished by flashlight-type batteries having too little power to be dangerous. The level of noise produced could be a concern if involving constant, long-term exposure, but this is not likely with school projects. The level of pressure created by a model rocket is not enough to cause explosions, an attribute of liquid fuel devices rather than a model rocket's solid fuel. Nevertheless, the danger of fires caused by flammable exhaust are significant, so care must be taken.

9. C: Chemicals are usually provided with a safety data sheet. Liquid paint thinner fits this definition and so is required by law to have appropriate warnings, although the information provided with consumer products is not likely to be as copious as with substances sold for commercial industrial use. The other options do of course contain chemicals of one kind or another, but the information given in the question does not make this necessity as likely as for the paint thinner.

10. C: Video commonly uses a red/green/blue color wheel, while the others are used for printing and for traditional artwork. The reason for this is that the human eye has particular attenuations that are not exactly the same as the theoretical attributes of light wavelengths themselves. Video is designed to produce as realistic a picture as possible, and so must be engineered to follow human characteristics as closely as possible. Human eyes can perceive differences in shades of green more accurately than shades of yellow.

11. B: The downward flow of water from a dam spins turbines to produce electricity. This requires the water to be above the turbines, so that gravity pulls the water downward. Many other forms of electricity generation using water function by means of steam pressure, where the heat from combustion, radiation, or geothermal sources turns water into steam. In such case the steam rises upward rather than downward, against and in spite of the force of gravity. In both scenarios, pressure against the turbine is exploited to make the turbine spin.

12. C: Deposits of petroleum and coal are the mineralized remains of life dating from the distant past. Intact fossils of bone or plant impressions are in fact often found in coal deposits, but this alone does not identify a given sediment as coal or other fossil fuels. Nor is it the definition of a coal deposit: a fossil fuel deposit might not contain any recognizable organisms. Fossil fuels can be stored without spoilage for long periods; however, this does not pertain to the term. Likewise, the advancement of renewable resources could someday render fossils fuels, but this is not the meaning of the term.

13. B: The term "light sweet crude" means raw petroleum with relatively few impurities such as sulfur. This makes it easier and less costly to refine. While fewer impurities means that more energy-yielding fuel may be derived from it, the end products are similar in energy potential. Likewise, in terms of pollution: a greater mass of by-products is produced when petroleum with more impurities is refined, but this does not necessarily reflect the pollution potential of the end product. Neither does the difficulty of extracting the petroleum from the ground necessarily correlate to this classification.

14. A: The information in the question is stated in terms of width, but width itself is not given. Therefore, the provided actual measurement, length, must be divided by 3, and then multiplied by 1.5. Alternately, 3 could be compared to 1.5 to find the ratio of length to depth, 2:1. The incorrect options are derived from applying the information incorrectly, or by transposing the data for width with the data for length. Other mistakes could include multiplying when the information calls for division, or reversing the numerator with the denominator of a ratio.

15. D: Current passes though the filament of a conventional electric bulb, meeting resistance from the composition of said filament. This resistance produces both heat and light on the non-visible portions of the spectrum, both of which are usually undesirable by-products, and visible light, the intended product. Oxidation and combustion are prevented from interfering with the process by enclosing the filament into the near-vacuum of a glass bulb. Electrical fluorescent light bulbs generate light by the excitation of gases with an electric current passing through it, producing fewer by-products and consuming less power.

16. D: The question describes a way of saving wind power, generated when the wind is blowing, for use when the wind is insufficient for consumer needs. The large-scale demand by consumers is the motivation for building this system, rather than a limitation. The system is intended to produce power without the copious pollution of other systems, such as burning fossil fuels. The limits of the system are ultimately the amount of water available as well as the capacity of the dam and of natural waterways downstream to accept the outflow without flooding.

17. C: The Engineering Method is an overview of design and testing processes, which usually includes application of the Scientific Method. Therefore, any element of the Scientific Method, such as creative input, evaluation of data, or testing a hypothesis, may be considered part of the Engineering Method as well, rather than something which distinguishes the two concepts. The difference is that the Engineering Method revolves around solving problems, such as filling a need for a new kind of machine, or overcoming a specific difficulty or failure. The Scientific Method does not explicitly address such needs.

18. A: All of the listed options could conceivably be used to retrace the steps taken by an engineering process. Expense accounts could show how resources are allocated, personnel records may show who was involved in a specific project, and orders from customers could be compared to steps taken in filling those orders. However, these are all incidental uses which may or may not be useful. An engineer's logbook is specifically intended to allow retracing the steps taken in a project.

19. B: A circuit board is built on a flat substrate. While it often may contain some overlap of components, the majority of components are aligned on a single two-dimensional plane. All of the listed options can be and commonly are depicted in two dimensions, but require a greater extent of cross-sections to depict all relevant details. An architectural plan for a building could include a series of flat blueprints, side views, and three-dimensional models. The engine and oven might be suitably depicted by a series of exploded views as well as flat plane views.

20. A: The vast majority of modern electronic computers are binary. All values are expressed as "on" or "off." As numerals, this is shown as 0 or 1. Subsequently, all values are combinations of powers of two. All other numerical values, such as the base-10 system in common usage, must be derived or translated from base-2 numbers. Base-12 or base-60 (sexagesimal) numbers are a traditional form still used for the degrees of a circle, longitude and latitude, and clocks. A binary must translate binary values into these systems if needed.

21. C: The term "hardware" refers to the physical components of a computer; "software" refers to the applications and files that reside on the disk drives or elsewhere in the computer's memory. Both the monitor and the printer are physical objects, and are therefore hardware. The word processor application and the operating system are both intangible programs residing in computer memory, and are therefore software.

22. A: Thermal heat sources, whether artificially made or taken from natural sources, are usually turned into electrical power by heating water into steam, which rises under pressure to spin a turbine, producing electricity from physical rotation. Thermal diodes are experimental devices that generate electricity with solid-state electronics, but this is to date purely experimental. Transduction refers to one kind of signal being converted into another type of signal, rather than the generation of usable energy, although the signal itself may require energy such as electricity.

23. A: Most braking systems operate on a principle of applying friction to a spinning disc. Friction causes heat, which may prove to be excessive, particularly if the components are poorly maintained, or if the system is used in situations which exceed the design specifications. A vehicle moving down a steep slope may find itself in such a situation of being compelled to apply the brakes in an overly forceful manner, but this is an indirect cause. Many braking systems employ power to operate, so a power failure could cause the system to operate improperly, but this does not the primary cause of overheating per se.

24. C: Many electrical systems rely on grounding, the directing of excess current into the earth (or in the case of airplanes an inert portion of the vehicle), in order to prevent overload. The term may also refer to a base value of voltage, but again this is a term applying to electrical systems. Plumbing and construction projects or systems frequently employ electrical systems which in turn require grounding, but these applications are secondary to the electrical systems themselves. A malfunctioning airplane may be "grounded," or prevented from flying, but this is not referred to as "proper grounding."

25. D: Civil engineering refers to large-scale projects that are used by many segments of society, such as roads or sewer systems. Many of these are government-directed and government-financed, then contracted to private industry. A civil engineer may be employed by either party. The other options are professions which do not involve road or bridge construction at all, except in the secondary sense that an agricultural engineer may plan a farm which includes a bridge, or a chemical engineer may contribute to the development of construction materials.

26. C: A design department might purchase materials for experiments or demonstrations, but not for the actual use of the product for customers, in which case it would be more than a design department. Marketing and sales are both areas concerned with selling products or finding potential customers, but not in acquiring materials. An operations department is concerned with using or implementing products, so the acquisition of materials is central to its mission.

27. A: Deviation means variance from a central tendency such as mean, median, or mode. That is, results that do not match the results defined in this way. Standard deviation is a measure of how many results fit the central tendency versus how many do not and by what margin. In particular, the measure is useful when most results are clustered around the center and drop-off in either direction. The range of results, as well as the most or least likely results, relate mathematically to standard deviation but are not by definition the same as the term itself.

28. C: The format for specifying a range of cells, such as the highlighted cells in this example, consists of the first and last cells in the range separated by a colon. It is necessary to fully specify both cells by row and column (such as B9); just the row or column for the last cell (such as just B or just 9) is not sufficient. (However, it is possible in Excel to specify entire rows or columns with just the letter or number, such as "B:B" or "9:9".)

In this case, using a formula to count the cells may seem pointless, since it's easy to just count them by eye. However, the COUNT formula may be useful for large ranges or for ranges that may change, either by having rows or columns inserted or deleted or by having individual cells blanked or filled in—note that the COUNT formula only counts the number of cells in the range that contain numerical values, not the total number of cells. (A similar formula, COUNTA, counts the cells in the range that have *any* content, numerical or otherwise, but still excludes blank cells.)

29. D: Iron that is alloyed with carbon in the manufacturing process is stronger and retains its shape better than other varieties such stainless steel. A sharp blade is an example of this shape retention. The other options are examples of situations requiring the attributes of stainless steel: heat resistance is generally superior to high-carbon alloys, as is ease of welding. While neither variety is harmful to food, the ease of cleaning stainless steel is an advantage in the context of food preparation. Carbon steel must be protected from moisture, which is often accomplished with oils that should not contact food.

30. A: The gram, as well as related metric terms such as kilogram or microgram, is defined by the SI (International System) as measuring only mass, not weight. Newtons are the unit for considering both mass and gravity in the form of weight. In the U.S. customary system, ounces measure weight rather than mass. Joules are a measure of energy, not weight or mass, although relativity physics compares mass to energy. Nevertheless, it is common to find grams described as measuring weight in casual usage, so making the distinction for students is important.

31. C: A radian is a portion of a circle's circumference equal in length to the radius, although the radius is a line segment while the radian is a curved arc. The radian is the SI (International System) preference for measuring circumference, although the sexagesimal 360-degree circle is still in common use. Radius x 2 x pi is equal to the full circumference. Circumference ÷ pi equals two radians, so this option would read circumference ÷ pi ÷ 2 if correct. Circumference by itself is equal to one radian x 2 x pi.

32. D: Significant digits are sometimes described as non-zero values, although this may or may not be the case. The difference is whether zero is an exact amount or the truncated portion of an estimate. If we read "five million cars" in an article, it can be usually be assumed that the amount is not really an even 5,000,000, but simply shorthand for an approximate amount. Trailing zeroes after a decimal are usually omitted entirely, but are sometimes used to note statistical accuracy. Although this means that results of 308.01 are improbable, it is not the same as an actual value.

33. A: Many if not all schools of engineering are concerned with finding lightweight materials in some context. In the construction of a building for instance, if the first story of a building can support a given weight, the second story can be bigger it the materials used to construct it are lighter. In agriculture, the particular composition of cropland may support vehicles of a certain weight, but heavier machines become bogged down. However, the priority for lightweight materials in aerospace is of primary importance, because the available energy to a flying craft is very limited.

34. A: Operations departments are typically charged with implementing, using, and maintaining the designs and solutions of engineers. This may involve for instance the actual operation of a power station, updating components of a computer server, or similar hands-on tasks. Management often is involved only peripherally with these activities, while sales departments usually have little to do with such operations. The distinction is important to technology education because students should pursue careers where they will feel comfortable. Familiarity with the actual daily activities of persons in a profession will help students make an informed choice.

35. A: Logarithmic or semi-logarithmic grids have, instead of the identical squares found in a conventional Cartesian grid, rows of progressively compressed rectangles with units to match. The purpose of this arrangement is to allow non-linear expressions to be graphed as a straight line, which results in more information to be placed upon a single sheet of paper (or computer screen). Otherwise, expressions containing exponents of two or greater would be curves, which would require an inordinately large graph to depict fully in a way that could be easily used.

36. A: Traffic barriers, such as plastic barrels, posts, or metal bars, are designed to crumple upon impact, much as the front and rear sections of a car have "crumple zones" designed to do the same thing. Such a violent collapse absorbs considerable energy, which is that much less destructive energy passed on to the occupants of the vehicles. The question specifies public roads because privately constructed barriers are often made without such considerations, sometimes being intended to stop thieves from crashing through the glass walls of a retail store, rather than accidental impacts.

37. C: All of the listed options are concerned with customer satisfaction to some extent; however, marketing is the department that explicitly exists for this purpose. Management decides the priorities of marketing, accounting determines the economic implications of a project, and sales finds the customer. Marketing is a topic appropriate for technology classes, because engineering exists to fill needs or wants. Marketing personnel thus often work with engineers to find a feasible solution to the demands of customers and are included as engineering-related career paths.

38. B: Discussion group posts are good for finding exhaustive information not available elsewhere, but are altered frequently. Therefore, they might not be there when you need the information later. User-created encyclopedias have similar advantages and drawbacks, and both can be unreliable sources. Video gaming sites could be a resource for student investigation of computer-graphic techniques, but would be a distraction in most other contexts. A relevant manufacturer's site can be an ideal source for technical information. Competency 009

39. C: Expressions without exponents (having only powers of one) are said to be linear because they produce straight lines when graphed on a Cartesian grid. A second-degree expression (or equation or inequality or function) produces a curved parabola, while a third-degree expression (so named for the highest exponent in any term) produces an S-shaped graph. Some graphing programs can produce both a graph and an equation for a given set of data, although real-life data is often too messy to show the underlying principles clearly for educational purposes.

40. B: All of the options contribute in some way to the propulsion of the vehicle. Until about a century ago, it was thought that the exhaust hitting the open air was the site of this physical reaction. The nozzle leading from the combustion chamber to the exhaust creates a low-pressure area which allows the vehicle to be propelled in the opposite direction, but it is the forward portion of the combustion chamber where the high pressure builds, moving the vehicle forward. The oxygen delivery system contributes to this, but is only a portion of the said high-pressure region.

41. C: Wood tends to warp in certain directions, which are determined by the grain. When pieces of wood are set together with the grain alternating in perpendicular directions, the warping of one piece is compensated by adjacent pieces warping in other directions. In the case of plywood, this is not outwardly visible and so does not function as a design element. While low cost is often an incentive to use plywood, it does not contribute to this practice, nor is vulnerability to rot affected.

42. A: Because liquids cannot be compressed, they convey pressure very effectively. That is, the volume of a liquid body cannot change by mechanical pressure alone. When liquid on one end of a tube is pushed inward, an equal amount of liquid is pushed out of the other side (if we assume that the tube has perfect integrity). Thus, it is subject to pressure but not to compression. Ionization (affecting electrical balances) and vaporization (liquid becoming gas) are possible but not directly relevant to the operation of hydraulics.

43. B: All of the options are potential and real descriptions of the operation of assembly lines. The adoption of outsourcing has increased the amount of product moving from factory to factory before completion; some functions are so specialized that a given single worker may be required at different location. However, the fundamental principle of this manufacturing method is that products are more efficiently moved than are workers or their work stations and tools.

44. B: Kerf refers to the gap left by a saw as it moves through the material being cut. A thin saw produces a thin kerf, while a thick saw with compound rows of teeth results in a wide kerf. The exact relationship of kerf to saw thickness is also affected by vibrations or unwanted motion, but these are minor differences. The other options are minor factors when compared to saw thickness as well.

45. C: Architectural plans are most commonly printed on paper measuring about one square yard. A residential house, measuring perhaps 20-60 feet across, would need to be scaled down by a ratio of 1:20 to 1:100 in order to fit on the paper. This range therefore includes the scales most commonly used by the construction industry. A plan drawn to a scale of 1:50 fits within the range, while a scale of 1:200 would be more appropriate for larger buildings or complexes. Scales of 1:3 or 1:10 might show a small part of the building.

46. B: Casting is the process of liquefying a material, usually accomplished by heat, and then pouring the liquid into a mold. As the liquid cools, it turns into a solid which retains the shape of the mold. Essential to the process is a material which can be liquefied. Resin is a term referring to substances traditionally derived from tree sap, but also including synthetic plastics that behave in a similar manner. Cloth and wood would burn rather than melt if heated in an oxygen atmosphere, while most kinds of stone would crack before melting.

47. B: Early bar code scanners used simple mirrors to bounce a laser beam into the proper angle for crossing a bar code. However, in this set-up the bar code must be held at the exactly correct angle, which is difficult for human operators to accomplish. The use of a holographic surface instead of a mirror splits the single beam into many beams, thus providing many different acceptable angles for passing the bar code. The code itself is not usually a hologram, nor are protection against counterfeit codes or user injury significantly affected.

48. A: There are many appliances sold in the United States with 240-volt rather than 120-volt outlet power requirements. The key differentiating statement in this item is the word consumer, which indicates a domain of products other than industrial or business machinery. Appliances intended to be frequently plugged in and unplugged by the non-expert consumer are usually sold in a 120-volt configuration, including most desk computers, small to mid-sized home or office photocopiers, and vacuum cleaners. Air conditioners, including small window units, are usually sold in a 240-volt configuration.

49. C: A capacitor stores an electric charge, often a very low charge, for electronic components and circuits. The purpose of such a function is to maintain a constant, regulated charge of current when other components on the circuit would otherwise cause undesired variance. The other options include changing instead of maintaining voltage, a function of transformers; the resistance function of resistors; and the production of light, which may be accomplished by a variety of mechanisms such as a light-emitting diode or an incandescent bulb.

50. A: Solder is melted to a temperature of 90 to 450 degrees Celsius, or 200 to 840 degrees Fahrenheit. However, a temperature of 180 to 190 degrees Celsius is the range most typically used. The reason is that the process is usually used to join electrical components or conducting wire. These components would melt or be otherwise damaged if the temperature is too high or alters too rapidly. Higher-end and professional-use soldering guns have a temperature-control mechanism to prevent this, while heat sinks (simple metal clips) are placed around the area to be soldered as a way of absorbing excess heat.

51. C: Excess heat from any source, be it from electrical current or ambient temperature, will damage electronic components; the smoke produced by a fire can do more damage still. Excess cold and dryness could, in certain circumstances, be harmful as well, but these are not common effects, nor are they the result of excess current. Moisture is a common hazard but is not an effect of excess current. Current that is excessive in terms of voltage, wattage, or the ratio of the two produces heat, which is one of the most common causes of component failure.

52. D: The correct answer may seem counter-intuitive but is a process common to proper use of concrete. The concrete (composed of cement powder mixed with water) must dry out, but doing so too rapidly results in cracks. Therefore, an essential step is to continually spray the drying cement with water when ambient moisture is insufficient, or even to suspend a reservoir of water above the cement to be drained upon it as needed. A warm temperature speeds the process and increases strength and is thus desirable. However, this option is not as essential as the presence of adequate moisture.

53. B: A cold saw is a circular saw blade designed to transfer the friction-based heat of cutting to the small bits of metal being sawed away, rather than to the piece of metal being sawed, or to the saw itself. This characteristic is beneficial because otherwise both components become too hot to touch and would otherwise experience the distortion in size and shape that occur when metal is heated. Chainsaws and rip saws are usually designed for cutting wood, while a hand saw could be designed for a variety of uses (although wood is the most common application in this case).

54. D: Although the term solid state was originally intended to distinguish tube-based electronics from modern forms such as transistors, it is commonly used to mean any electronic device with no moving parts. This is an advantage held by USB and other solid-state flash memory devices in contrast to disc or tape drives, which move the storage medium over a reader. Unlike random access memory, a constant current is not required, and unlike read-only memory the medium may be written over many times.

55. D: The degree of accuracy required for the large-scale frames of houses is not very great when compared to most other forms of woodworking. The material is fairly pliable, the lengths involved are large enough to exploit that pliability, and the joints themselves are uncomplicated: the end of one piece is laid against the side of another, while metal struts provide reinforcement. Therefore, the accuracy needed, about 1/4 inch, is less exacting than most other kinds of construction or craftwork. The options other than 1/4 inch are appropriate for finer woodwork or for mechanical parts.

56. A: The primary building advantage of concrete is its resistance to high pressures, allowing large loads of weight to be rested upon it or anchored by it. Tensile strength is poor, often requiring use of rebar (joined metal struts centered inside the mass of concrete). Even when rebar is used, the concrete is still very brittle, subject to cracking or breaking off when loads are not properly balanced or become excessive. Extreme temperatures may affect concrete, but are in any case not a factor that distinguishes use of the material.

57. A: The term carbon steel is a reference both to the presence of carbon as an alloy as well as to the relative absence of other alloying substances such as copper. The presence of carbon helps prevent the dislocation of atoms within the steel. The surface finish of products made with these alloys is irrelevant to the term itself, as are the magnetic properties. Use of the term carbon in the context of reproduction was commonly used to refer to carbon paper, an obsolete process predating modern photocopiers.

58. A: A miter joint involves two diagonally cut pieces of wood joined at an angle of about 45 degrees, linking the pieces themselves at an angle typically of 90 degrees. The purpose of such a join is primarily aesthetic rather than functional. This is characteristic of finished pieces, particularly the visible outer surface of these pieces. Shipping crates and warehouse pallets are roughly constructed, while the frame of a wall is usually concealed under plaster, drywall, and paint. Finished pieces of furniture or a picture frame are the most common applications.

59. D: While all of the options are possible results of engineers certifying their work, the specific purpose of this practice is to verify that the engineer is properly certified and otherwise qualified to perform the work, and that the work has been executed in proper fashion. This is commonly accomplished by use of ink stamps, or by a simple signature or initials. The other options are essentially potential beneficial results which could happen as a result of following these conventions, but are not usually the primary means of ensuring such goals.

60. B: All of the options are hazards common to arc welding and other forms of welding. However, it is the brightness of the light created that is dangerous over a distance. Persons who are present in a room or area where arc welding is conducted should wear eye protection. If this is not practical, such as when many persons are present or when the welding is conducted for a brief time, all persons without appropriate eye protection should be required to look away from the light produced by the welding process.

61. B: Leather, or similar materials such as synthetic leather substitutes, is recommended for use with power tools as protective although not invulnerable safety gear. Cotton gloves are used with hand tools and similar labor to prevent simple abrasions rather than forcible cuts or pinches, while rubber, vinyl or similar non-permeable, non-woven materials are used for handling chemicals. However, none of the other options provide the strength to stand up to the possible stresses resulting from common power tools.

62. A: In modern buildings, the frame supports are most commonly held in place by concrete. The concrete may contain steel rebar and stone aggregate, but these are not the primary or definitive components. The employment of a packed-soil foundation alone is an archaic construction method, although soil and rubble infills are often used to buttress the concrete. Steel girders are used extensively as frame supports, but are held by the foundation rather than being the main component of the foundation itself. Stone blocks continue to be used as foundation material in modern times, but are less common than poured concrete.

63. C: The primary component of drywall sheets is a plaster made of gypsum; hence, the common terms gypsum board or plaster board. The gypsum is refined from calcium sulfate and mixed with additives, which may include paper fiber and potash or similar ash-like substances, but these are not the primary component, nor are the sheets of paper which line the side. Cement, when used as a generic term, may describe adhesives used but these are not the main ingredient of the product.

64. B: A building made entirely above the frostline, or lowest depth at which groundwater typically freezes in cold weather, may suffer foundation damage as a result of pressure from expansion and contraction in the surrounding soil as water freezes and unfreezes. Extending the building below this area prevents such damage and is an important reason why basements are more commonly built in cold climates than in warm ones. The copious presence of groundwater would be a disincentive to building a basement.

65. B: Large buildings with visible exteriors made almost entirely of glass are often considered to be designed as such for aesthetic architectural purposes, although there are practical advantages. One of these is the insulating property of glass, a particularly useful aspect on very tall buildings, where the ambient outside temperatures and wind patterns are irregular and undesirable. Little support is provided by glass walls, so these buildings usually have a core of steel girders. Decoration is by definition not a practical purpose, nor does glass help issues of tenant privacy.

66. D: A multitester (or multimeter) is a handheld electronic instrument used to test several measurements of electrical current, and sometimes other physical phenomena. A great variety of electronic multitesters have been designed and sold for many different specialties of the field. However, most instruments bearing the name are intended to measure voltage, wattage, and resistance. Temperature, humidity, and light are all parameters measured by certain specialized models, but are by no means present on the most common multitesters available.

67. A: A printed circuit board is an example of a substrate, or underlying support layer, although the non-conductive core is technically the substrate while the imprinted copper is the layer above (and possibly below) it. Varnish and paint would be the opposite of a substrate, being on the surface rather than the lowest or centermost layers of an assembled product. Devices that are located underground may rest upon "substrates" in the geological sense of the word, but even in this context are not the substrates themselves.

68. A: The registration of a patent means that the invention becomes publicly known, and its commercial use may be licensed to interested parties. When an invention is retained as a secret, it is not subject to legal expirations and thus may be used as such indefinitely. Or, the secret to be kept from competitors is that a commonly known technique is being used for a specific purpose. Some forms of processes, such as most recipes for food, cannot be patented at all.

69. C: The vernier compass was invented to distinguish the magnetic pole of the Earth from the center of the Earth's rotation, the latter being considered true north for the purpose of creating and reading maps. The other options are all other kind of surveying instruments: the theodolite measures vertical and horizontal angles; a transit is a special invertible kind of theodolite; and a wye level establishes the flat base angle of the Earth's surface by gravitation, and is held in place by wye rings.

70. D: An industrial standard is a measure of quality or best practice and is typically established by professional organizations or national/state law. Individual manufacturers can and do create standards of their own, but the term industrial standard primarily refers to industry-wide conventions. Consumer protection groups may also create standards, but these are observational rather than the guiding force of the actual work or product being observed. International standards may be adopted, but any legislative mandate is created nationally or by state and local governments.

71. B: A new machine costs $1,000 and lasts ten years before obsolescence, or in other words costs $100 a year. The older machine costs only $50 a year to maintain until reaching its obsolescence, a cheaper option. Keeping the older machine for ten years is not a viable option, as this would take it beyond the point where it becomes obsolete. Likewise, retaining it for an indeterminate period of time would cause the same problem, and so this is also not the best answer. Based on the information given, the five-year option is less costly, while addressing the issue of obsolescence.

72. A: The term biotechnology in a broad sense can mean primitive and traditional methods of using plant or animal products, but usually refers to certain innovative applications. Of these, the applied science of genetics is by far the most commonplace. As technical literacy requires understanding what is being discussed, an understanding of probable intentions is important. Methods of sealing wood could involve such technology, but this is not specified. Biomechanical designs are a narrow subset of the general term.

73. D: Plotter printers draw lines, while most other printing techniques compose images from series of dots. Raster graphics are an example of dot composition. The terms font and typeface are generic terms for symbols that may be generated by a variety of methods, not only or mainly plotter printers. Vector graphics are composed of solid lines; the term can refer to both types of printing, such as the plotter printer, and to image displays such those as used in monitors known as vectorscopes.

74. C: When a saw begins a cut on the edge of a board, there may be little need for guides to be cut beforehand, although notches are sometimes utilized. However, a cut in the middle of a board needs a space to allow the jigsaw blade access to the full thickness of the board. Additionally, the evenness of the final cut is improved immensely by defining a definite beginning and end. The steps of sanding the board, applying varnish, and attaching accessories are final steps after the primary structure of the piece is done.

75. C: A dust mask is of course intended to stop dust from entering the respiratory system of the user. Therefore, the answer to the question involves a dust-producing activity. The application of paints, as well as the chemicals used for tanning leather, often produces vapors that require ventilation; a dust mask is not designed for vapors. Cutting metal may produce sharp flying shards, but a dust mask is not strong enough to be of help. Sanding wood, especially if done by machine, can produce clouds of small particles that cause irritation if inhaled, thus requiring the protection of a dust mask.

76. B: The best option given is the pacing and scheduling of work, as this is usually a business decision. All the other options require greater input technical expertise, although management would make the final decisions in any event. Customer relations are the responsibility of marketing, sales, and similar customer service departments. Deciding on materials requires the input of management to arbitrate on the basis of economic realities and likewise decisions of personnel. However, the managerial input for scheduling is greater than for the other options.

77. A: The interchangeability of identical parts is seen as a hallmark of the modern manufacturing process, from the beginning of the Industrial Revolution through present times. The remaining options are also characteristic of the same modern, assembly line-oriented systems. However, they do not specifically address the question, which asks about assembly of parts, rather than design and planning, or what happens after the assembly is complete and the product is used by consumers.

78. A: It is important to avoid discrimination against students and parents from lower socioeconomic backgrounds. This necessitates consideration of access to expensive appliances and services such as the internet or even telephones. While in many situations these are adequate for reaching an entire student population or most individuals in that population, consideration must be given to economically disadvantaged households. The remaining options represent subjective decisions that may be relevant to certain situations.

79. B: While any level of quality could be chosen for video, and any other level for corresponding audio tracks, the most commonly used ratios are usually in the low hundreds. This practice is founded on the concept that video information inherently contains about two hundred times the information of audio, although this of course is to some extent an arbitrary distinction. Thus, the ultimate basis of the ratio rests in large part upon the expectations of the viewers, who may otherwise be expected to find other ratios distracting, or may lead to an impression of low quality.

80. B: Radio transmissions, including those used for television and wireless telephones, are regulated and primarily enforced at the federal level. The application of fume-producing surface treatments is also subject to federal safety regulations, as well as regulation of the disposal of waste products resulting from application. Local ordinances may add to these regulations but are not the primary regulatory means. Combustion-propelled model rockets are often restricted within city limits by ordinances similar to those restricting fireworks.

81. A: All of the options are oft-cited justifications for including humanities courses, such as for literature and history, with engineering-oriented degree plans. However, the remaining options are subsets of the correct answer. The question asks for the best answer, which in this case is the most inclusive answer. A better understanding of client priorities and communication might, for instance, lead to better recognition of environmental priorities, and would most certainly require adequate skills of grammar and spelling.

82. B: Modern technology education is often described as a laboratory rather than a workshop, with a greater emphasis on the underlying science of technology than in the past. However, the theoretical science must pertain to an applied use in a technological context. Of the options given, only the production of video games specifically mentions such an application. The remaining options could be tied into applications, but these are not mentioned. Standardized assessments for students of these courses are uncommon, particularly at the state-sponsored K-12 level.

83. B: Biological catalysts can be harvested from bacterial colonies and other organic sources for the purpose of industrial applications. This represents a major category of use for the innovative modern techniques, often but not exclusively involving genetic engineering, known as biotechnology. In particular, it is an application beyond that of biological systems: the catalysts are not used to directly affect living things or the products of living organisms, which is the subject of the remaining options.

84. A: Many innovative systems for producing mechanical power, such as the propulsion of an automobile, employ hybrids of both petroleum-based fuels and electrical motors, such as a motor powered with electricity generated by an internal combustion engine. However, the energy savings derived from these systems comes from sources such as energy recovered from braking, powering down when the vehicle is idling, and similar devices. No mechanical device is 100% efficient, so adding more steps means more wasted energy. Diesel engines are generally more energy efficient than gasoline power.

85. D: Total quality control is a term for evaluating how effective a company's standards are. The other options presume that standards have been set, and that sufficient or insufficient performance is derived from these established norms. Company quality examines the human interactions which may affect quality. Failure testing involves the generation of actual data regarding a product, while statistical control takes these results and derives a relevant meaning such as how likely a given product is to fail under conditions of use.

86. C: The task of a marketing department is to find out what customers want and how much they are willing to pay. These parameters are then passed on to other departments such as management and engineering. The engineers must then create designs that reflect those needs and economic realities. All of the options are similar practical considerations, but cost is the best choice because it directly involves evaluating customer requests or needs.

87. A: Of the listed options, the American National Standards Institute deals with the most diverse range of products, including consumer products such as printer paper. The Institute of Electrical and Electronic Engineers, as well as the Institute of Nuclear Materials Management, can be discounted because of the specific industries mentioned in their names. This leaves a choice between the American National Standards Institute and the National Institute of Standards and Technology. Of these two, the name of the latter has a greater connotation of high tech and industrial applications.

88. D: Push-button combination locks are primarily found mounted on doors, rather than simply attached by the locking mechanism itself. Compact electronic keypad locks are available, but expensive and excessive for the stated use. Multiple dial locks are easy to use but are notoriously easy to break, leading to the common choice of self-contained, single dial locks for most student use. Latches of lockers are often made specifically to accommodate this variety of lock.

89. B: The nominal size of lumber refers to boards that have not yet been planed or sanded into the regular rectilinear shapes necessary to fit one board tightly against another. Reference charts made for this purpose assume that a half-inch or three-quarters of an inch will be lost to planing, so woodworkers must plan for such differences. The difference is only relevant to width and depth, not to the length of a board. The length is commonly equal to or a little longer than the stated dimension.

90. B: The oscillations referenced by the term oscilloscope typically mean repeating waves of energy, such as radio signals or similar applications of electricity or light. Literal rotations of mechanical parts may be adjusted by devices such as the strobe lights used to adjust the timing of belts. The finding of surface defects may be addressed by a magnifying glass or microscope, while periscopes are used to see into the recessed and otherwise inaccessible interiors of machines.

91. D: The electrostatic charge functions much like the way dust collects. Static electricity causes dust to cling onto the surfaces of electrical appliances and similarly charged objects, such as carpets or furniture. By intentionally creating such a charge during the painting process, adhesion is improved. Demagnetization would involve an effectively opposite process. The paints used vary in terms of resolvability. Corrosion resistance is only one of several benefits derived from improved paint adhesion.

92. A: Oxygen is a corrosive, highly reactive element. Often in the manufacturing process, these characteristics are particularly undesirable. However, simply removing the surrounding air would be both costly and would subject materials to stress from the pressure changes required to create a vacuum. Air-like mixtures without oxygen are therefore employed. Barring extraordinary laboratory conditions, argon reacts with nothing. Nitrogen is relatively nonreactive and is cheaper than argon, and so usually constitutes the greater part of these mixtures.

93. B: Fiber optics are most commonly used for communicating data. Other uses do in fact involve magnification, using the optical cable as a kind of periscope to inspect the interiors of machines or even medical uses within a patient's body, but this means that the image conveyed is subject to magnification after leaving the optical cable itself. Textiles and agriculture use other kinds of fibers in various applications, but these generally do not use the optical image transmissions of images or of light patterns.

94. C: While this problem could be solved with mathematical operations, there is an easier method, one which has led to the common use of certain scale ratios. There are 12 inches to a foot, with most rulers dividing an inch into sixteenths. Because 12 times 16 is 192, 1/16th of an inch equals 1 foot in a 1:192 scale. We may thus read sixteenths as feet without any further calculation. The arithmetic for this problem is 3 x 192 = 576, or 576/16th inches. 576 / 16 = 36 inches; 36 divided by the 12 inches in a foot equals 3 feet.

95. D: Computer semiconductor chips are composed of thin films over a thin substrate, so even without specific familiarity with the process of chemical vapor deposition, the correct answer may be inferred. Increasingly obsolete methods of motion picture production use film, hence the term films meaning movies, but this is not specifically relevant to the topic of the question. Some methods of finishing furniture and the surfaces of automobiles use film-like substances, not typically in the deposition process mentioned.

96. D: Gear ratios are expressed in consideration of the origin of power, that is, which gear is turning which. The pinion, the often smaller gear which transmits power from an engine or other source, becomes the denominator (if the information is expressed as a fraction). That is, for each revolution of the larger gear mentioned in the problem, the power-conveying pinion gear revolves 1.44 times. The information could theoretically be expressed in opposite terms, yielding a ratio of 0.69:1, but this is not the common convention of usage.

97. B: In analog video, the camera is adjusted to be insensitive to green or blue light, while modern digital video simply removes the designated color from each bit of information. A superimposed picture-within-a-picture is a related technique, but is not specifically mentioned in the question or prompt. Focal length is not directly relevant. The overall effect is to remove green light, not to bathe the subject in green light visible to the viewer.

98. C: Lubrication is the primary function of water when used with sandpaper. Sealing is often undertaken to prevent water from contacting and degrading a surface. The common use of water as a cleaner is not directly relevant, nor is the role of the water jets that are used in mining operations to remove debris from the path of a drill. Some modern forms of stonecutting use jets of water to produce cuts in a block of stone, but this is not relevant to sandpaper.

99. C: Epoxy adhesives are supplied to the consumer in two parts, an adhesive and a hardener for the adhesive. The two portions react chemically when mixed, forming a single durable compound. Depending on the variety used, some contraction or expansion may occur, but this is generally minimized in order to allow close fitting of parts to be bonded together. Some adhesives must be melted or otherwise softened prior to use, but this is not directly relevant to the question.

100. C: The question refers specifically to improved crops, meaning plants and their edible or otherwise usable produce. Within this classification, the transference of genes is a major technique for altering the plants. The remaining options are peripheral factors that contribute to the quality of crops but do not contribute as closely, or that cannot be considered a part of the plants themselves.

Soil treatments affect the plants but are not identical to the plants, while irradiation of the produce occurs after the produce is separated from the living plant.

How to Overcome Test Anxiety

Just the thought of taking a test is enough to make most people a little nervous. A test is an important event that can have a long-term impact on your future, so it's important to take it seriously and it's natural to feel anxious about performing well. But just because anxiety is normal, that doesn't mean that it's helpful in test taking, or that you should simply accept it as part of your life. Anxiety can have a variety of effects. These effects can be mild, like making you feel slightly nervous, or severe, like blocking your ability to focus or remember even a simple detail.

If you experience test anxiety—whether severe or mild—it's important to know how to beat it. To discover this, first you need to understand what causes test anxiety.

Causes of Test Anxiety

While we often think of anxiety as an uncontrollable emotional state, it can actually be caused by simple, practical things. One of the most common causes of test anxiety is that a person does not feel adequately prepared for their test. This feeling can be the result of many different issues such as poor study habits or lack of organization, but the most common culprit is time management. Starting to study too late, failing to organize your study time to cover all of the material, or being distracted while you study will mean that you're not well prepared for the test. This may lead to cramming the night before, which will cause you to be physically and mentally exhausted for the test. Poor time management also contributes to feelings of stress, fear, and hopelessness as you realize you are not well prepared but don't know what to do about it.

Other times, test anxiety is not related to your preparation for the test but comes from unresolved fear. This may be a past failure on a test, or poor performance on tests in general. It may come from comparing yourself to others who seem to be performing better or from the stress of living up to expectations. Anxiety may be driven by fears of the future—how failure on this test would affect your educational and career goals. These fears are often completely irrational, but they can still negatively impact your test performance.

> **Review Video: 3 Reasons You Have Test Anxiety**
> Visit mometrix.com/academy and enter code: 428468

Elements of Test Anxiety

As mentioned earlier, test anxiety is considered to be an emotional state, but it has physical and mental components as well. Sometimes you may not even realize that you are suffering from test anxiety until you notice the physical symptoms. These can include trembling hands, rapid heartbeat, sweating, nausea, and tense muscles. Extreme anxiety may lead to fainting or vomiting. Obviously, any of these symptoms can have a negative impact on testing. It is important to recognize them as soon as they begin to occur so that you can address the problem before it damages your performance.

> **Review Video: 3 Ways to Tell You Have Test Anxiety**
> Visit mometrix.com/academy and enter code: 927847

The mental components of test anxiety include trouble focusing and inability to remember learned information. During a test, your mind is on high alert, which can help you recall information and stay focused for an extended period of time. However, anxiety interferes with your mind's natural processes, causing you to blank out, even on the questions you know well. The strain of testing during anxiety makes it difficult to stay focused, especially on a test that may take several hours. Extreme anxiety can take a huge mental toll, making it difficult not only to recall test information but even to understand the test questions or pull your thoughts together.

> **Review Video: How Test Anxiety Affects Memory**
> Visit mometrix.com/academy and enter code: 609003

Effects of Test Anxiety

Test anxiety is like a disease—if left untreated, it will get progressively worse. Anxiety leads to poor performance, and this reinforces the feelings of fear and failure, which in turn lead to poor performances on subsequent tests. It can grow from a mild nervousness to a crippling condition. If allowed to progress, test anxiety can have a big impact on your schooling, and consequently on your future.

Test anxiety can spread to other parts of your life. Anxiety on tests can become anxiety in any stressful situation, and blanking on a test can turn into panicking in a job situation. But fortunately, you don't have to let anxiety rule your testing and determine your grades. There are a number of relatively simple steps you can take to move past anxiety and function normally on a test and in the rest of life.

> **Review Video: How Test Anxiety Impacts Your Grades**
> Visit mometrix.com/academy and enter code: 939819

Physical Steps for Beating Test Anxiety

While test anxiety is a serious problem, the good news is that it can be overcome. It doesn't have to control your ability to think and remember information. While it may take time, you can begin taking steps today to beat anxiety.

Just as your first hint that you may be struggling with anxiety comes from the physical symptoms, the first step to treating it is also physical. Rest is crucial for having a clear, strong mind. If you are tired, it is much easier to give in to anxiety. But if you establish good sleep habits, your body and mind will be ready to perform optimally, without the strain of exhaustion. Additionally, sleeping well helps you to retain information better, so you're more likely to recall the answers when you see the test questions.

Getting good sleep means more than going to bed on time. It's important to allow your brain time to relax. Take study breaks from time to time so it doesn't get overworked, and don't study right before bed. Take time to rest your mind before trying to rest your body, or you may find it difficult to fall asleep.

> **Review Video: <u>The Importance of Sleep for Your Brain</u>**
> Visit mometrix.com/academy and enter code: 319338

Along with sleep, other aspects of physical health are important in preparing for a test. Good nutrition is vital for good brain function. Sugary foods and drinks may give a burst of energy but this burst is followed by a crash, both physically and emotionally. Instead, fuel your body with protein and vitamin-rich foods.

Also, drink plenty of water. Dehydration can lead to headaches and exhaustion, especially if your brain is already under stress from the rigors of the test. Particularly if your test is a long one, drink water during the breaks. And if possible, take an energy-boosting snack to eat between sections.

> **Review Video: <u>How Diet Can Affect your Mood</u>**
> Visit mometrix.com/academy and enter code: 624317

Along with sleep and diet, a third important part of physical health is exercise. Maintaining a steady workout schedule is helpful, but even taking 5-minute study breaks to walk can help get your blood pumping faster and clear your head. Exercise also releases endorphins, which contribute to a positive feeling and can help combat test anxiety.

When you nurture your physical health, you are also contributing to your mental health. If your body is healthy, your mind is much more likely to be healthy as well. So take time to rest, nourish your body with healthy food and water, and get moving as much as possible. Taking these physical steps will make you stronger and more able to take the mental steps necessary to overcome test anxiety.

Mental Steps for Beating Test Anxiety

Working on the mental side of test anxiety can be more challenging, but as with the physical side, there are clear steps you can take to overcome it. As mentioned earlier, test anxiety often stems from lack of preparation, so the obvious solution is to prepare for the test. Effective studying may be the most important weapon you have for beating test anxiety, but you can and should employ several other mental tools to combat fear.

First, boost your confidence by reminding yourself of past success—tests or projects that you aced. If you're putting as much effort into preparing for this test as you did for those, there's no reason you should expect to fail here. Work hard to prepare; then trust your preparation.

Second, surround yourself with encouraging people. It can be helpful to find a study group, but be sure that the people you're around will encourage a positive attitude. If you spend time with others who are anxious or cynical, this will only contribute to your own anxiety. Look for others who are motivated to study hard from a desire to succeed, not from a fear of failure.

Third, reward yourself. A test is physically and mentally tiring, even without anxiety, and it can be helpful to have something to look forward to. Plan an activity following the test, regardless of the outcome, such as going to a movie or getting ice cream.

When you are taking the test, if you find yourself beginning to feel anxious, remind yourself that you know the material. Visualize successfully completing the test. Then take a few deep, relaxing breaths and return to it. Work through the questions carefully but with confidence, knowing that you are capable of succeeding.

Developing a healthy mental approach to test taking will also aid in other areas of life. Test anxiety affects more than just the actual test—it can be damaging to your mental health and even contribute to depression. It's important to beat test anxiety before it becomes a problem for more than testing.

> **Review Video: <u>Test Anxiety and Depression</u>**
> Visit mometrix.com/academy and enter code: 904704

Study Strategy

Being prepared for the test is necessary to combat anxiety, but what does being prepared look like? You may study for hours on end and still not feel prepared. What you need is a strategy for test prep. The next few pages outline our recommended steps to help you plan out and conquer the challenge of preparation.

STEP 1: SCOPE OUT THE TEST

Learn everything you can about the format (multiple choice, essay, etc.) and what will be on the test. Gather any study materials, course outlines, or sample exams that may be available. Not only will this help you to prepare, but knowing what to expect can help to alleviate test anxiety.

STEP 2: MAP OUT THE MATERIAL

Look through the textbook or study guide and make note of how many chapters or sections it has. Then divide these over the time you have. For example, if a book has 15 chapters and you have five days to study, you need to cover three chapters each day. Even better, if you have the time, leave an extra day at the end for overall review after you have gone through the material in depth.

If time is limited, you may need to prioritize the material. Look through it and make note of which sections you think you already have a good grasp on, and which need review. While you are studying, skim quickly through the familiar sections and take more time on the challenging parts. Write out your plan so you don't get lost as you go. Having a written plan also helps you feel more in control of the study, so anxiety is less likely to arise from feeling overwhelmed at the amount to cover.

STEP 3: GATHER YOUR TOOLS

Decide what study method works best for you. Do you prefer to highlight in the book as you study and then go back over the highlighted portions? Or do you type out notes of the important information? Or is it helpful to make flashcards that you can carry with you? Assemble the pens, index cards, highlighters, post-it notes, and any other materials you may need so you won't be distracted by getting up to find things while you study.

If you're having a hard time retaining the information or organizing your notes, experiment with different methods. For example, try color-coding by subject with colored pens, highlighters, or post-it notes. If you learn better by hearing, try recording yourself reading your notes so you can listen while in the car, working out, or simply sitting at your desk. Ask a friend to quiz you from your flashcards, or try teaching someone the material to solidify it in your mind.

STEP 4: CREATE YOUR ENVIRONMENT

It's important to avoid distractions while you study. This includes both the obvious distractions like visitors and the subtle distractions like an uncomfortable chair (or a too-comfortable couch that makes you want to fall asleep). Set up the best study environment possible: good lighting and a comfortable work area. If background music helps you focus, you may want to turn it on, but otherwise keep the room quiet. If you are using a computer to take notes, be sure you don't have any other windows open, especially applications like social media, games, or anything else that could distract you. Silence your phone and turn off notifications. Be sure to keep water close by so you stay hydrated while you study (but avoid unhealthy drinks and snacks).

Also, take into account the best time of day to study. Are you freshest first thing in the morning? Try to set aside some time then to work through the material. Is your mind clearer in the afternoon or evening? Schedule your study session then. Another method is to study at the same time of day that you will take the test, so that your brain gets used to working on the material at that time and will be ready to focus at test time.

STEP 5: STUDY!

Once you have done all the study preparation, it's time to settle into the actual studying. Sit down, take a few moments to settle your mind so you can focus, and begin to follow your study plan. Don't give in to distractions or let yourself procrastinate. This is your time to prepare so you'll be ready to fearlessly approach the test. Make the most of the time and stay focused.

Of course, you don't want to burn out. If you study too long you may find that you're not retaining the information very well. Take regular study breaks. For example, taking five minutes out of every hour to walk briskly, breathing deeply and swinging your arms, can help your mind stay fresh.

As you get to the end of each chapter or section, it's a good idea to do a quick review. Remind yourself of what you learned and work on any difficult parts. When you feel that you've mastered the material, move on to the next part. At the end of your study session, briefly skim through your notes again.

But while review is helpful, cramming last minute is NOT. If at all possible, work ahead so that you won't need to fit all your study into the last day. Cramming overloads your brain with more information than it can process and retain, and your tired mind may struggle to recall even previously learned information when it is overwhelmed with last-minute study. Also, the urgent nature of cramming and the stress placed on your brain contribute to anxiety. You'll be more likely to go to the test feeling unprepared and having trouble thinking clearly.

So don't cram, and don't stay up late before the test, even just to review your notes at a leisurely pace. Your brain needs rest more than it needs to go over the information again. In fact, plan to finish your studies by noon or early afternoon the day before the test. Give your brain the rest of the day to relax or focus on other things, and get a good night's sleep. Then you will be fresh for the test and better able to recall what you've studied.

STEP 6: TAKE A PRACTICE TEST

Many courses offer sample tests, either online or in the study materials. This is an excellent resource to check whether you have mastered the material, as well as to prepare for the test format and environment.

Check the test format ahead of time: the number of questions, the type (multiple choice, free response, etc.), and the time limit. Then create a plan for working through them. For example, if you have 30 minutes to take a 60-question test, your limit is 30 seconds per question. Spend less time on the questions you know well so that you can take more time on the difficult ones.

If you have time to take several practice tests, take the first one open book, with no time limit. Work through the questions at your own pace and make sure you fully understand them. Gradually work up to taking a test under test conditions: sit at a desk with all study materials put away and set a timer. Pace yourself to make sure you finish the test with time to spare and go back to check your answers if you have time.

After each test, check your answers. On the questions you missed, be sure you understand why you missed them. Did you misread the question (tests can use tricky wording)? Did you forget the information? Or was it something you hadn't learned? Go back and study any shaky areas that the practice tests reveal.

Taking these tests not only helps with your grade, but also aids in combating test anxiety. If you're already used to the test conditions, you're less likely to worry about it, and working through tests until you're scoring well gives you a confidence boost. Go through the practice tests until you feel comfortable, and then you can go into the test knowing that you're ready for it.

Test Tips

On test day, you should be confident, knowing that you've prepared well and are ready to answer the questions. But aside from preparation, there are several test day strategies you can employ to maximize your performance.

First, as stated before, get a good night's sleep the night before the test (and for several nights before that, if possible). Go into the test with a fresh, alert mind rather than staying up late to study.

Try not to change too much about your normal routine on the day of the test. It's important to eat a nutritious breakfast, but if you normally don't eat breakfast at all, consider eating just a protein bar. If you're a coffee drinker, go ahead and have your normal coffee. Just make sure you time it so that the caffeine doesn't wear off right in the middle of your test. Avoid sugary beverages, and drink enough water to stay hydrated but not so much that you need a restroom break 10 minutes into the test. If your test isn't first thing in the morning, consider going for a walk or doing a light workout before the test to get your blood flowing.

Allow yourself enough time to get ready, and leave for the test with plenty of time to spare so you won't have the anxiety of scrambling to arrive in time. Another reason to be early is to select a good seat. It's helpful to sit away from doors and windows, which can be distracting. Find a good seat, get out your supplies, and settle your mind before the test begins.

When the test begins, start by going over the instructions carefully, even if you already know what to expect. Make sure you avoid any careless mistakes by following the directions.

Then begin working through the questions, pacing yourself as you've practiced. If you're not sure on an answer, don't spend too much time on it, and don't let it shake your confidence. Either skip it and come back later, or eliminate as many wrong answers as possible and guess among the remaining ones. Don't dwell on these questions as you continue—put them out of your mind and focus on what lies ahead.

Be sure to read all of the answer choices, even if you're sure the first one is the right answer. Sometimes you'll find a better one if you keep reading. But don't second-guess yourself if you do immediately know the answer. Your gut instinct is usually right. Don't let test anxiety rob you of the information you know.

If you have time at the end of the test (and if the test format allows), go back and review your answers. Be cautious about changing any, since your first instinct tends to be correct, but make sure you didn't misread any of the questions or accidentally mark the wrong answer choice. Look over any you skipped and make an educated guess.

At the end, leave the test feeling confident. You've done your best, so don't waste time worrying about your performance or wishing you could change anything. Instead, celebrate the successful completion of this test. And finally, use this test to learn how to deal with anxiety even better next time.

Review Video: 5 Tips to Beat Test Anxiety
Visit mometrix.com/academy and enter code: 570656

Important Qualification

Not all anxiety is created equal. If your test anxiety is causing major issues in your life beyond the classroom or testing center, or if you are experiencing troubling physical symptoms related to your anxiety, it may be a sign of a serious physiological or psychological condition. If this sounds like your situation, we strongly encourage you to seek professional help.

Thank You

We at Mometrix would like to extend our heartfelt thanks to you, our friend and patron, for allowing us to play a part in your journey. It is a privilege to serve people from all walks of life who are unified in their commitment to building the best future they can for themselves.

The preparation you devote to these important testing milestones may be the most valuable educational opportunity you have for making a real difference in your life. We encourage you to put your heart into it—that feeling of succeeding, overcoming, and yes, conquering will be well worth the hours you've invested.

We want to hear your story, your struggles and your successes, and if you see any opportunities for us to improve our materials so we can help others even more effectively in the future, please share that with us as well. **The team at Mometrix would be absolutely thrilled to hear from you!** So please, send us an email (support@mometrix.com) and let's stay in touch.

> **If you'd like some additional help, check out these other resources we offer for your exam:**
> **http://MometrixFlashcards.com/NYSTCE**

Additional Bonus Material

Due to our efforts to try to keep this book to a manageable length, we've created a link that will give you access to all of your additional bonus material:

mometrix.com/bonus948/nystceteched118